PESHWA BAJIRAO I

&

MARATHA EXPANSION

PESHWA BAJIRAO I

&

MARATHA EXPANSION

BY

V.G. DIGHE, M. A., Ph. D.

FOREWORD BY

SIR JADUNATH SARKAR

GYAN

Published by

Gyan Publishing House
5, Ansari Road
Daryaganj, New Delhi-110002
Phone: 011-47034999, 9811692060
E-mail: books@gyanbooks.com

Distribution Network
gyanbooks.com
India, USA, Canada, UK, Australia

ISBN: 978-93-6433-195-1 (HB)
First Published, 1944

2nd Impression 2024

Printed at: Gyan Press, Delhi.

PESHWA BAJIRAO I & MARATHA EXPANSION
Author: V.G. DIGHE, SIR JADUNATH SARKAR (FOREWORD)

PESHWA BAJIRAO I

(By courtesy of the Bharat Itihas Samshodhak Mandal, Poona)

PESHWA BAJIRAO I
&
MARATHA EXPANSION

BY

V. G. DIGHE, M.A., Ph.D.

FOREWORD BY

SIR JADUNATH SARKAR

KARNATAK PUBLISHING HOUSE

BOMBAY 2

1944

To

RAO BAHADUR

G. S. SARDESAI,

Historian of the Marathas

IN

VENERATION & GRATITUDE

CONTENTS

FOREWORD

In the long and distinguished galaxy of Peshwas Baji Rao Ballal was unequalled for the daring and originality of his genius and the volume and value of his achievements. He was truly a Carlylean Hero as King —or rather as "Man of action." If Sir Robert Walpole created the unchallengeable position of the Prime Minister in the unwritten constitution of England, Bajirao created the same institution in the Maratha Raj at exactly the same time.

And yet no worthy study of such a career was written in English before this volume, and indeed no full and correct history of Bajirao could be written before 1930, in which year the vast mass of Peshwa State Papers (in Marathi) preserved in the Poona Daftar began to be published and a few years later Chevalier P. S. Pissurlencar and Dr. Braganza gave to the world the invaluable original documents of that time in the Portuguese language, and the Jaipur Maharaja's archives were ransacked yielding the best raw material for the history of the Maratha penetration into Northern India during those years, mostly in the Persian language. Before that date our knowledge of this great Peshwa and his times had been confined to Grant Duff's book composed a century and a quarter ago at the dawn of Maratha historiography, which was supplemented merely by the Persian sources on some special campaigns used by Irvine in his *Later Mughals* and some Marathi historical letters printed by Parasnis (viz. the correspondence of Brahmendra Swami) and Rajwade (relating to the Janjira Campaign).

But the revolution in Maratha historiography which has been created by the discovery and publication of original sources in diverse languages in the life-time of the present generation, had not before this been represented by any attempt at presenting a synthesis of these materials. That much needed work has been now done by Dr. V. G. Dighe in the present thesis composed in 1940-41 and by Rao Bahadur Sardesai in his new *Marathi Riyasat*, Vol. V, published a year later.

Dr. Dighe's work of which I was an examiner, impressed me so much by its outstanding merit that I moved the Bombay University to assist in printing it and placing it before the vast English reading public. This has now been done and the students of Indian history will be thankful to the University for its liberality to scholarship and to Dr. Dighe for presenting us with a scientifically written and full history of one of the most momentous epochs in the life of the Maratha race.

As the title of the book indicates the author's main subject has been the expansion of the Maratha power during those eventful years (1720-1740), and naturally the details of the internal affairs of Maharashtra have been crowded out by the bigger issues of foreign policy and military adventure which had to be minutely and critically studied here. But even in the domestic or constitutional sphere a valuable contribution of Dr. Dighe is his fresh and penetrating analysis of the relations between Raja Shahu and his great minister by which much popular misconception has been corrected. Dr. Dighe has made a compact presentation of the subject and touched up salient features with a commendable economy of words. But the chapters on the Janjira Campaign and the capture of Bassein in this volume are the most detailed and documented accounts of these two heroic achievements of the Maratha race to be found in any language and they lead the reader by clear steps through the tangled maze of war and diplomacy and their interaction. Here is new light presented in its full splendour.

This volume will form a very valuable addition to the growing literature on Maratha History, and long continue as a standard authority in its own field.

JADUNATH SARKAR

PREFACE

The Marathas, a war-like people, inhabit the western part of the Deccan. Their early history is lost in dim antiquity. From the 5th century onward rose mighty kingdoms in the land, the Chalukyas, the Rashtrakutas and the Yadavas which knit the Marathas into a homogeneous people. Under the aegis of these native dynasties the Marathas attained prosperity beyond measure : they developed their free institutions, built lovely temples, perfected their language and enriched their literature. After that for four centuries the tide of Islam swept every thing before it. Alauddin Khilji's warriors carried the crescent to the southernmost corner of India and with the fall of the great Vijayanagar empire in 1565 under the hammer-blows of the Deccan sultanates, disappeared the last vestige of independent Hindu power in the south. Islam became triumphant throughout the length and breadth of this land.

The defeats of their armies in the field, the destruction of centuries-long dynasties and the ruin that followed in the social structure of society, brought on the children of the soil a feeling of despair and deep frustration and created in their mind a sort of inferiority complex that they were no match for the foreign invaders, that they were in no way worthy to administer their affairs and that it was wise to reconcile themselves to the change of rulers and bend to the wishes of their new masters. It is to the glory of the Marathas that they were the first to shake off this intellectual paralysis and strike boldly for the liberation of their homeland. Their early struggle for swaraj under Shivaji's leadership is now familiar to students of history in the works of Sir Jadunath Sarkar, Prof. Rawlinson, Mr. Chintaman Waidya, the two Kincaids and the essay collection published by the Shivaji Karyalaya. The consolidation of Maratha power and its expansion beyond the limits of Maharashtra under Bajirao I is a less known chapter of Maratha history and the present work is the first attempt of its kind to place it before readers in a scientific manner.

Bajirao is looked upon as the greatest personality after Shivaji in Maratha history and the story of his career has an abiding interest. His achievements may be summed up as the establishment of Maratha supremacy in the Deccan and of political hegemony in the north. When he was called to the Peshwaship in 1720 the Maratha state was in a perilous condition. It was a house divided against itself, menaced on the east by the great Nizam-ul-mulk, its march southward barred by the same power and large part of its territory on the western seaboard yet in foreign hands. At his death he left the nation strong and united, its friendship solicited by Rajputs and Bundelas and its alliance courted by the Mughal rulers. The policy of northward drive the Peshwa pursued so vigorously soon brought the Marathas to the gates of the imperial city and made them dictators of imperial policy. These stirring events are unfolded in the following pages.

The present work was submitted to the University as a thesis for the Ph. D. degree in 1941 and is now being published in a somewhat modified and abridged form. I take this opportunity to express my gratitude to my guide Sir Jadunath Sarkar without whose help and encouragement the work would never have been attempted. Thanks are due to Major Dr. Maharaj Kumar

Raghubir Sinh of Sitamau for allowing me the use of valuable Persian MSS. in his possession and Father Candes of the Portuguese Church in Poona who kindly read with me the Portuguese records on the subject. Prof. Potdar at great inconvenience to himself went through the manuscript and made valuable suggestions. My friends Messrs. Khare, of the Itihas Samshodhak Mandal, and M. V. Gujar were likewise helpful to me in the preparation of the work. Lastly I must acknowledge my indebtedness to the University of Bombay for the substantial financial help it has granted towards the cost of the publication of this work.

Bombay, V. G. DIGHE
1st. Nov. 1944.

CHAPTER I

FAMILY AND EARLY LIFE

Two personalities loom large in the history of the Marathas, Shivaji the founder of the independent Maratha Power and Peshwa Bajirao I, the founder of their empire. They tower head and shoulders above their contemporaries: their policies and actions completely influenced and moulded the shape of things to come.

Bajirao the eldest son of Balaji Vishwanath Bhat, was born on 18th August 1700.[1] The Bhat family came of the stock of Konkanastha Brahmins who are even at present known for their intellectual acumen, industry and perseverance. Bajirao's forefathers were the hereditary Deshmukhs or revenue collectors of Mahal Danda Rajpuri and Adhikari of Shrivardhan in the Janjira State.[2] This office may have been acquired by the family at least a century before Bajirao's birth.[3] Except for their connection with this tract very little is known of the earlier generations of the Bhat family.[4] The first man to emerge from obscurity was the father of Bajirao, Balaji Vishwanath. With the foundation of Shivaji's power in Maharashtra began a migration of adventurers and career-seekers to his kingdom and the Bhats were no exception. Their sympathies and

---

1. Bh. Itihas Samshodhak Mandal Quarterly, Vol. XVI, No. 3, p. 72 prints a horoscope from which this year is taken.

2. Ait. San. Sahitya III, pp. 113-26, gives information of the Peshwa's Watans.

3. Varshika Itivritta, Shake 1837, p. 96.

4. The Hakikat of the Bhat family printed in rumal No. 2 by Bhave, says that the grand-father of Balaji Vishwanath was a Sardar of two thousand troops under Shivaji. The Hakikat was prepared in the 19th century and has no value as a contemporary record. It gives no authority for the statement, which must therefore be discarded.

connection with the Angrias[5] brought them into trouble with the Sidi of Janjira in whose territory lay Shriwardhan. To escape from the harassment of the Sidi Chief, the Deshmukh of Shriwardhan, Balaji Vishwanath left his homeland and settled at Saswad. His knowledge of revenue matters made his services welcome to the Maratha chiefs.[6]

The times following Shivaji's demise were stormy. The Revenue had to be collected not in a settled country, but from a territory which was overrun and occupied by armies.[7] This kind of work required a man who knew not merely the intricacies of revenue problems, but could cajole the peasantry and Mughal officials or fight the latter when necessary. Balaji Vishwanath's qualities eminently fitted him for this task. He is first mentioned in 1696 as Sabhasad of Prant Poona.[8] From 1699 to 1702 he acted as Sar Subahdar of Poona[9] and in 1702 is found defending Sinhagad under the command of Dhanaji Jadhav.[10] Between 1704 and 1707 he worked as Sar Subahdar of Prant Daulatabad.[11] An old Bakhar represents him as mediating for the release of Shahu by back-door methods in 1705.[12] It was quite natural that in his capacity of Sar Subahdar Balaji Vishwanath may have made contact with the

5. Peshwyanchi Bakhar p. 5. Duff. I, p. 342, and S. P. D. VII 40. The latter paper says that Balaji Pant Nana emigrated to the Desh country and later acquired the Peshwaship. If he had left his homeland much earlier, in Shivaji's time, how could he have established an intimate connection with Kanhoji Angria which was so helpful to him in 1713? The cordiality between the two families is also exemplified by the letters passing between them. How could Balaji establish these cordial relations with Angria if his family had long before left their homeland? Angria rose into prominence in 1698.

6. Bhat Peshwe Gharanyachi Hakikat, p. 73, MSS. record.

7. It was probably Double Government: See Khafi Khan in Elliot & Dowson, Vol. VII, p. 374.

8. S. P. D. XXX, No. 1.

9. Itihas Samgraha, Peshwe Daftarantial Mahiti, pp. 122-24, Purandare, I, No. 12.

10. Purandare Daftar I, No. 21.

11. Itihas Samgraha, pp. 124-26, and Purandare Daftar.

12. Tritiya Sammelan Vritta, (1837) pp. 86-90.

royal prisoner. In 1707 he appears to have risen to the post of Diwan of the Senapati[13], and with Khando Ballal persuaded his master to espouse the cause of Shahu who had returned to the Deccan, and thus helped his king to win his first important victory at Khed.[14] Shahu on his coronation in January 1708 conferred on Balaji the title of "*Senakarte*"[15] maker of armies, showing the high estimation in which he was even then held by his royal master. Dhanaji Jadhav died in June 1708 and was succeeded by his son Chandrasen. When a dispute broke out between the Senapati and Balaji Vishwanath, the Sovereign supported the latter as against the Senapati,[16] giving another instance of his confidence in Balaji. The fortunes of Shahu reached their lowest ebb in 1712 : he was abandoned by his Senapati ; his Sarlashkar was disaffected towards him ; Kanhoji Angria threatened to march on Satara ; and his supporter Zulfiqar Khan was no more. In this critical hour he was saved by the genius of his "Senakarte." Raising a fresh army Balaji Vishwanath defeated Chandrasen Jadhav, fought the minor rebels and for crippling the power of Tarabai, appears to have fomented a revolution in the Kolhapur camp.[17] Kanhoji Angria he conciliated later by leaving him in possession of his conquests and recognising the Konkan as his sphere of influence. As the ablest servant of the sovereign, he was appointed Peshwa in November 1713[18] and held that post till his death in 1720. He scored his greatest diplomatic triumph when he concluded the treaty with Husen Ali Sayyid, the Subahdar of the Deccan securing to Shahu Shivaji's conquests and legitimatising the

13. Rajwade, II, p. 7.

14. Rajwade, IV, p. 33 ; Peshwa Bakhar, (Sohoni), p. 3 ; Bhat Peshwyanchi Hakikat, (Bhave), p. 73.

15. MSS. records. The account of Chaskar Joshi says it was conferred on him while Shahu was conducting operations against Rangna : also S. P D. XXX 2.

16. Shahu Bakhar, pp. 28-29.

17. Kincaid and Parasnis II, p. 151 : there is however no direct evidence to prove Balaji's complicity in the revolution at Kolhapur which according to Bawda Daftar, I, occurred in 1714.

18. Shahu Rozkird, p. 42.

Maratha claims of Chauth and Sardeshmukhi over the six Subahs of the Deccan. In pursuance of this agreement he accompanied Husen Ali to Delhi,[19] had the treaty ratified by an unwilling monarch[20] and returned to the Deccan in 1719.

Bajirao was trained under his father in diplomacy and war. The education of a Brahmin boy in reading, writing, accounts and a little Sanskrit was a matter of course, and the Second Peshwa underwent this formal education. But he did not remain long confined to his books. From very early times he showed a special aptitude for the military profession and accompanied his father in several expeditions. He was with his father when the latter was tracked down like a hunted animal by the infuriated Senapati in 1710;[21] in 1716 he shared his father's imprisonment at the hands of the rebel Damaji Thorat when he had to subsist on parched rice and gur.[22] During the last two years of his father's premiership he held an important military command under him[23] and visited the Delhi Court.[24] After his return he marched towards Kolhapur.[25] He thus knew at first hand the currents and cross currents of home as well as foreign politics and was far better equipped to shoulder the responsibilities of his post than any other person at the Court when called to the Peshwaship.

The several problems that confronted the young Peshwa were a legacy of his father's policy. It had not been possible for Balaji in the short space of six years of his Peshwaship to bring the great feudatories under the effective control of the Sovereign or define their relations with the central authority closely. All over the country these chiefs raised forces, and fought and harassed the Mughal officials. Their actions to be

---

19. S. P. D. XXX. pp. 224-265.
20. The text of the treaty is given by Mawji and Parasnis, in treaties, Engagements and Sanads, No. 1.
21. Shahu Bakhar, p. 28.
22. Ibid, p. 35, and Rajwade II, p. 29.
23. Shahu Roznishi No. 108. The correct year for this is 1718.
24. S. P. D. XXX, pp. 260-62.
25. Balaji Bajirao Roznishi, Bajirao's itinerary, p. 219.

effective required to be backed by an organized authority and animated with a common purpose. By the exigencies of the situation Balaji Vishwanath had been forced to make a departure in favour of these chiefs ; they were left free to manage affairs in their conquests in return for their recognition of Shahu's authority. But it was necessary that the Royal authority, if it was to be effective, should be strong enough to override that of the feudatories and bend them to its will.

Maratha supremacy in the Deccan had been conceded by the defeated Mughals and recognized in the treaty of March of 1719. That treaty however had been concluded by the Sayyids who were out of favour with the new Emperor, and within a year their party was overthrown at Delhi and their rivals came into power. The Deccan was seized by the Nizam, the most capable among the Mughal chiefs. He was not likely to respect an agreement concluded by his opponents which made a mockery of his authority. A part of the Swaraj territory was yet in the hands of Mughal officials like the Sidi of Janjira and had to be wrested from them. The civil war with the Kolhapur party was only in abeyance, the faction of Sambhaji refusing to accept a subordinate position.

Added to this were the Maratha claims on Malwa and Gujarat which had not been admitted by the Mughal Court. As a reply to the Mughal offensive against their homeland, the Marathas had crossed into these provinces to cut off the rear of the enemy and had made inroads as far as Sironj and Kalabagh even in the days of Aurangzeb. These had been repeated with greater boldness in the second decade of the 18th century. Important outposts like Songarh had been seized in Gujarat, while in Malwa the Marathas fought the Imperial Subhadars with varying fortunes. But these attempts, not being backed by organized authority, could not produce the impression necessary to establish the Maratha claims over these tracts. The Peshwa was determined not to lose the advantage of the ground thus prepared, but to consolidate the gains and make a further advance. He had seen enough of the Mughal Durbar to convince him of its weakness. The parties anxious to dominate at the Court were bidding against each other for Maratha co-operation and the young Peshwa was too shrewd not to perceive the advantage such a situation gave him. The material necessary for making the preponderance of his state felt in the imperial councils was ready at hand. The war of liberation had taught every Maratha peasant and villager to wield a weapon and roused the martial instincts of the nation as never before. These Maratha warriors had not only withstood the enemy's onslaught, but worn him out. The time had come to carry the war into the enemy's camp ; the nation was ready for a soldier to lead its myriads of horsemen for conquest.

Thus the situation though bristling with difficulties, was full of promise. It was handled by the young Peshwa with bold imagination and consummate skill. During the twenty years of his Peshwaship he had established beyond challenge Maratha supremacy in the Deccan by defeating Nizam-ul-mulk at Palkhed, overawed the lesser chiefs by destroying the Senapati at Dabhai, recovered Maratha territory from the Sidi and the Portuguese, while in the north he laid firmly the foundation of Maratha power in the provinces beyond the Narbada, and paved the way for a further advance.

CHAPTER II

SUPREMACY IN THE DECCAN

The first serious problem that confronted the Peshwa was the security of the Maratha homeland. After a bitter struggle with the Mughals the Marathas had succeeded in driving them out and regaining their independence. But that independence was not safe so long as the enemy continued to hold posts in Maratha territory and encircle it completely. The conquered countries of Bijapur and Golconda with the subah of Daulatabad (representing the old Mughal conquests) had been consolidated into one big province and placed under a Governor from Delhi. The extent of the territory and wealth of that province made it a source of potential danger, and afforded the enemy a base from which to launch a fresh offensive against the Marathas. So long as this danger near home was not mastered and brought under control the independence of the Maratha state must always be in peril.

The war of liberation had rid the Marathas of this nightmare and the position had been further consolidated by the growing weakness of the empire. The superior claims of the Marathas had been tacitly recognised by Zulfiqar Khan when he granted them the Chauth and Sardeshmukhi of the six subhas of the Deccan: His successors—Nizam-ul-mulk (1713-15) and Husen Ali Sayyid (1715-18) who had attempted to follow a strong policy had failed miserably and the latter had found his safety in coming to an understanding with his erstwhile enemies by not only surrendering the whole of the territory in Maharashtra belonging to Shivaji (Swarajya), and recognising the new conquests made by Parsoji Bhonsle in Gondwan and Berar, but also granting their claims to Chauth and Sardeshmukhi over the revenues of the Mughal Deccan.[1] A political revolution at Delhi soon destroyed the Sayyids' party and transferred power to the Turanis: (the province of the Deccan came to be ruled by the Nizam, the ablest of the Turani or Mughal chiefs, who was unfriendly towards Maratha aspirations and unwilling to compromise with them. He was not likely to surrender his authority without a contest) and his course required to be closely watched.[2]

The Deccan had a peculiar fascination for the Nizam. Having spent his early years there in the southern campaign of the Emperor Aurangzeb, the Nizam knew no other country or people better than that of the Deccan. On the fall of Zulfiqar Khan in 1713 he was called to Court by Farrukh Siyar and was sent to the Deccan with the title Nizam-ul-mulk.[3]

1. Khafi Khan, pp. 467-8.
2. *Ibid.*, pp. 488-508 and 512-17, Irvine II, 40-9.
3. Dr. Khan's Nizam-ul-mulk, pp. 42-65, Irvine I, pp. 270-1.

The first period of the Nizam's Governorship lasted from May 1713 to June 1715 and did not pass uneventfully. It may in fact be said that the policy he later followed towards the Marathas was formulated during his first viceroyalty of the Deccan. Separated from the heart of the Empire by a long distance, the province offered great possibilities to an ambitious man and the Nizam was not slow to perceive them. The only effective opposition to the establishment of his power came from the direction of the Marathas and to check their power and keep it in effective bounds became the watchword of his policy. But the Nizam had not forgotten the lessons of Aurangzeb's fruitless campaigning of twenty-five years. He knew that the Marathas were too strong to be attacked in their homeland and he could not expect to succeed where the Emperor backed by the resources of the empire had ignominiously failed. He directed his energies to prevent their expansionist activities by repudiating their claims to the revenue of the province under his command.

He understood full well that the repudiation of these claims was a challenge to the Marathas and would involve him in a long protracted struggle with them for which he was not at all prepared. In order to divert their pressure therefore, he took advantage of the dissensions prevailing among them. His diplomacy went a long way in disrupting Shahu's authority; he was however soon recalled to Delhi and was succeeded by Sayyid Husen Ali. The Sayyid in 1718 in order to defeat the machinations of the Court sought an understanding with the Marathas granting them Chauth and Sardeshmukhi over his govt. and bowing to their superior authority.[4]

The ratification of the treaty took place in March 1719, but within a year the Sayyids' influence at the Court was completely subverted by their opponents. Nizam-ul-mulk who was then holding Malwa as Subahdar and who had long nursed thoughts of revenge against the Sayyids, revolted openly and

4. Khafi Khan, pp. 466-68.

marched south. He destroyed one army of the Sayyids at Pandhar and proceeded to face another moving in his direction.

It was at this time that Bajirao was appointed Peshwa in succession to his father. Immediately on his appointment to the Peshwaship he hurried with his contingent to join Alam Ali Khan, the Sayyids' deputy, then marching against the rebel Nizam-ul-mulk. On 9th June Bajirao effected junction with Alam Ali's troops at Sawarde in pargana Undangaon;[5] on 15th July he came up with the Nizam's troops near Pohur; on the day of the final action (a 31st July) he was posted at Nimbgaon in Pargana Balapur.[6] Despite Maratha aid Alam Khan went down before his opponent. Bajirao retired with his army intact through Khandesh and in October reduced Baramati.[7] He remained in the neighbourhood for over a month and then returned to Satara. Taking counsel with the Maharaja, he invaded the Khandesh district to collect the dues of chauth; on 4th January 1721 took place the first meeting between the Peshwa and the Nizam near Chikhalthan.[8] On 28th January the Peshwa had moved to Aurangabad and from Aurangabad he entered Khandesh. On 17th February he arrived at the westernmost point of Khandesh and in April was back again in Balaghat. The two districts were laid under contribution, and only late in June the Peshwa reported himself at the capital.[9] The party of the Sayyids supported by the Marathas had suffered a total eclipse and it was necessary not to allow the hard won claims to lapse by falling into disuse.

Bajirao repeated his visits to the Khandesh Balaghat region in April 1722 and the year after that. In the meanwhile the Nizam had gone back to Delhi to assume the office of the Vazir vacated by the death of his cousin Amin Khan. In his absence the Deccan came to be administered by his Deputy Mubariz Khan who would not conceal his dislike for the

---

5. S. P. D. XXX, p. 265.
6. Balaji Bajirao Roznishi, p. 220.
7. Idem & S. P. D. XXX, 26; also Peshwa Shakawali.
8. S. P. D. XXX, p. 266.
9. Balaji Bajirao Roznishi: Bajirao's itinerary at pp. 220-22.

Marathas, defied their claims and completely estranged them.[10] He had to pay a heavy price when two years later he fought the Nizam as a rival for the prize of the Deccan.

In 1724 affairs took a sudden and unexpected turn. The Nizam, a man advanced in years and austere in habits did not quite fit in in the gay life of the Imperial Court. His administration of affairs created for him powerful enemies among the Emperor's boon companions: his policies and actions were distrusted and when the Nizam added Gujarat and Malwa to his own charge in 1723, grave suspicions began to be expressed that he was strengthening his position with a view to overawing the Emperor and establishing a permanent tutelage over him like that exercised by the Sayyids. Without support of the Emperor, surrounded by courtiers who hardly concealed their enmity to him, the Vazir thought it wise to retire to his Deccan principality. On the pretext of ill health he left the capital and reached Ujjain in February 1724.[11]

The Emperor however would not allow him to withdraw peacefully to assume independence. He was immediately deprived of his subahdari of Malwa and Gujarat and even his deputy in the Deccan was encouraged to oppose him and destroy his army, if possible. He was egged on to this by an imperial farman appointing him to the province. It was believed that Mubariz Khan marching from Hyderabad would soon possess himself of Aurangabad, the capital of the province and from thence move northward into Malwa, where he would be joined by reinforcements from Delhi and the combined armies would then hurl themselves against Nizam-ul-mulk.

As a counterpoise the Nizam called the Peshwa to meet him near Dhar, made friendly professions and on 18th May entered into a pact with him.[12] Besides recognising the imperial grants of chauth and Sardeshmukhi of the Deccan, the Nizam agreed

10. Shahu Roznishi, 4, 9; Hadiqat-ul-alam p. 136, & Khafi Khan.

11. Khafi Khan, pp. 523-25; Irvine, II, p. 141.

12. S. P. D. XXX, p. 269 and Mss. record.

to subsidise Bajirao's army.[13] As a result a Maratha army kept the field throughout the monsoon and continued to co-operate with the Nizam.

The Nizam reached Burhanpur in May and occupied Aurangabad at the end of June 1724. Mubariz Khan also prepared for the struggle and joined by the Pathan Nawabs, advanced in the direction of Aurangabad to give battle. He manoeuvred for a position where his opponent would be unable to bring his superior artillery into action. He was however foiled by the Maratha horse under the Peshwa. They challenged his passage at every step and arrested his progress. On 30th September the Peshwa captured Mubariz Khan's outposts on the Purna and drove him to the shelter of Shakar Khera.[14] In the final action on the next day (1st October) the Khan's army was annihilated, the Khan himself being among the slain. A few weeks later the Nizam moved south and persuaded the Khan's son Khwaja Ahmad to surrender (1725 January). The roads were cleared, the turbulent element was put down, and order was soon restored. The Emperor to save his face, accepted the *fait accompli*, pardoned the Nizam and on 20th June 1725 sent him farmans establishing him in the Subahdari. The Nizam was now firmly entrenched in his position and began to weave plots against the Marathas.[15]

Before we take up further narrative a few doubts must be answered. The Nizam had declared his inveterate hostility to the Marathas during his first viceroyalty of 1713-15; his second term of 1720-21 was marked by no friendly sentiments towards his Maratha neighbours. His deputy during his absence had shown himself impatient of Maratha encroachments and had obstructed them whenever he could. During his term of office as Vazir he had shown himself a bigot—an enemy of all Hindus by pressing for the renewal of the Jaziya levy. In

13. Peshwa Rozkird mss. and Dr. Pawar's paper at the I. H. Commission, 1940 Session, pp. 204-15, Vol. XVII.
14. S. P. D. XXX, 33, 34; also pp. 270-1.
15. Khafi Khan, p. 526, Hadiqat-ul-alam, pp. 136-37.

addition to his viceroyalty of the Deccan he had Malwa and Gujarat transferred to himself. His territory thus bounded that of the Marathas on three sides and a contest with them looked imminent. Under these circumstances does it not appear strange, unwise and impolitic that the Marathas instead of trying to defeat his object, should have taken up his cause and actively helped him with men and money? All accounts agree that the Maratha horse contributed materially to the Nizam's victory. It was the Maratha cavalry that foiled Mubariz Khan's march to Aurangabad and forced him to give battle in a disadvantageous position. The Nizam was not an unknown character when the Peshwa helped him win the war. He was a veteran statesman, with whom it behoved the Marathas to deal tactfully. That he won them over to his side was a success of his diplomacy.

He had early established personal contact with the young Peshwa Bajirao, a man of imperious nature and impetuous temperament. They had met in January 1721 at Chikhalthan, and in 1723 February at Badaksha (or Bolasha?) near Jhabua. The Nizam's position as Vazir being risky, he was on the look-out for allies who could help him when the time came to withstand the might of the empire. What could be more natural than that an alliance with the Marathas or shall we say particularly with Bajirao[16] should have suggested itself to him? It was easy to win the Peshwa over by holding out promises of greater gain at the cost of the Empire. A rebel is always more liberal to his allies than the *de facto* ruler in power. He has staked his all on his rebellion and is anxious to win at any cost. If the rebel wins, the power that is defeated has to make amends to the rebel as well as to his ally; if he loses, his ally can claim nothing from him. He is thus in a position to outbid the *de jure* authority in inviting allies.

16. There is ground to believe that Bajirao had not secured the consent of King Shahu when he assisted the Nizam. See Rajwade, VI, Nos. 18, 19. Shahu's orders to his commanders are to keep themselves neutral. See Shahu Roznishi, No. 12.

Such an attempt was made by both parties—the Nizam and Mubariz Khan—in the dispute. Letters were sent to Mughal officers and Rajahs in the south to oppose the Nizam, and Mubariz Khan was authorised to open fresh negotiations to gain allies. An important paper[17] has come to light which sets forth the terms demanded by the Marathas. In addition to the confirmation of the former grants of Chauth and Sardeshmukhi of the six Subahs, the new demands stipulated for Chauth from Malwa and Gujarat, for the relinquishment of the tribute which the Raja had agreed to pay for the Sardeshmukhi claim, asked for the restoration of several forts in Maharashtra which still remained under Mughal authority, further asked for the province of Hyderabad to be made over to Fatesingh Bhonsle, for the Maratha territory taken by the Sidi to be restored, and on the top of it all, was the demand to dictate the appointment of the Deccan Subahdar. The terms were staggering, and it was impossible that Mubariz Khan could accept them ; they were rejected by the Khan. The Nizam on his side held out fair promises to the Marathas, and though their exact nature is not known there is ground for believing that in addition to recognising their former grants he agreed to encourage their claims on Malwa and Gujarat and to subsidise their army.[18] He met Bajirao at Nalcha on 18th May 1724 when negotiations were perfected and since then large sums were received by the Peshwa for his military expenses. The Nizam was intent on winning the war and had really no intention to keep his promise. His actions were soon to belie his words.

The Marathas in the meanwhile were thinking of other grandiose plans. Trusting to the friendship of their new ally they turned to utilising it for establishing their claims on the Karnatak. The Peshwa was advised by his mutaliq to settle the preliminaries of a joint Maratha-Nizam expedition.[19]

17. See S. P. D. X. 1.

18. Peshwa Diary for 1724. unpublished. Vide Dr. Pawar's paper.

19. Purandare Daftar, I, 77 ; Rajwade, VI, 22.

An army led by the Pratinidhi, the Peshwa and the Sarlashkar left Satara in November 1725 and invaded the western Karnatak marching by way of Nira Narsingpur, Pandharpur, Bijapur, Bawnagar, Bidargi, Kolhapur, and Hanumant Sagar. The petty state of Sonda was levied under contribution. The expedition arrived near Chittaldrug on 20th March 1726, and then retired reaching their own capital on 23rd May.[20] The Nizam who looked on the Marathas as dangerous rivals, had sent secret instructions to his commander Iwaz Khan to thwart their plans and obstruct the progress of their arms.[21] The hostility of their ally and the inability of the Maratha commanders to sink their mutual differences and work harmoniously defeated the object of the expedition.

The next year's expedition was commanded by the Peshwa and the Senapati, and took a more westerly route, marching right across Kolhapur territory by way of Wai, Wadgaon, Patan, Kognoli, Samangarh, Nessari, Belgaum, Rani Bennur, Sonda, Hasan and Seringapatam.[22] The convulsions in Karnatak caused by the war between the five nawabs of this region and the Raja of Mysore attracted Maratha armies to this quarter. Though terrible hardships were suffered in the march, the Peshwa succeeded in levying Chauth and Sardeshmukhi from the rulers of Mysore and Arcot.[23]

In the meanwhile events nearer home were moving swiftly to a climax. The Nizam as soon as he had triumphed over his rival began to look round for means to free himself from the shackles of Maratha demands. The first step he took in this direction was the removal of his capital from Aurangabad to Hyderabad, a place distant from Maratha territory and possessing a more centrical situation for his subah of the Deccan. Aurangabad lay on the direct route from the south to the north

20. Balaji Bajirao Roznishi, pp. 225-6.
21. Dr. Khan's Asaf Jah, p. 184.
22. Balaji Bajirao Roznishi, pp. 226-28.
23. Wilks' Mysore, Vol. I, p. 141 ; S. P. D. XXVIII, 9, 10 ; Ait. Tipanen 11, 44.

and was easily accessible to Maratha armies. Hyderabad henceforth became the capital of the Nizam.[24]

Another measure of safety that he took was to secure the territory round his capital from Maratha exactions. He successfully negotiated through the Pratinidhi for the exemption of the province of Hyderabad from chauth and Sardeshmukhi. allowing them in exchange their claims over the mahals held by him in personal jagir in the Balaghat Gangathari region.[25] The negotiations were opposed by the Peshwa, but the counsel of the Pratinidhi (who had been seduced by the grant of a jagir in Berar[26]) prevailed and the exchange of territory was effected in the beginning of 1726. Shahu had not yet fathomed the deep laid plans of the Nizam, and being himself a man of conciliatory disposition and no politician at all, he wanted to live at peace with his neighbours. He was soon to receive a rude awakening.

While the Nizam was thus secretly improving his position, the two Karnatak expeditions played into his hands. The activities of Shahu's armies in the south roused the enmity of his cousin Sambhaji of Kolhapur. Shahu did not like to be harsh towards his cousin and had so far left him undisturbed in his territory. The Kolhapur Raja had viewed the all round expansion of Shahu's power in Maharashtra with an envious eye, and when Shahu's troops crossed the Krishna, Sambhaji began to concert measures to prevent further encroachments on what he regarded as his own sphere of influence. He demanded of Shahu to define clearly their respective territories and spheres of influences. There is extant a paper dated 30th Dec. 1725 which contains the terms of a draft treaty between the two parties.[27] According to the treaty Shahu was to let the country from Wai between the Krishna and the Ghatprabha

24. Life of Shahu Chhatrapati by Chitnis. pp. 71-2.

25. *Ibid*. Dr. Khan speaks of exchanging Indapur Jagir for Hyderabad Chauth. I follow Chitnis. Indapur was given to Shahu by Aurangzeb.

26. S. P. D. X, 39 and XXX, 66 would support this statement.

27. Kavyetihas Samgraha No. 14 (1930 ed.)

remain in the possession of his cousin and share with him his southern conquests. This apparently did not satisfy Sambhaji who soon made common cause with the Nizam.

The negotiations between the Kolhapur party and the Nizam were undertaken by Chandrasen Jadhav[28] who had early deserted Shahu and sold himself to the Mughals for a jagir. A mutilated letter from Sambhaji of Feb. 1726 helps not a little to unravel the tangled skein of this plot and eminently supports the account of Chitnis,[29] wherein Chandrasen Jadhav is referred to as the "traitor." Through Chandrasen Sambhaji sent overtures to the Nizam to secure his recognition for himself as the head of the Maratha state and to oppose Shahu's all-pervading claims of Chauth. To quote the letter Sambhaji says, "I asked your aid to oppose the Pratinidhi's expedition in this quarter. The Nizam from Adoni has invited me to join him. I am stopping at Torgal to meet him. You must continue pressing my claims with the Nizam. You have rendered me great services in persuading the Nawab to break with Shahu."[30]

Sambhaji's proposals were most acceptable to the Nizam. He knew that his safety lay in fomenting civil war between his two Maratha neighbours and thus diverting and wearing out their strength. His recent friendship for Bajirao and Shahu had gained him his object ; his Muslim rival was crushed and the Delhi Govt. had sufficient trouble to engage them in Malwa and Gujarat and had confirmed his appointment as Subahdar of the Deccan. He had now no longer any use for the Maratha alliance and determined to use this occasion to shake off the hated claims of Chauth and Sardeshmukhi. He unfolded his scheme to Sawai Jai Singh in one of his letters. He wrote, "With a view to carrying out the Emperor's order I have with God's help, called to my side Rajah Sambhaji (of Kolhapur) who is Shahu's rival, conciliated him and engaged in

28. Hadiqat-ul-alam, Vol. II, p. 139.
29. Chitnis : Life of Shahu, p. 75.
30. Jadhav Gharanyachi Kaifiyat, p. 81.

punishing and exterminating Shahu. Sultanji Rao[31] who was the General of the enemy's army, came and saw me and was appointed to command Rajah Sambhaji's army. By the grace of God, I am hopeful that other partisans of Shahu would desert him for my side and his party would cease to exist according to our heart's desire." He prided himself on "having taken on his shoulders this grand enterprize than which nothing else could in the estimation of the Emperor, be a proof of his truth, loyalty and devotion. Had it not been so it was highly inexpedient for him to make a rupture with the Marathas at a time like that : in spite of the fact that in the reign of Aurangzeb the Marathas did not possess so much strength, predominance and numbers, vast treasures were spent in the war against them and mighty troops employed : and now the strength and power of the Marathas had increased beyond all limits and they had dug their claws in all imperial territory, he had challenged them to battle out of reliance on the grace of God and the Emperor's favour and aid.[32]"

Shahu had so far shown himself willing to live in amity with his neighbours. Towards his cousin he had never expressed ill-will, though he had power and resources sufficient not only to defeat him, but even to extirpate him completely. He had believed in the friendly professions of the Nizam and had only a year back consented to the exchange of his claims over Hyderabad in spite of the opposition of the Peshwa. Unaware of the dangerous alliance forming against him, he had repeated the expedition to Karnatak to complete the task left over. But as soon as the Raja's main army under the Peshwa had passed beyond striking distance of the Nizam's territories the confederates showed their fangs. The armies of the Nizam and Sambhaji began to move ominously[33] and the Nizam declared himself unwilling to abide by the pact he had recently signed

31. Sultanji Nimbalkar Sarlashkar deserted to the Nizam in 1727.
32. Mss. letter (Sir Jadunath Sarkar's collection).
33. Shahu Roznishi, Nos. 22-26, 32, 39, 212, 187.

with Shahu till, as he gave out, the dispute about the rival claims of the cousins was settled ; in pursuance of this policy he dismissed Shahu's officers and asked him to submit his claims to his arbitration.[34]

Shahu was dumb-founded ; his ablest generals were far away in the south and his enemies had caught him napping. Hurriedly he sent orders to his officers to hold to their posts, and courier after courier galloped south recalling the Peshwa and Senapati by command of the King, who had in the meanwhile been advised by the Pratinidhi to open negotiations and yield to the arbitration of the Mughal Viceroy.[35]

In keeping with Maratha character, Shahu was unwilling to effect a participation of his kingdom and share his rights with his cousin as independent sovereign.[36] The Peshwa on his arrival in May 1727 opposed the arbitration, which he easily perceived, challenged Shahu's superior authority over the Maratha state and aimed at weakening his power. On 1st August orders for a general mobilisation were given ;[37] forts were warned to be on the defensive ;[38] on the expiry of the monsoon a large Maratha army consisting mainly of light cavalry and led by Bajirao, the ablest leader and exponent of guerilla warfare invaded the Nizam's territory towards Aurangabad.[39]

As the Maratha army was plundering Jalna, the Nizam taking Raja Sambhaji with him set out to punish the Marathas. On 6th November 1727 a skirmish took place and the Marathas avoiding a contest now turned in the direction of Burhanpur. To save the place the Nizam hurried towards Burhanpur, but failed to come up with the Peshwa owing to his baggage and equipment. The Peshwa then struck in the direction of

34. Hadiqat-ul-alam, p. 138.
35. Dr. Khan's Nizam-ul-mulk, p. 185.
36. Chitnis Life of Shahu, p. 75 ; see clause to this effect in the treaty, S. P. D. XV, pp. 90-91.
37. Shahu Roznishi No. 33.
38. Itihas Samgraha, Peshwa Daftar, p. 23.
39. Bajirao's itinerary ; B. B. Roznishi pp. 228-29.

Gujarat towards the Nizam's jagirs in Surat to draw his army to a hilly country. Near Songarh he was joined by the Gujarat troops under Udaji Pawar.[40] "The Nizam turned rein from the pursuit and set his face towards Poona[41] for destroying the place of the Peshwa's abode;" his advance guard under Turk Tazkhan, Rambhaji Nimbalkar and Thorat went devastating as far as Lohgarh, but meeting with resistance fell back on Poona. By this time the main army under the Nizam came up and encamped at Anjanpur. Jawale, Talegaon, Sikharapur surrendered. Udapur and Narayangarh near Junnar were prepared for defence, but gave up at the first summons. The Nizam advanced on Poona by way of Awsari, Pabal and Khed. There he celebrated the marriage of Sambhaji with a princess of the Ramnagar Chief. Supa, Patas and Baramati were occupied and the Mughal army marched on Pedgaon when news arrived of the Peshwa having re-entered Gandapur and Baizapur parganas. Leaving his baggage in Ahmednagar (22 Feb.) the Nizam by the Kasar Bari pass retired to meet the Peshwa.[42]

The Kasar Bari route[43] passes through a mountainous region difficult for passage of an army and here the Peshwa blocked the Nizam's path. His Maratha allies on whose aid the Nawab had placed great reliance proved utterly worthless and lacking in daring and initiative.[44] Grain and forage could not reach his army and water became scarce. Avoiding a close contest for which he was but ill-equipped, the Peshwa by his clever strategy brought the Nizam into a difficult situation from which he was unable to extricate himself. On 25th Feb. was fought an engagement near Palkhed in which the Nizam was worsted, but which was not decisive.[45] The

40. S. P. D. XXX, p. 282.

41. Hadiqat-ul-Alam, p. 139.

42. S. P. D. X, 50.

43. Kasar Ghat is twenty miles due east of Manmad and the same distance North of Baizapur.

44. Shahu Bakhar, Chitnis, p. 78.

45. S. P. D. XXX, pp. 282-83. Palkhed—12 miles east of Baizapur and 20 miles west of Daulatabad.

distress of his army growing the Nizam at last sued for peace and a treaty was concluded on 6th March 1728 at Mungi Shevgaon, by which he agreed not to oppose Shahu's claims of Chauth and Sardeshmukhi over the six subhas of the Deccan and to offer no protection to Sambhaji the Kolhapur prince.[46]

The Nizam's attempt to challenge Maratha supremacy in the Deccan was defeated in a decisive manner. Maratha expansion to the south and east now became a matter of time and its legality was never called into question. The Nizam had invaded Maratha territory not to recover this province or that district, but to aim a deadly blow at Shahu's authority. By this defeat of the Great Mughal Chief the Peshwa won for himself a place of confidence in the Raja's counsels which nothing could shake. The Kolhapur prince having lost the support of the Nizam could no longer resist the superior claims of Shahu. He was defeated in 1730 and was at last persuaded to accept the position of an honourable vassal by the treaty of the Warna concluded in 1731 April.

CHAPTER III

MARATHAS IN GUJARAT

Peshwa—Senapati struggle (1700-37.)

Gujarat excluding Kathiawar forms the northern division of the present Bombay Presidency. To the north lies the Marwar desert; mount Abu and the spurs thrown out by the Aravali form the north-east boundary of the province. The east is marked by forest land rugged in the north with wide spurs of the Vindhyas, more open towards the central highway and southward again roughening into the off-shoot from the main range of the Satpuras. The hilly tract of Dharampur separates it in the south from Maharashtra, while to the west stretch the Kathiawar Peninsula and the Arabian Sea.

46. S. P. D. XV, pp. 90-91.

Gujarat was a valued possession of the Mughal Empire since its conquest by Akbar in 1573. Handicrafts and commerce were the main sources of the wealth of the province. "All the merchandise of the rich inland districts of Khandesh, Malwa, Berar and even upper India had to cross Gujarat for shipment abroad. On its coast stood the famous ports of Broach and Surat" which were the emporium of India even in 1st century A. D. They were likewise the most convenient and most frequented entrances to India for southern Asia and East Africa. "Through Surat passed the enormous volume of Muslim pilgrims to the holy cities of Arabia. Travellers, merchants, scholars, fortune-hunters and political refugees from Persia, Arabia, Turkey, Egypt, Zanzibar and even Khurasan and Barbary used to enter India through the Gujarat ports."[1] Gujarat was thus pre-eminently the 'beauty and ornament of India' as remarked by Aurangzeb in one place.

The hand of the Maratha invader fell early on this rich province lying immediately to the north of Maharashtra. Surat was sacked completely by Shivaji in January 1664 and again in October 1670.[2] In 1672 by reducing Jawhar and Ramnagar[3] Moro Trimbak extended the Maratha State till it impinged on the southern border of Gujarat. From this safe and convenient base Maratha bands occasionally carried raids into the province. The long war Aurangzeb waged against the Marathas in the south had an adverse effect on the fortunes of this tract. Unable to meet the Mughals in the open the Marathas retaliated by attacking the outlying provinces of Gujarat and Malwa. The Marathas were reported to have levied contribution on Surat in 1702 and again threatened it in 1704* ; but no major invasion

1. Sarkar's *Aurangzeb*, Vol. V, p. 426.

2. *Jedhe Shakavali in Shiva Charitra Pradeep*, pp. 22 and 25 ; Orme, mss., Vol. 263, pp. 23-24 and *English Factories in India*, Vol. 11, pp. 298-303. *Factory Records, Surat*, Vol. III p. 94. *Patra Sar Samgraha* also gives accounts from these and other sources.

3. *Patra Sar Samgraha*, 1474-77.

* *Manucci*, III, p. 491.

occurred till 1705. Late in that year Dhanaji Jadhav at the head of a strong force burst into south Gujarat, defeated the local forces and laid the country waste. The Deputy Governor sent a force against the raiders which was attacked by Jadhav near Ratanpur and dispersed, two of the Mughal commanders were captured and held to ransom ; the Mughal camp was completely plundered (15 March 1706). The Deputy Governor now advanced with another army. He met with no better fate. He was surrounded at the Baba Piarah ford and his army annihilated. Chauth was levied on the province and those towns which failed to pay were plundered by the Maratha horse.[4]

The Marathas repeated their expedition next year (1707) when they entered east Gujarat marching by way of Jhabua and Godhra where they met with little resistance. From Godhra they passed on to Mahuda in Kaira and threatened Ahmedabad. Their presence spread consternation throughout, and the Governor was glad to buy them off for a sum of Rs. 2,10,000.[5] In 1711 a Maratha force was engaged by the Governor of Surat near Anklesar and dispersed.[6]

In 1716 the Marathas won an important success over the Mughals in the Tapti region which fixed their hold on the Surat Athavisi. Khanderao Dabhade who held the country of Baglan and Khandesh under fee had built a chain of forts on the road from Burhanpur to Surat, garrisoned them and exacted Chauth from caravans passing that way. In 1712 he plundered a rich caravan of treasure escorted by Muhammad Tebrezee and had continued his career with great daring making that highway impassable unless he received the tribute. Sayyid Husain Ali, when he came to the Deccan as Viceroy could not allow this state of things to remain for long. He sent a strong expedition under his Bakhshi Zulfiqar Beg, to

4. *Mirat*, I. 379-88 & *Manucci* IV, 246-7 ; Also Sarkar, *Aurangzeb*, V, pp. 431-32.

5. History of Gujarat in *Bombay Gazetteer*, Vol. I, part I, pp. 296-97.

6. *Ibid*, p.297.

clear up the road and expel the Maratha chief. Retiring before the Mughal force Khanderao drew the luckless Zulfiqar into the wild jungles of Baglan. In the defiles the Mughal force was surprised and totally defeated. Zulfiqar Beg with a number of his followers fell on the field. "It is commonly said that not one bullock, camel or horse belonging to that army was saved."[7]

Muhkam Singh the Diwan of Husain Ali marched with another force to retrieve Imperial fortunes and bring Dabhade to book. Dabhade eluded the pursuit[8] and his posts held against the Imperialists.

In 1719 Pilaji Gaikawad, Dabhade's able Lieutenant, marched on Surat and defeated the Imperial troops commanded by Sayyid Akil and Muhammad Panah and exacted Chauth from the city from which even the English merchants were not exempted.[9] Pilaji soon established himself at Songarh[10] and began to raid the adjacent territory and lay it under contribution. He cultivated the goodwill of the border tribes of Bhils and Kolis and with their aid began slowly extending his conquests, while his master, busy in the affairs of the Court, was engaged on distant expeditions to Delhi, Aurangabad and elsewhere.

From 1719 Maratha incursions into Gujarat assumed a new aspect. In that year the Marathas had marched to Delhi as auxiliaries of the Sayyid brothers and for their co-operation, had been rewarded with the Imperial Grants of Swaraj, Chauth

7. Khafi Khan in Elliot & Dowson, Vol. VII, p. 463 & Rajwade. Vol. II, p. 28.

8. S. P. D. XXX, pp. 234-41.

9. Gaikwads of Baroda, English Documents, ed. Gense and Banaji pp. 1-2.

10. Songarh is on the western skirts of the Dang forests, about 50 miles east of Surat. About the importance of Songarh Arthur Wellesley observes :—'The fort of Songarh is most important for the defence of the Athavisi and for the security of Surat itself.' In another place he remarks, 'the districts depending on Surat can be entered by an army from the eastward only by the road which leads to Songarh.'

and Sardeshmukhi. The Swaraj grant restored to their authority the territory that was formerly Shivaji's kingdom, the grants of Chauth and Sardeshmukhi established their claims over a (25 plus 10 per cent.) share of the total revenues of the six Subahs of the Deccan. Though Raja Shahu had likewise included the cession of the Chauth of Gujarat in the draft treaty drawn up by him,[11] no concessions were obtained with regard to this demand at this time. The Imperial Court felt it was yet in a position to stave off Maratha advance in that quarter and another decade was to pass before its hands were forced. The history of Gujarat for the next twenty years is therefore the story of Mughal Maratha struggle in this region, which becomes complicated on account of the jealousies and rivalries not only of powerful Maratha commanders, but also of the succeeding Mughal Subahdars and their deputies, the powerful families of the Babis and Jhaloris, and of the Governors of Surat, Broach and Cambay.

Leaving out of account the two attacks of Shivaji on Surat it will be noted that regular Maratha incursions into Gujarat began from 1705 and the Dabhade contingent formed the spearhead of the attack. Dabhade's family had early distinguished itself in the service of the State. The founder of the family Yesaji Dabhade, Patil of Talegaon, had served in the household establishment of the great Shivaji. His sons Khanduji and Shivaji accompanied Rajaram in his flight to Jinji and were instrumental in effecting his escape when that fortress was reduced by Zulfiqar Khan in 1698. Family tradition says that Shivaji Dabhade collapsed while carrying the royal fugitive back to Maharashtra. The father escorted the royal ladies, but was unable to rescue his own family from that doomed place. On his arrival in Maharashtra in 1699 Rajaram honoured his faithful servant with the command of a paga and the dignity of Senakhaskhel.[12] Khanderao Dabhade

11. *Life of Chatrapati Shahu*, by Chitnis, p. 51, ed. 1924.
12. Dabhade Senapati Yanchi Hakikat, pp. 2-3, Rajwade, III. 166.

fought with conspicuous bravery under Dhanaji Jadhav in the battles of Ratanpur and Baba Piarah ford in 1706. In 1707 he joined Shahu's cause on the advice of Dhanaji Jadhav.[13] His loyalty was divided when civil war broke out between Shahu and Tarabai, the consort of his old patron.[14] His services in the Baglan region from 1712 to 1716 however secured him the confidence and won him the esteem of the Raja who appointed him commander-in-chief, the highest post which a soldier would covet.[15] When the father's rank was elevated in 1716 his former dignity was conferred on his able son Trimbakrao. In the December of 1716 he beat back the Sayyid's army and relieved the capital.[16] In August 1717 he led an expedition in the Mughal territory and plundered Ahmednagar.[17] His contingent distinguished itself in the Delhi expedition of 1718-19, as also in the battle of Balapur (Aug. 1720), when the Marathas fought against the Nizam as the allies of the Sayyids.

Khanderao was now advanced in years. The active life in the field for over thirty years had impaired his constitution and of late he had developed a kidney trouble. He continued to attend Court affairs in a languid manner. Though present in the Karnatak expedition of 1726-27[18] and the battle of Palkhed (1728) he was a dying man and was in no way responsible for the glorious success against the Nizam. He died on 27 Sept. 1729.[19]

From the beginning of the century Dabhade arms had penetrated into Gujarat by successive incursions and the influ-

13. S. P. D. XII, 1.

14. Iti. Samgraha, Pesh. Daft. Sanads, etc. p. 12, Aitihasik Patravyawahar, n. 5.

15. Shahu Rozkird No. 155 gives the date of the appointment of Khanderao Dabhade to the Senapati's post as 13 Jan. 1717; but from the entry in S. P. D. XXX, p. 237 it would appear that Dabhade is working in that capacity in Dec. 1716.

16. S. P. D. XXX, pp. 238-40;

17. *Itihas Samgraha*: Peshwa Daftar, p. 16.

18. S. P. D. XXX, pp. 276-7.

19. *Kesari* dated 3 March 1934.

ence of the Senapati in that region was acknowledged in the scheme of demarcation of fields of operations. Baglan and Gujarat were recognised as the special sphere of the Dabhade.[20] Though age and ill health prevented Khanderao from participating in the expansionist activities, his lieutenants were by no means inactive. In 1723 (Dec.) Surat and the adjoining territory were once more laid under contribution by Pilaji Gaikawad,[21] while another Maratha Chief entered Gujarat from the side of Dohad.[22] This was according to Mirat the first year in which the Marathas imposed a regular tribute on Gujarat. In June 1724 Trimbak Rao Dabhade was reported to be active in the Surat Athavisi.[23]

The political situation in Gujarat added to the confusion caused by Maratha incursions. During the reigns of Bahadur Shah (1707-12) and Farrukh Siyar (1713-19) except for temporary disturbances created by the border tribes and occasional raids of Maratha horse, the province remained comparatively quiet and peaceful. The fall of the Sayyid brothers and the political upheaval at Delhi changed the situation in Gujarat. The Subhadar Ajit Singh Rathor, the nominee of the Sayyids, had to make way for Haider Quli Khan (1720-22) an intrepid soldier and a favourite of the new party at Delhi. Haider Quli Khan's activities in Gujarat made him unpopular with the Court and roused the suspicion of the Vazir, Nizam-ul-mulk; he dismissed him from the province and transferring the viceroyalty to himself sent his uncle Hamid Khan to administer the territory (Feb. 1723). Nizam-ul-mulk did not long retain the governorship; he was replaced by Sarbun-buland Khan, Mubariz Ul-mulk (July 1724)[24] when he abandoned the Vizarat and retired to the Deccan. The succession

20. Chitnis, p. 47, and Duff I, p. 373 (1912 ed.).
21. S. P. D. XXX. 349, p. 371, *Bombay Gazetteer*, Vol. I. Part I, pp. 303-4.
22. This was probably Kanthaji Kadam Bande. No. 3 XIII S. P. D. would confirm this conjecture. The correct date of this paper is May 1723.
23. S. P. D. XXX, No. 354, p. 373.
24. *Irvine*, Vol. II, p. 170.

of the new Governor to his appointment was in each case contested by the retiring office-holder. The attempts of Haider Quli to raise revolt against Vazir Nizam-ul-mulk did not succeed for want of sufficient following. The Nizam's deputy Hamid Khan, however successfully challenged the new Governor and calling in the Marathas to his aid, gave him no peace for over a year. As the Marathas were involved in the contest between the retiring deputy Governor and his successor it becomes necessary to trace the narrative in greater details.

When Nizam-ul-mulk crossed the Narbada and marched into the Deccan the ruling faction at Delhi deprived him of his governorship of the two provinces of Gujarat and the Deccan, incited the local officials there to revolt against him and oppose his march. To counteract the intrigues of his opponents the Nizam advised Hamid Khan, his uncle and deputy in Gujarat, to secure the help of the Marathas by offering them Chauth of the province and resist the new regime. Hamid Khan immediately arranged terms with Kanthaji Kadam Bande who was near in Khandesh and with his help defeated and slew Shujaat Khan, the new Governor's nominee, within sight of the walls of the capital, (Dec. 1724). Rustam Ali Khan, the brother of the unfortunate man and the deputy Governor of Surat, prepared to bring to book the rebel Hamid Khan: he won over Pilaji Gaikawad for a price and proceeded to meet his adversary. In the battle of Arras on 8th February 1725 the new ally of Rustam Ali refused to fight, contenting himself with plundering the baggage of the Khan. Rustam Ali came out victorious at the end of the struggle, but his baggage being lost, was unable to pursue the advantage gained by him. Hamid Khan after his defeat retired to the camp of Kanthaji to renew the struggle. The confederates were now joined by a force of the Peshwa led by Pawar and Baji Bhivrao who had invaded Gujarat to take advantage of the utter confusion and disorder prevailing in the province consequent on Shujaat Khan's death.[25] The overwhelming superiority of numbers

25. S. P. D. XXX, No. 312.

enabled the Marathas to take the offensive. They surrounded the small force of Rustam Ali, cut off its supplies of grain and fodder and impeded the progress of its march at every step. The Khan's little force could take no shelter from the fire of the guns which daily played on it. Gradually the army melted away ; at last on 11th February at Basu, 25 miles from Ahmedabad, the remnant which attempted to fight out its way was cut down almost to a man.[26] With the destruction of Rustam Ali's force in succession to the defeat of Shujaat Khan imperial rule broke down in Gujarat. The cause of the rebel had triumphed beyond expectation and his allies, the Marathas, now shared in his triumph. The Chauth for the lands on the Ahmedabad side or north of the Mahi was granted to Bande, that on the side of Baroda and Surat to Pilaji Gaikawad, while the Peshwa's force took a share from the parganas of Sunth, Tala, Nidkavad, Jhalod and Parolia bordering on the province of Malwa.[27] Taking advantage of the unsettled condition and civil war the Marathas reaped a rich harvest and completely undermined the existing Mughal authority. They secured an influence in the province which the successive Governors were unable to shake off. With no body to control their activities or check their movements, Bande and Gaikawad went round collecting whatever they could from the undefended province. So secure did they feel themselves that they came to blows over the division of spoils near Cambay where Kanthaji defeated Pilaji Gaikawad and forced him to retire (April 1725). He then levied tribute from the town, to which the English were forced to contribute 5,000 rupees. On the approach of the rains the Marathas retired to their country promising Hamid Khan to return in the fair season.[28]

The Imperial Government could no longer remain quiescent to the loss of its authority over one of its major provinces.

26. S. P. D. XXX, 312 ; Irvine, II, pp. 170-71 ; *Bombay Gazetteer*, Vol. I, Part I. pp. 304-5.

27. Idem.

28. Surat Factory Diary II, 672, (Gaikawads of Baroda. English Documents, pp. 8-9.)

Sarbuland Khan, the new Governor was equipped with an efficient force, a large chest of 50 lakhs of rupees and was asked to proceed immediately to his charge. The province was being ravaged by the Marathas and the bordering Koli tribes were in no peaceful mood. The task which presented itself to the new Viceroy was the most difficult one : though Hamid Khan the Nizam's deputy, soon withdrew from the struggle at the instance of his master his Maratha allies had no mind to give up their hold over the province. Kanthaji Kadam saw his friend safely across the Mahi and then returned to the attack. On his way he was joined by Pilaji Gaikawad and they now set about harassing the troops of the new Governor. They plundered right upto the gates of Ahmedabad, following Cossack methods. They were however brought to bay near Sojitra in pargana Petlad and defeated by the Governor's troops (Jan. 1726). From Petlad the Marathas carried the struggle to another centre Kapadwanj where they did not fare better. Accustomed to guerrilla warfare they were unable to hold their own against regular troops. They therefore retired to the hilly country of Ali Mohan to renew the struggle.[29]

While Sarbuland Khan's troops were pursuing Kanthaji Bande towards Ali Mohan another body of the Marathas descended into Gujarat by way of Idar and laid siege to the rich town of Vadnagar. This was the Peshwa's force led by the veteran Udaji Pawar working in close cooperation with Ambaji Purandare, Baji Bhivrao and Antaji Pant Bhanu. The Viceroy had no troops to spare to fight this new menace and he capitulated by granting them for the year the Chauth previously assigned by Hamid Khan to Bande and Gaikawad.[30]

29. This account is based mainly on Irvine's chapter on "Marathas in Gujarat upto 1730" pp. 155-207 and *Bombay Gazetteer*, Vol. I, Part I, pp. 302-318. Both use Mirat-i-Ahmadi as their principal authority. References in S. P. D. are specially indicated.

30. *Bom. Gazetteer*, Vol. I, Part I, p. 307, Entry No. 105 Shahu Chatrapati Diaries ; p. 118, *Itihas Samgraha* ; History of the Pawars of Dhar, pp. 16-30.

Vadnagar paid four lakhs in ransom, but before it could settle down, it was visited by the troops of Bande and thoroughly ransacked. Umreth suffered a similar fate shortly afterwards. Bande's operations in this region met with disapproval at Satara and he was asked to withdraw[31].

With the return of the fair weather Bande took the field early in Oct. 1726. His position as well as that of Gaikawad had been assailed by the recent activities of the Peshwa's force and they were determined to resist any further attempt at encroachment and started their operations vigorously. From the irruptions of Bande and Gaikawad the Governor sought refuge in an agreement with the Peshwa. On 20 Feb. 1727 he concluded with the Peshwa's representative, on the line of the last year's pact, a treaty granting Raja Shahu through the Peshwa Chauth and Sardeshmukhi of the province on condition that the latter would take it upon himself to expel other disturbers of the peace, a clause mainly directed against Bande and Gaikawad.[32] Udaji Pawar was asked to dislodge Bande and Gaikawad. From Lunawada Bande fell back and joined Pilaji Gaikawad near Baroda.[33] Udaji Pawar advanced to meet the confederates and support the operations of the Faujdar of Baroda against them. Bande and Gaikawad outmanoeuvring Pawar forced him to retire. The Faujdar of Baroda, Sadr-uddin was no longer able to retain the important posts of Baroda and Dabhai which thus passed into the hands of Gaikawad (1727 April) and with these important posts southern Gujarat with the exception of the port of Surat came under Maratha sway. Sarbuland's force of 8000 was no match against the

31. S.P.D. XXX, No. 312 p. 276.

32. S.P.D. XV, No. 86, pp. 84-85. The full text of the treaty is printed at pp. 84-86, S.P.D. XV; the correct date of the two grants is 20 Feb. 1727 and not 9 Feb. 1728 as given by the editor. Mirat says the Governor did not consent to these proposals. But in view of several orders issued by Raja Shahu based on this treaty the statement of the author is open to doubt.

33. S.P.D. XII, 28-30: I place these papers in 1727 and not in 1729 as done by the editor. In 1729 the Peshwa was busy in Malwa and Bundelkhand, and in 1728 was fighting the Nizam.

numerous horse of the confederates and when they asked of him to confirm the grants of Chauth and Sardeshmukhi in their favour, the Governor had them transferred. Pilaji Gaikawad secured the right of realising revenue from the country south of the Mahi (Baroda side) and Bande from that of the Ahmedabad side.[34] Bande also secured Pawagarh, a place of great strategic importance which was surprised by Krishnaji Kadam.[35]

The success of the confederates was reflected in the new orders dated 1st Aug. 1727 issued by the Satara Raja granting the half share of Gujarat revenues held by Chimaji Appa on behalf of the Peshwa to Dabhade Senapati.[36] Gujarat now became the happy hunting ground for the Marathas. Imperial authority was at a low ebb. Foreign invasion and internecine war of the last three years had lowered Imperial prestige. The bordering Koli tribes raised their heads; there was utter lawlessness and disorder everywhere. Revenue ceased to flow into the treasury and with the dwindling revenues the Governor was unable to keep a large standing army. The remedies he resorted to, proved worse than the disease itself. Additional taxation made the Governor unpopular in the province; while the confiscation of estates held by Delhi nobles made him disliked at the Court. The cession of Chauth to Bande and Gaikawad added to his unpopularity. The military went in arrears and lost all sense of discipline. Maratha revenue officials spread every where for the collection of their various claims.[37]

While the Governor was reducing the Koli chiefs in the cold weather of 1727-28 he was visited by Kanthaji's agents

34. Watson in *Bombay Gazetteer*, Vol. I, Part I, pp. 308-9; Irvine II, pp. 194-96; S.P.D. XII, Nos. 28-30 and XV, No. 86. The movements of the various chiefs are so obscure owing to the scanty material that it is well nigh impossible to disentangle the maze. I have kept before me the treaty of 20 Feb. 1727 as the guiding star and have tried to fit the bits of information to suit this event.

35. *Idem*.

36. Shahu Roznishi, Entry No. 159.

37. *Irvine*, Vol. II, pp. 194-7.

and matters connected with the Chauth were settled.[38] About the same time the province was visited by the Peshwa himself in the course of his fighting with the Nizam and tribute demanded.

In 1729 December the province was invaded by Chimaji Appa with a picked force on behalf of the Peshwa. Appa crossed the Tapti at Khara Nala on 11th December, forded the Baba Piarah ford on 23rd December and on the new year's day struck at Pawagarh, then held by Bande.[39] Pawagarh capitulated within a week;[40] Bande's garrison marched out and Chimaji began his advance on the Capital of Gujarat. The Governor was just then engaged in a costly expedition against Cutch and had no reserves left to repel the Peshwa's attack. The cities of Petlad and Dholka were sacked (22 March 1730) almost under the eyes of the Governor.[41] Reports spread of Kanthaji Kadam returning with a large force to protect his claims. The situation became most alarming. Sarbuland Khan being detested at Delhi could not count on drawing support from the Court and the enemy began knocking at the door. The desperate situation required a desperate remedy and the Khan sought it in coming to an agreement with Chimaji Appa by renewing the treaty concluded in 1727 Feb. Since then the Peshwa had added immensely to his prestige by his victories over the Governors of the Deccan (1728 March,) and of Malwa and Bundelkhand in 1728 Nov. and 1729 April respectively. By granting Chauth and Sardeshmukhi once for all to the premier Maratha chieftain, the Mughal Governor hoped to escape the claims and exactions of Bande, Gaikawad and others, who were ravaging his possessions. The negotiations had been opened as early as 1726, and now backed up by a powerful force under

38. *Ibid*, p. 198.

39. Chimaji Appa's itinerary is given in S. P. D. XXX, pp. 295-96.

40. S. P. D. XXX, p. 297.

41. Gaikawads of Baroda, p. 10; Peshwa Rozkird, Mss.

Chimaji, were concluded on 23rd March 1730.[42] Sardeshmukhi or ten per cent of the whole revenue, both of the land and customs with the exception of the port of Surat and the district around it, and the Chauth or one fourth of the whole collections on the land and customs, excepting Surat and 5 per cent on the revenues of the City of Ahmedabad, were granted to the Peshwa ; it was stipulated in the deeds that for these cessions the Peshwa was to maintain 2,500 horse for keeping peace in the province ; no more than two or three persons were to be placed in each district to collect the Maratha dues, no extra demands whatever were to be made on the ryots, and every aid was to be given to maintain Imperial authority. The Peshwa was bound on the part of Shahu Raja to prevent Maratha subjects from siding with or in any way supporting disaffected Zamindars or other disturbers of public peace in the Mughal dominions, a clause, which was specially aimed at Pilaji Gaikawad, the deputy of Dabhade, who from his position at Songarh commanded the principal route from the Deccan into Gujarat and exercised great influence over the Bheels and Kolis of the country.[43]

The agreement concluded by Chimaji Appa was a bombshell to Trimbak Rao Senapati and all those who worked in his behalf. From the beginning they had detested the Peshwa's interference in Gujarat, hated the preponderance he was claiming in the counsels at the Court and had voiced their disapproval in no uncertain manner. A weak and vacillating monarch swayed by the advice of elderly courtiers then occupied

42. A summary of the agreement is given at p. 82 op. S.P.D. XV. Sarbuland Khan first granted Chauth to the Peshwa in 1726 (Shahu Roznishi, No. 105). This agreement was repeated in Feb. 1727. (S.P.D. XV, 86, pp. 84-85) and finally ratified in 1730 March.

43. S.P.D. XV, No. 86, p. 82 gives the agreement in summary. Grant Duff in his history gives it at p. 412, Vol. I, 1912 Ed. He adds in a foot-note that the original deeds from the records of the Peshwas were made over to him. The year 1729 of the conclusion of the agreement given by him is obviously a mistake.

3

the throne of Satara and this man was now called upon to give law to his warring chiefs and to pacify them. He was called upon to decide a question which would have tried the abilities of the ablest of rulers. His growing kingdom sprawling out in all four quarters was the handiwork of a band of war-lords and not his own. He had risen to authority not by the power of his sword, but by granting to his chiefs whatever they acquired by their prowess. To the present Peshwa (and his father) he was specially indebted for his exalted position, and over his activities he could therefore wield but nominal control. As premier of the realm the Peshwa claimed to hold the guiding authority over the activities of other chiefs. This claim reduced the other war-lords to a subordinate position and was naturally resented by those whose interests it affected. The Senapati became the centre of revolt for the disaffected elements and round him therefore gathered these chiefs, Pilaji Gaikawad, Kanthaji Kadam Bande, Udaji Pawar, Kanhoji Bhonsle and others. The party counted on being supported at Court by the Pratinidhi and Sumant.

The agreement with Sarbuland Khan was concluded in the last week of March and Chimaji Appa returned to Poona on 8th July 1730 and from there proceeded to Umbraj to explain to the Raja the implication of the treaty. A concession was made by assigning to the Senapati the Chauth (Mokassa) of the province and collection of a part of the Sardeshmukhi.[44] But the interference by the Peshwa in his sphere roused in the Senapati's heart burning hatred which no terms or adjustment could pacify. He challenged the Peshwa's claim of judging his acts or of interposing his authority over him.

The family account of the Dabhade Senapati puts the issue in a clear and lucid manner.[45] "Peshwa Bajirao opened negotiations with the Senapati that they should share their

44. *Grant Duff*, Vol. I, p. 412. I accept this because it is hard to believe that the Senapati was expelled from the province or altogether excluded from sharing its revenue.

45. *Dabhade Hakikat*, P. 8.

conquests in Malwa and Gujarat mutually. The Senapati declined pleading the order of the Maharaja. He said Malwa was given over to the Peshwa and Gujarat to the Senapati for conquest. He had no mind to invite others to his sphere." By his persistent efforts Dabhade had established a firm grip over the province and it was only natural he should decline sharing his influence with the Peshwa. All along he had resisted the Peshwa's insidious attempts at dividing their spheres. The first attempt was defeated in 1727 August in the life time of Khanderao Dabhade when Bande and Gaikawad drove Pawar out of Baroda and Shahu secured to the Senapati the half share claimed by the Peshwa.[46] But since then the Peshwa's position had improved immensely.

With his power increased and prestige enhanced the Peshwa returned in 1730 to the charge of Gujarat—a province that presented the appearance of an apple ripe for the plucking. The Senapati's position, on the other hand, had deteriorated comparatively ; Khanderao Dabhade had been an invalid, for the last five or six years of his life and died in Sept. 1729. His son Trimbak Rao Dabhade though an intrepid soldier, yet lacked his father's experience and prestige. Raised to the Senapati's dignity in Jan. 1730[47] he was all of a sudden confronted with the loss of his authority over his father's conquests and that stung him to the quick. Apprehending that he would get no justice from the monarch, young Dabhade looked round for means to retaliate and thought of seeking aid of the Nizam, of making common cause with the inveterate enemy of the Marathas. Proposals were sent by Dabhade to the Nizam's Court in the first week of October,[48] asking for his support against the Peshwa. The Nizam was not likely to let slip an opportunity to harm his enemy. He felt he could once more with impunity withhold the Chauth of the six Subahs of the

46. Shahu Rozkird, No. 159.
47. Shahu Rozkird, p. 78.
48. S.P.D. X, 72 ; Nos. 59-73 in this selection deal with the Dabhade-Nizam intrigues.

Deccan, take away the means which enabled the Peshwa to raise large forces and thus altogether reduce his strength without involving himself in hostilities.[49] He refused to discuss several outstanding questions with the Peshwa's agents, brought charges against the Peshwa of befriending rebels from his state and threatened reprisals.

Information reached the Peshwa of the secret intrigues between the Senapati and the Nizam and to prevent a junction of their armies he took the field early (Oct. 1730)[50] and advanced into Khandesh. Kanthaji Bande was then threatening to stop the Peshwa's collections in that district and sharp orders were issued by the Maharaja asking him to hold his hands.[51]

The Nizam marched into Khandesh on the pretext of subduing some of his rebel chiefs, but really with the intention of watching at close quarters the Peshwa-Senapati dispute. The Satara Court had been apprized of the serious state of affairs and became alarmed at the prospect of the Senapati going over to the enemy and declaring war. The Raja who had only a month back agreed to the commutation of the Gujarat Chauth for a sum of 15 lakhs of rupees consenting to the expulsion of Gaikawad, Bande and Dabhade,[52] and had seriously discussed assigning the collection to the Peshwa,[53] thought it wise to revise his decision. To appease the Senapati the Raja restored to him the collection of the Chauth of Gujarat. (15 Dec. 1730).[54] This decision of the Court had been taken under the stress of circumstances and the Peshwa refused to submit to it. Advancing into Gujarat, he met the new Governor Abhay Singh at Shahi Bag in Feb. 1731, renewed the pact concluded

49. S.P.D. X, p. 67.

50. S.P.D. X, 67, XII 42; The Peshwa's itinerary from Oct. 1730 upto 1732 is given at the end of the Roznishi of Balaji Bajirao.

51. Shahu Rozkird, No. 49.

52. S.P.D. X, 66, The Nizam's talk with Deepsingh.

53. S.P.D. XII, 39.

54. S.P.D. XXX, p. 299.

last year, "agreeing to accept 13 lakhs of rupees in lieu of Chauth ; six lakhs were paid immediately and the remaining sum, it was stipulated, would be paid on his leaving the parts and on condition that he would expel Gaikawad and Bande from Gujarat.[55] 'By this arrangement the Viceroy hoped to get rid of Pilaji Gaikawad who had entrenched himself in Surat Athavisi, while the Peshwa imagined that by driving out this able representative of the Senapati he would fix his hold over the province.[56] With a contingent of the Rajputs and Mughal artillery to assist him the Peshwa advanced in the direction of Baroda then held by Pilaji Gaikawad.

A pact was thus made with the Mughal Governor contravening the decision of the Raja and once more challenging the rights of the Senapati and his chiefs in Gujarat. An appeal to arms became inevitable. Putting himself at the head of 10,000 horse[57] Trimbak Rao marched into Gujarat (1730 Dec.). On the way he was joined by the Nizam's contingent under

---

55. Surat Factory Diary, p. 614. Daniel Innes to Henry Lowther :—7 April 1731 "Chimna Raja has lately had a very considerable advantage over the joint forces of Pilaji and Kanthaji. The former has agreed with the Maharaja (Abhay Singh) for 13 lakhs of rupees, the quarter part for all Gujarat. Six of which the Maharaja paid him down the remainder to be paid on his leaving these parts, but conditionally no other Ganim power besides Chimnaji shall enter into Gujarat, which Chimnaji promised to hinder, should Pilaji's or Kanthaji's force attempt it. Some days since they came to an engagement within 3 or 4 miles of Baroda wherein Chimnaji had the advantage. Kanthaji fled, Pilaji is wounded and run into Dabhoi fort with 2000 or 3000 men ; Trimbak Rao, a great general is killed ; Pilaji's son killed ; 4 or 5000 men killed of Kanthaji and Pilaji ; and Chimnaji is said to have lost 1000 men. 17 elephants, it is said, Chimnaji has taken with 10 camels of treasure and four or five thousand horses without their riders with their tents and baggage...... Khan's son, nephew to Chin Kilich Khan (Nizam) who, it is said, commanded 5000 Moor men belonging to Chin Kilich Khan in the lascar of Kanthaji and Pilaji, is likewise said to be killed, etc."

56. *Bombay Gazetteer*, Vol. I, part I, p. 312.

57. S.P.D. 42 XII.

Mominyar Khan and Kuwar Bahadur, and later by Bande and Gaikawad with their levies of Kolis and Bhils.[58]

The Nizam in the meanwhile was thinking of other grandiose plans for avenging his defeat at Palkhed. He felt that once he could destroy the Peshwa, he would dethrone Shahu and place his protégé the docile Sambhaji on the musnud and break up the shackles of Maratha claims that made the existence of his state precarious. Not feeling secure in the fidelity of his new ally he opened correspondence (Dec. 1730) with Muhammad Khan Bangash who had then been appointed Governor of Malwa and invited him to meet him on the Narbada to concert measures against the growing power of the Marathas. Malwa was then engulfed in the tide of Maratha advance and Muhammad Khan required little persuasion to listen to the proposal of common action against them. In the last week of March 1731 the two Governors met on the Narbada and held several discussions for evolving plans of joint action.[59]

With the Nizam's attitude clearly hostile and his army hanging on his left flank it was unwise of the Peshwa to delay the attack and allow himself to be encircled. His army though numerically inferior[60] to that of the Senapati was made up of veterans and led by such able captains as Pilaji Jadhav, Ranoji Sindhia, Dhamdhere and, others, and on Thursday 1st April 1731 he struck at the Senapati's army. The battle was sanguinary and lasted over six hours. The Senapati was seated on an elephant and led his army in person shooting arrows into the ranks of the enemy. The Peshwa led the charge on horse back. In order that his elephant might not be swept in the surging tide of the battle the Senapati had had the animal

58. Dabhade Ballad. This is the only source giving the movements of Trimbak Rao Dabhade.

59. Irvine in *J.A.S.B.* 1878.

60. Surat Factory letter of 7th April 1731 places it at 15,000; while Chitnis gives the strength of the Peshwa's force as 25,000. The enemy according to these two sources had mustered over 50,000 troops.

chained[61] and that proved his undoing. Perched on the elephant he offered an easy target to the enemy's marksmen and when the two armies closed, a bullet pierced his head and the Senapati fell dead in the howdah. With the death of the General a panic ensued, and the army fled leaving its camp standing. The defeat of Dabhade was complete.[62]

The Peshwa-Dabhade contest has become a matter of controversy between historians; one school of thought looks upon the Senapati as a rebel and a criminal, and feels that he met the fate of a traitor which he richly deserved; another would look upon the Peshwa as the aggressor who drove the hapless Senapati into the arms of the arch enemy of the Marathas. There is hardly room for doubting the existence of an understanding which extended to a full military alliance between Dabhade and the Nizam.[63] But it is clear from an examination of the evidence that Dabhade's intrigues were mainly directed against the assumption of superior authority by the Peshwa, and that the Nizam gave a willing ear to his overtures because the Peshwa represented to him the obstacle that stood between him and complete independence. He was interested in the intrigues for no altruistic motive, but only in so far as they enabled him to take advantage of the internal dissensions of the Maratha leaders, evade payment of Chauth and thus reduce the strength of his troublesome neighbour. The stand taken by Dabhade Senapati appears to be, as remarked by Duff, that "he was proceeding to protect the Raja's authority." Supposing the intrigue to be directed against the Raja, what are we to make of his attempts to appease the Senapati by sending him special

---

61. *Dabhade Hakikat, and Chitnis Bakhar*, pp. 66-68.

62. S. P. D. XII, 46. There is no proof of the Peshwa having brought about the death of the Senapati treacherously. Bhau Singh Toke was a Sardar under the Nizam and had recently transferred his services to the Peshwa. If the bullet that killed the Senapati came from one of Toke's troopers it cannot be called an instance of treachery. Beyond the statement in the family account of the Dabhade there is nothing to show that low cunning and treachery were used by the Peshwa to bring about the end of his adversary.

63. Chitnis Bakhar and S.P.D., X, 59-73.

envoys, Naroba Mantri and Purandare,[64] and restore to him the collections of Gujarat by his order of 15th December 1730? Dabhade's revolt was directed mainly against the Peshwa and not against the Crown. If the Raja looked on him as a rebel conspiring against the throne his sorrow over the Senapati's death and his attempts to conciliate the family after that event[65] must be understood to be nothing more than effusions of a sentimental heart, and place him in further unfavourable light. There is no ground to believe that the Raja had ordered the execution of the Senapati and the Peshwa merely carried out the sentence. In a letter to a Maratha Sardar Chimnaji Appa says "We killed Dabhade. What harm could the Raja do to us?"[66] Would anybody carrying out the royal sentence refer to it in this defiant tone?

The consequences of the defeat of the Peshwa would have been disastrous to the Maratha cause. The Nizam looked on Bajirao, and rightly, as the bulwark of Maratha resistance; the destruction of his power would have caused a serious split in the Maratha ranks and realised the Nizam's long cherished dreams of crippling the Maratha State and reducing it to a third rate power.

The defeat of the Senapati thus put an end to a formidable rebellion and foiled the Nizam's scheme of sowing dissension in the ranks of his enemy. Pursuing the Peshwa southward the Nawab tried to engage him near Surat, but the Peshwa's horse proved too elusive for the slow moving Mughal columns. Bajirao crossed the Narbada at Ankalesar[67] and reached the Deccan. Afraid to continue the struggle single handed the Nizam returned to his capital and soon came to an understanding with the Peshwa on several questions of policy.[68]

---

64. S.P.D. XII, 42.
65. *Br. Ch.*, App. 188 and Shahu Roznishi No. 110.
66. S. P. D. XVII, 30.
67. *Br. Charitra*, Nos. 352, 359. The Nizam speaks of having gained a victory over the Peshwa near Surat. Sarkar Mss.
68. *Siyar-ul-Mutakherin*, p. 235 (Calcutta Ed.), *Grant Duff*, I. p. 416.

While Maratha affairs in Gujarat were thus in a disorganized state Abhay Singh, the Mughal Subahdar, thought of recovering south Gujarat by a swoop on Baroda and Dabhai. Inviting Pilaji Gaikawad to a friendly meeting he had him assassinated and attacked his force on the night of 23rd March 1732. The Marathas were taken by surprise and dispersed in confusion. They abandoned the important post of Baroda and fell back on Dabhai where the enemy followed them. Unable to make any impression on the place Abhay Singh had to retire to the capital with the setting in of the monsoon.[69]

Vigorous measures were taken by Uma Bai Dabhade to avenge the death of her General. Taking with her her young sons and Damaji Gaikawad, the son of the slain General, she marched on Ahmedabad and laid siege to the place.[70] (Feb. 1733). The Maratha horse harassed the country round and cut off supplies from the capital. A Rajput of note was killed in the fighting and the Governor came to terms by agreeing to pay the Senapati 80,000 rupees from the revenue of Ahmedabad in addition to the Chauth and Sardeshmukhi of the province. Soon after this Abhay Singh retired to Marwar, leaving Ratan Singh Bhandari to carry on the Gujarat affairs as his deputy. Bhandari struggled manfully against the advancing tide of Maratha expansion, but he could not hope to succeed where better men had failed. In 1734 in the absence of its commandant, Sher Khan Babi, Baroda was surprised by Mahadaji Gaikawad, and recovered by the Marathas,[71] and it has remained in the possession of the Gaikawad family upto now. The same year Idar and north Gujarat were visited by Malhar Rao Holkar and Ranoji Sindhia who had been invited by the brothers of Abhay Singh to assist them against Jawan Mard

69. Jodhpur letters mentioned in the report of the Indian Historical Records Commission 13th Session; also Shahu Rozkird No. 161.

70. S.P.D. XIV, 1 and Br. Ch. app. 190. Also *Bombay Gazetteer*, Vol. I, part I, p. 314.

71. History of Gujarat, *Bombay Gazetteer*, Vol. I, Part I, pp. 314-5.

Khan Babi.[72] In 1735 the Chauth of the northern half of Gujarat passed to the Gaikawad after he had defeated Bande at Anand Mogri 25 miles S. E. of Kaira and expelled him from that district.[73] In 1735 December fighting between Ratan Singh and the Gaikawad was again reported ; Damaji's agent Rangoji was pressed hard and fell back on Viramgaum. Ratan Singh on being informed that another force was advancing on Ahmedabad, gave up the pursuit of Rangoji and hurried to the capital. Rangoji then marched into Kathiawar to levy tribute.[74]

The year 1737 proved still more glorious for the Gaikawad arms. The Viceroyalty of the province was transferred to Momin Khan, but this man, lacking means to effect anything by himself, called in Damaji to his aid. Damaji agreed on condition that half the revenue of the entire province was ceded to him. The terms were accepted and the confederate army laid siege to the capital. Bhandari resisted for over six months ; but at last despairing of succour, capitulated on 26th May 1737 and marched out of the city. Maratha influence now became supreme in Gujarat ;[75] the last vestiges of Mughal rule disappeared when Ahmedabad was captured by the Marathas in 1753.

The conquest of Gujarat by the Marathas was thus mainly the work of two families—the Dabhades and their assistants the Gaikawads. The later progress was directed by Damaji Gaikawad as Trimbak Rao Dabhade's younger brothers proved utterly incompetent and worthless. The life of Baburao Dabhade was that of a drunkard and the Raja's remonstrance fell on deaf ears.[76] Yashwant Rao Dabhade Senapati had no heart for fighting and showed no anxiety to lead armies. He gradu-

72. *Idem.*
73. *Ibid*, p. 316 and Shahu Roznishi, 223.
74. *Bombay Gazetteer* Vol. I, Part, I, pp. 315-18 and S. P. D. X, 93 and XIV, 43.
75. S. P. D. XII, 88, 96, 98, The Gaikawads of Baroda, p. 26.
76. S. P. D. XII, 52, 54, 65, 66.

ally faded into insignificance.[77] The Gaikawad's services were recognised by the Raja who conferred on him the dignity of Senakhas Khel after the death of Baburao Dabhade (Dec. 1736)[78]. In 1751 the Peshwa made a division of Gujarat with the Gaikawad and completely wiped out the influence of Dabhade Senapati.

CHAPTER IV

CAMPAIGN AGAINST THE SIDI OF JANJIRA

The Peshwa's first offensive

(April 1733 to Dec. 1733).

Konkan or the strip of territory lying along the west coast from Daman to Goa though separated from the Desh country by the western ghats, forms a part of the Maratha homeland and had early engaged the attention of Shivaji. He overran the northern districts then known as the Subah of Kalyan Bhiwandi as early as 1657, occupied Kalyan and drove out the Adilshahi garrison. He pushed his conquests further south where he found a powerful ally in the Sawant of Wari. But it was not till 1661 that Tal or South Konkan felt the full brunt of his armed might. In that year a powerful Maratha force marched in that country, defeated the Adil Shahi forces, reduced the rich cities of Dabhol, Sangameshwar, Rajapur and Kharepatan and established Shivaji's power in South Konkan.

The expansion of his rule in Konkan districts brought Shivaji in contact with the maritime powers of the west coast. The Portuguese then held Daman, Bassein and the island of Salsette in the north (designated by them the Province of the North) and the settlement of Goa in the south. The English had factories in Surat and Bombay. Further south were the Sidis of Janjira, the Sawant of Wari and the Dutch. While

77. S. P. D. XII, 67.

78. This is a surmise based on the papers printed in S. P. D. XII, esp. 90-95.

the English and the Dutch contented themselves with commerce and clung to their factory stations the Sidis with the Portuguese held considerable territory inland and were over a long period, locked in struggle with the Marathas.

The Sidis came from the east coast of Africa. In the days of the Bahamani Sultanate it had become a fashion to bring into India Abyssinians and other Africans and employ them in service. Brave warriors and skilful mariners as these Abyssinians—the Sidis[1]—were, their services were particularly prized by the Deccan Sultans and many of them by their courage, energy and ability rose to high positions under them.[2] When the island of Janjira was reduced by Sultan Ahmad Nizam Shah in 1490[3] he appointed an Abyssinian as its Governor, and thus began the long line of its alien rulers, one of whose descendants still holds sway over the place.[4] The situation of the district beyond the western ghats and the low state into which the Nizamshahi Sultanate fell in the later decades of the sixteenth century made the Sidi Admirals virtually independent of the central authority.

On the dissolution of the Nizamshahi Sultanate in 1636 the west coast south of the Nagothana creek was transferred to the Bijapur Sultan.[5] Adil Shah continued the Sidi admiral of Janjira in command of the coast, gave him the title of Vazir and placed the entire sea-board from Nagothana to Bankot in his charge. Thus when Shivaji came down sweeping the west coast districts in 1657 he found his way blocked by the Sidi of Janjira and had to direct his energies to the reduction of the Sidi's power. Though Janjira could not then be taken, a large

---

1. A corrupt form of Sayyids.

2. Malik Ambar, so famous in the history of the Deccan, originally was a Sidi slave. For the origin of the Sidis see Kolaba Gazetteer, pp. 432-4 ; Orme, Hist. Fragments, p. 56.

3. Bombay Gazetteer, XI, Kolaba, pp. 433-34 and Ferishta III, 198-9. Local tradition says it was treacherously captured from Rama Koli.

4. For the early account (not very reliable) of the Sidi Governors of Janjira see Bharat Varsha, and Ferishta.

5. Aurangzeb I, p. 38 ; Cambridge History IV, p. 267.

part of the Sidi's territory was seized and he was fenced round by a ring of fortlets at Birwadi, Tala, Ghosala, Surgarh, Sudhagarh and Rairi.[6] The campaign was renewed two years later when the Sidi lost practically the whole of his land possessions[7] from which he drew his sustenance. Throughout his reign Shivaji directed his energies to reduce the island castle of Janjira and ferret the troublesome neighbour, but for want of an efficient artillery and a strong navy, failed to make any impression on the place.[8] About 1670 when the Sidi was in his last straits he transferred his allegiance to the Mughal and thus secured powerful assistance in his struggle with the Marathas.[9] In 1673 the Sidi recovered Danda Rajpuri from Shivaji and advanced in the interior 'burning Tull and other great towns of Sevagees'.[10] In 1675-76 Shivaji renewed his

---

6. Shivapur Daftar Yadi in Shiva Charitra Pradeep, p. 50, and Shiva Bharat, 48, 58. The Yadi contains the laconic entry that in July (Shravana Shud 1) 1657 Raghunath Pant went to Rajpuri. But in Shiva Bharat Afzul Khan while recounting the aggressions of Shivaji is made to say ..." you have surrounded the Lord of Janjira." Jedhe while noting the capture of Kalyan, Bhiwandi in Oct. 1657, makes no reference to the progress of Maratha arms further south that year. Pissurlencar in his Shivaji tells of the Governor of Goa having strengthened the garrison of Cheul in the cold season of 1657 owing to the disturbances caused by Shivaji in the northern districts. Also Ali Adil Shah's farman dated 16 June 1659; Sabhasad p. 66 (1923 ed.).

7. Shiva Bharat, 18, 48, 58; English Factories in India, X, (1655-60), p. 250, ... "promising that if we would lye with our ships before Danda Rajapore castle, that Sevagyes men should assist us ashore, hee having already taken the town of Danda Rajapore, but not the castle". (10 Dec. 1659). Revington to the Co.

8. Patra Sar Samgraha 791, 848, 959, 1268, 1314, 1317, 1395, 1409, 1416, 1418, 1420.

9. Khafi Khan, p. 290; Sir Jadunath while accepting the account of the revolution at Janjira expresses doubt about the date. In 1672 the Sidi is referred to as the admiral of the Mughal, P. S. 1512. Also Fryer I, p. 249.

10. Khafi Khan, p. 292, and F. R. Surat, Vol. 106, pp. 25-7. According to Dr. Balkrishna [Shivaji III, pp. 320-4] the account of the recapture of Danda Rajpuri is greatly exaggerated by Khafi Khan.

attempts to take the place, but met with no better success than in his previous attacks.[11] To circumscribe the Sidi's power he fortified in 1679 the neighbouring island of Khanderi and in 1680 built another castle at Kolaba.[12]

Unable to meet Shivaji in the field, the Sidi chiefs made descents on his coastal towns, burnt standing crops and laid waste the country side. Misusing the hospitality of the English at Bombay they often used it as a base from which to sail up the Nagothana creek and ravage the lowlying tracts on the mainland opposite Bombay, seize the peasantry, decapitate them or often sell them into slavery. The Maratha navy vainly attempted to get at the Sidi, but returned discomfited owing to the heavy keels of the Sidi's fleet and superior gun fire.[13]

Aurangzeb's advent in the south in 1681 excited the Sidi to commit great excesses on Maratha territory. In December of that year he burnt the town of Apta on the Patalganga. Sambhaji, resolved to root him out, came down to Rajpuri with a force of 20,000 in January 1682 and for a month shelled the castle of Janjira continuously from a nearby height. Unable to reach the island he tried the mad project of filling the narrow strip of water that separated it from the mainland. The Mughal invasion of North Konkan obliged him to turn elsewhere leaving only a small force to press the operations. After his departure the siege was abandoned.[14]

The fall of Raigarh and the disintegration of the Maratha state following the death of Sambhaji in 1689 considerably strengthened the hands of the Sidi. Not only did he recover his former districts wrested from him by Shivaji, but in addition he was put in possession of the important fortresses of

11. P. S. 1645-6, 1779, 1791, 1866.

12. P. S. 2118-37, 2144, 2147, 49, 2154, 2164, 65, 2208 and Cheul Chronicle in Rajwade III, p. 510.

13. Sabhasad 68 ; P. S. 1575, 1579-80, 1585-86 etc : Orme, Hist. Fragments, pp. 107, 109, and MSS. 3779, 3870 quoted by Sir Jadunath Sarkar in his Shivaji at p. 268.

14. Orme, His. Fragments, p. 110 (1805 ed.) also Sambhaji Charitra by Chitnis, Itihas Samgraha, Junya Ait. Goshti.

Raigarh, Mandangarh, Anjanwel and Ratnagiri. In the struggle that raged to the north of Rewdanda creek between Mughal troops under Matabar Khan and Maratha garrisons at Sagargarh, Rajkot and Pali, the Sidi fought on the side of the Mughal and seized the two important ports of Rewas and Thal which enabled him to dominate Maratha shipping in the Pen river and at Kolaba. The inland forts in the subah of Cheul were occupied by the Mughals and it was only the daring and energy of Kanhoji Angria that kept the Maratha flag flying aloft at Khanderi and Kolaba and obliged the Subahdar to share the revenues of the province with him.[15]

In 1701 a determined attack was made on Alibag by the Sidi. The Bombay Factory recorded on 14th January that "the Sidis lately had several hot skirmishes with the Marathas who are very strong........ The Sidi having blocked up by sea the entrances to Kanhoji Angria's castle, he being then abroad with his gallivats, took his opportunity whilst he was thus employed to the southward, to come to Thal and lay it waste with other places and continues in these parts plundering and carrying away booty and people ; he had with him 40 gallivats ; the Marathas have demanded half the revenues of Matabar Khan's jurisdiction, which he at first withstood but at last granted them 1/3rd. So at present he sits quiet."[16] On 6th March it was reported that the Sidi was lying full before Kolaba and Kenery.[17] The attack was beaten back but good understanding had not been restored in April of 1701 when a skirmish between the two parties took place and the Sidi having suffered greatly in casualties called for a surgeon from Bombay to treat his wounded.[18] In 1714 a joint assault by the Sidi, the Portuguese and the Mughal Subahdar on Angria's territory was defeated with the assistance of Peshwa Balaji Vishwanath.[19]

15. Cheulchi Bakhar in Raj III, p. 511, Aurangzeb V, 150-55.
16. Secretariat Outward letter-book VII, pp. 110-1.
17. *Ibid*, 132.
18. Sec. Out. letter-book VII, p. 140.
19. Shahu Maharaj Yanche Charitra p. 40, Rajwade II, pp. 23-25.

The treaty of 1718 concluded by Husain Ali with the Peshwa while recognising Shahu's right to the Swaraj (the conquests of his grand-father) did not immediately put him in possession of all the territories comprising it. It left him free to recover them from local Mughal officials, some of whom especially in the outlying provinces, had dug themselves in and refused to surrender without a struggle. The Konkan by the pact concluded by Peshwa Balaji Vishwanath with Kanhoji Angria in 1714 February[20] had been recognised as the exclusive sphere of Angria's operations. Though Kanhoji had successfully held his own against the Sidi he was unable single-handed to wrest the Swaraj territory from his grasp.

On Kanhoji's death in July 1729 events began to move rapidly. The guiding hand of the great Admiral being removed it was decided at home to strengthen royal authority in that quarter. The time chosen was most opportune ; the Nizam, the representative of the great Mughal, had been worsened in the contest with the Marathas at Palkhed and had been forced to abandon his ally, the Kolhapur Raja ; that prince who had challenged Shahu's supremacy finally gave up his claims by the treaty of the Warna and accepted the position of an honourable vassal. The rivalry between the Peshwa and the Senapati, though it ended disastrously for the Senapati's party, roused against the Peshwa almost national resentment and united against him the entire court, from whom the Peshwa could find protection only in the benignant influence of the throne. The King's prestige rose high ; his authority became supreme and he now chose to direct the nation's arms to the conquest of Konkan which had remained outside Swaraj territory in spite of Imperial grants and which Kanhoji had been unable to wrest completely from the Sidi's stranglehold single-handed. The Sidi's power from Janjira as centre had spread in a fan-like fashion and had thrust itself almost to the foot of the western ghats, covering the entire Kolaba district with the exception of

20. Treaties, agreements & Sanads, Edited by Mawjee and Parasnis, p. 197.

Pen and Alibag taluks and reaching Chiplun and Anjanwel in the south. His territory thus included Raigarh, the capital of the great Shivaji, a place of sanctity to the Marathas, which their racial pride and national honour would not allow them to be left in the hands of an alien. The expedition therefore was not of the nature of a new adventure but was directed to the recovery of Maratha patrimony that had been lost to the enemy during the interregnum of Sambhaji's death and Shahu's succession.

On his father's death Sekhoji Angria succeeded to the Admiralty receiving the investiture robes on August 5th, 1729.[21] He immediately yielded to the pressure from Satara and agreed wholeheartedly to support the expedition against the Sidi with his fleet. The attack on Janjira was, however, delayed by dissensions in the house of Angria. There was rivalry and ill-feeling between Sekhoji and his younger brother Sambhaji ; the latter was impatient of any authority and chose to remain away when the Admiral visited his liege-lord at Satara in 1731.[22] The conquest of Konkan was canvassed at Court and in consequence Bajirao visited Alibag in February, 1732, which visit was returned by Sekhoji in April next.[23] In December of the same year rapprochement with the Nizam was effected by a friendly meeting and plans were matured for surprising Janjira. The negotiations were entrusted to Yashwantrao Potnis who succeeded in seducing Shekhji, a powerful Sidi Sardar. Shekhji promised to transfer his allegiance to the Marathas on condition that he was put in command of the fleet, given a large portion of the territory under Janjira, and his brother appointed second in command at Raigarh.[24] While the Marathas were preparing

21. S. P. D. XXXIII, No. 1 ; Raja's order of bestowal is dated 21 July 1729.

22. Rajwade, Vol. III, Nos. 242, 244.

23. *Ibid*, 255. In Rajwade III, 10 there is a significant statement ये साली निश्चये उतरतात, from which the conclusion that the expedition was under discussion for some time.

24. S. P. D. XXXI, No. 165, Shahu Maharaj Charitra, p. 88, Duff., p. 427, Vol. I, 1912 Ed.

to strike at the enemy their plans were suddenly pushed forward by the death of Sidi Rasul of Janjira (February 1733) and the split among his commanders about the successor. The Sidi's eldest son Abdulla was murdered and his grandson Abdur Rahman fled to the Marathas for protection.[25] This was the opportunity the Marathas were long waiting for. An army of five thousand under the Peshwa accompanied by Fatesingh Bhonsle as royal representative was directed to descend into Konkan and deliver a blow at Janjira. Another under the Pratinidhi was to attack the Sidi's southern possessions. The Peshwa marched with a war chest of Rs. 28,000 by the shortest route through the mountainous Bhor country by way of Pali, Kolar near Surgad, Sikare, arrived before Rajpuri on the last day of Baishakha, (2 May 1733) completing his arduous march within a week.[26] The suddenness of the approach of the Marathas completely surprised the enemy. Rajpuri and Khokri on the mainland surrendered without striking a blow, as also the Sidi's fleet lying in the port.[27] Shekhji, the powerful Sidi Sardar, walked over to the Marathas and with him the Peshwa sat down at Bala Roza at Rajpuri[28] to conduct the operations of the siege.

The plan that had been suggested to the Peshwa and accepted by him for reducing the place was to secure the co-operation of the Angrian navy and attack the island castle of Janjira from land and sea. Shekhji, the Sidi's right hand man, was in the Peshwa's camp ready to guide the ships in the waters round Janjira. With the enemy's ranks split up, it was expected that his resistance would soon crumble and the castle pass into Maratha hands.

"The fortified island of Janjira lies just within the en-

25. Shahu Bakhar, p. 89, and Bom. Co. to Court of Directors dated 14 April 1733.

26. Bajirao Ballal Rozkird Mss.

27. S. P. D. III, 2. Purandare Daftar I No. 104 and Forrest, 'Home Series', Vol. II, p. 52, also Bom. Co. to Court of Directors, dated 18 Aug. 1733.

28. S. P. D. III, No. 2, XXX, No. 322.

trance of the Rajpuri creek, the mainland being half a mile distant to the east and a mile to the west. In shape it is irregularly oval, and is girt by walls which at high tide rise abruptly from the water to a height of from forty-five to fifty feet. On the east side opposite Rajpuri is a large and handsome gateway with steps leading to the water and on the west facing the open sea a small postern gate. The walls are battlemented, strongly loopholed and have their faces covered with nineteen bastions eight feet across and thirty feet deep, at intervals of about 90 feet."[29] The passage from Rajpuri to the castle was covered by artillery making the enemy's approach well-nigh impossible. The castle had weathered several attacks of the great Shivaji and had successfully stood two long sieges. Its capture could be secured only by an artillery that could silence its guns and blast away its walls or by a complete blockade that would starve out the garrison till it surrendered. The Peshwa followed different methods. As the opposition was disorganised he chose a strategy of lightning rapidity marching up to the castle before the enemy was aware of his presence and storming the place. On his way to Rajpuri he had invited Sekhoji Angria to meet him at Pali,[30] to devise plans for supporting his attack with the fleet.

The response of Angria was disappointing. Though the expedition was under discussion for some time Sekhoji was unaware when exactly he would be called upon to co-operate in the enterprise. When messengers from the Peshwa arrived, a part of his fleet was away south organising the recent conquest of Ratnagiri and the Admiral had to plead his inability to support the Peshwa before Janjira. The Arabian sea is particularly violent during the early months of the monsoon—May to July—when all small crafts are hauled ashore. The Admiral refused to risk his fleet in the dangerous waters.[31] Shekhji, the Sidi's Sardar, who was expected to take the Marathas inside the

29. Kolaba Gazetteer, p. 462.
30. Brahmendra Charitra, p. 48.
31. S. P. D. XXXIII, Nos. 10, 29.

fort could achieve little.[32] The two main props of the scheme having proved unreliable it had to be reviewed and revised.

Yielding to repeated advice from the Peshwa the Admiral at last met him on May 6th at Rajpuri and in personal discussions that lasted over a fortnight new lines of operation were devised.[33] The grandiose plan of the swift and total destruction of the Sidi and the establishment of Maratha authority on the entire sea-board appeared to Angria as chimerical. On the contrary he advocated an altogether different plan of action. According to him the Peshwa's force was to remain encamped before Janjira and watch its land communications. The Pratinidhi, he advised, should exert pressure at Anjanwel. He himself after bringing his ships ashore would negotiate with the Portuguese and the English to secure their neutrality and employ the monsoon months in reducing Thal, Revas, Chaul and such other coastal points from which the Sidi drew provisions and sent raiding parties to plunder his towns and villages. After the abatement of the monsoon his fleet would assault the isolated Underi island : his rear thus secured the Angrian fleet would then sally forth to the attack of Janjira.[34] Frankly Angria's vision was bounded by his small territory of Kolaba the security of which appeared to him his primary concern. In the drive against the Sidi he envisaged the opportunity of possessing himself of the several points of vantage from which the Sidi had long molested his territory.

Unused to sea-warfare, the Peshwa found himself in a strange atmosphere and unwillingly acquiesced in the new strategy proposed by the Admiral. While these discussions were progressing the enemy was not idle. The creek connecting the castle with Dighi and Rajpuri being left unguarded the Sidi garrison managed to secure provisions by means of its ships, made a bold front and absolutely declined to treat with the

32. Kavyetihas Samgraha, No. 22.

33. Purandare Daftar I, No. 104 and S. P. D. XXXIII, 11 and 15.

34. S. P. D. XXXIII, 15.

Marathas except on its own terms.[35] After a month's warfare the Peshwa saw the hopelessness of a rapid victory and realised that the enemy could be subdued only by an effective blockade by land and sea. The force he was commanding was unequal to the task and unless sufficiently augmented and aided by the navy could never hope to beat the enemy down to his knee. He therefore informed the authorities at Satara that his position was untenable unless assured of ample resources in men and money which he estimated at 15,000 infantry, half of which was to be armed with matchlocks.[36] Well aware of the weakness of the Marathas in this particular arm and the incapacity of the royal authority to organise effective measures he advised the King to abandon the expedition and patch up a treaty with the Sidi on his own terms,[37] or if the project was to be persisted in, to assist him adequately bearing in mind the magnitude of the project and the difficulties of the situation. Swift came the Maharaja's replies to hold on while reinforcements would pour in the Konkan through the southern passes, and through Bhor, from the Sawants of Wari and Gaikawad of Guzarat.[38] How empty these assurances were the Peshwa was to realise in the course of the campaign. A small force under the Pratinidhi, however, left the capital on its way to Janjira.

The Peshwa in the meanwhile was not having an easy time. The inland forts of the Sidi that had been abandoned on the approach of Maratha troops were now occupied and garrisoned by detachments from the small force the Peshwa was commanding, which was further reduced by desertions on account of the inclement weather of the Konkan. Outposts were established at Danda, Rajpuri, Nanivali, Kumbharu, points from which the Sidi was suspected of drawing provisions.[39] To seduce the garrison of Janjira the Peshwa was advised by

35. S. P. D. XXX, 95, XXXIII, 18-9.
36. Purandare Daftar, I. No. 102.
37. Purandare Daftar, I, 106.
38. Kavyethihas Samgraha Patren, etc., 22, Shahu Roznishi 58-9.
39. Purandare Daftar, I, 106.

Shekhji to declare that his intentions were limited to secure the succession of Abdur Rahman and establish lasting peace between the two neighbours.[40]

Capture of Raigarh.

The fort of Raigarh, perched on a spur of the Sahyadri, had been chosen by Shivaji as his capital for its particular situation and natural strength. After its surrender to the Mughals in 1689, Aurangzeb had transferred it to the Sidi for his valuable services in the war and since then it had remained in his undisturbed possession for the last 44 years. One of the main objectives of the present expedition, its surrender had been secretly negotiated by Yashwant Rao Potnis. A small force of 800 was detached by the Peshwa to exert pressure and occupy the place.[41] The garrison made overtures for surrender. The news unfortunately leaked out and the party that was carrying the treasure to be paid to the agents at Raigarh was surprised and plundered by Sidi's men.[42] The Peshwa could ill-afford to satisfy the demand from his own slender war-chest and wrote to Satara to supply him with funds to forward his negotiations. Before replies were received from Satara the Pratinidhi had arrived at Mahad (25 May), made fresh overtures through another channel and stole a march on the Peshwa by occupying for himself the place on 8th June.[43] The capture of Raigarh was hailed at Satara as a great exploit winning for the Pratinidhi warm praises from the Maharaja and the entire Court. While the Pratinidhi won laurels for his success the Peshwa remained encamped at Rajpuri, helpless before the barrier that lay between him and the island fort and chafing that his rival should have snatched from him the fruit of his labour.[44]

The occupation of Raigarh by the Pratinidhi cannot be ac-

40. S. P. D. XXX, 95.
41. S. P. D. III, No. 4. XXXIII, 27.
42. S. P. D. XXXIII. 20, 29, XXX. 95.
43. S. P. D. III, 7. According to XXX, 95 Fatehsingh and Baji Rao desired the Pratinidhi to meet them at Rajpuri : Purandare in 107 tells us that he avoided meeting the Peishwa.
44. Rajwade VI, 86 Purandare I 105.

claimed as a brilliant military feat. Neither the small detachment despatched by the Peshwa, nor the entire force of the Pratinidhi could have carried the place by assault, even if they had sat before it for a complete year. The Sidi was weak on land and had retired before the advancing waves of Maratha troops. Raigarh was isolated when its communications with Janjira were severed by the establishment of a Maratha outpost at Pachad. But the garrison could have held out if they had the will to do so. The place was too strong for the small Maratha force operating against it. But where Maratha arms would have failed their money and intrigues succeeded.

The success at Raigarh instead of forwarding Maratha plans gave a definite set-back to the entire project. The secret methods pursued by the Pratinidhi for defeating the Peshwa's plans exasperated the latter and widened the breach already existing between them. The Peshwa vowed vengeance against his old rival for refusing to meet him at Rajpuri and following him at Raigarh. The concealed enmity of the two was fanned to white heat and vitiated the future conduct of the campaign. Instead of joint action and co-operation there were to be complaints and counter-complaints and frustration of each other's plans.[45]

Angria opens the offensive in the north.

As decided in their discussions at Rajpuri Angria opened the offensive in the northern sector by capturing the Mughal post of Rajkot at Cheul, where Sidi's men often found shelter in their cruises from north to south. A detachment under Tukoji Kadu while on its way to the Peshwa's camp at Rajpuri, came across a party of the enemy commanded by Sidi Anol, followed it up to Rajkot, and successfully stormed the place destroying the last vestiges of Mughal power in Kolaba (2 June 1733).[46] The attack of Thal and Rewas next engaged the attention of Angria for which he begged the Peshwa to aid him

45. Rajwade VI, 86, S. P. D. XXXIII, 38, 48, 62, III. 19, 21, etc.

46. S. P. D. XXXIII, 22, 23.

with a few cavalry dreading the enemy's ravages in the country round Pen when his troops would be engaged at Thal.[47]

Thal is about six miles north of Alibag and had a small square fort 100 by 80 with a gate facing north. It was from this place that the garrison of Underi drew its provisions of food and water and was therefore peculiarly valued by it. Guns from the island covered it, and laid the attacking force open to a murderous fire. At this time the outer works were protected by a wooden palisade and by two bastions which commanded the gateway. Owing to rough conditions at sea the occupants of the garhi could obtain no aid from outside and were helpless before superior numbers.

About the 1st July arrived the cavalry detachment from the Peshwa under Keshav Lingoji and Anandrao Shirke. Two days were spent in perfecting the preparations for the attack and the small force moved on Wednesday at the dead of night towards its objective. Thursday morning revealed the attacking force to the garrison, who welcomed them with a brisk fire supported by artillery from the island. The shells burst in Angria's force wounding many and killing a horse the Admiral was riding. Braving the fire the men dug trenches in the sands and prepared batteries—three on the southern and one on the northern side and began to reply the enemy's fire. The outer works were soon demolished and the guns from the bastions silenced, the gunners all this while being exposed to the fierce fire from Underi. On Friday two more guns were drawn to the northern side and placed in position. On Saturday the whole day long a steady fire was maintained from both the batteries and worked havoc inside the walls. Two Sardars of note and a dozen soldiers were killed and many wounded. Realising the post could no longer be held, the enemy under cover of darkness escaped in boats to Underi setting fire to the magazines inside. Thal fell on Saturday, 7th July.[48]

Even more remarkable was the success of the detachment

47. S. P. D. XXXIII, 30, 37, 39.
48. S. P. D. 58, XXXIII.

sent against Rewas. The party left at night and reaching the little port within a few hours, scaled the walls and completely surprised the inmates of the garhi (4th July.). A few soldiers who offered resistance were cut down, but most of them were allowed to make good their escape.

Angria was now free to direct his arms against the last citadel of the enemy in his sector, the island of Underi.* The Maratha garrison on the nearby Khanderi island was instructed to watch the movements of enemy ships and prevent their egress or ingress. Batteries were prepared on the mainland and began sending shells in the direction of Underi when on 15th July twelve ships were sighted approaching the island. Angria's first surmise was they were the Sidi's vessels carrying succour from Surat to the beleaguered garrison and instantly the shore batteries opened against them. The surmise however proved false; the ships flew English colours and were carrying the British expeditionary force for the relief of the island.[49] The Bombay Government apprehending that "it will be impossible for any small embarkation or ships of little force bound to this port to escape Angria's gallivats, and consequently an end to the greatest part of their country trade" had decided "to use their utmost endeavours to prevent the island and fortress of Underi falling into the enemy's hands by succouring the same." Consequently an expedition consisting of two ensigns, four sergeants, four corporals, forty European musketeers, sixty topasses and a train of artillery, provision and warlike stores sailed under convoy of the 'Mary' on the 15th July, arrived off Underi on the 16th; taking a survey of the place and estimating it tenable they proposed to the Killedar the hoisting of the English flag, to which the Killedar agreeing to, the English flag, was accordingly hoisted on the 16th in the morning under the discharge of the artillery of the fort and the gallivats.

The Underi reversal.

* Underi, Khanderi or Henery, Kenery, sister islands to the south of Bombay.

49. S. P. D. XXXIII. 63-65.

when Angria from Khanderi and his batteries from Thal began and continued to fire pretty briskly at the fort of Underi for that and the several following days, but without doing any damage. On the 18th the gallivats and boats returned to Bombay with the families of the garrison."[50] Rather than let the island fall into the hands of the Marathas, the Sidis had invited the English to occupy it and hold it for them.

The occupation of the island of Underi by the English at this particular moment was clearly an infringement of international law. They justified their conduct by the exigency of the situation. With Rewas, Thal, Khanderi and Underi in his hands, Angria commanded the whole shipping of Bombay and was thus in a position to threaten the entire trade of the Company in western waters. By securing Underi from the Sidi the English had forestalled Angria. His agents were already in Bombay negotiating for the neutrality of the English and this was their reply to his request for their neutral attitude. The English clearly showed how little they valued Maratha friendship when their interests were threatened.

On the heel of the occupation of Underi news reached Angria of a dangerous combination between the Sidis, the English and the Portuguese;[51] that the transfer of Underi was the first outward sign of this alliance and that the allies were waiting for the monsoons to abate when they would open their counter offensive against him. The Portuguese, according to this plan, were to attack the Angria near Cheul, and the English at Kolaba. Pressure at these points, it was thought, would oblige Angria to recall his detachments from Rajpuri and Anjanwel : Janjira would be relieved and the allied force would then land at Rajpuri and attack the main Maratha army.[52] To counteract this dangerous move Sekhoji suggested to the Peshwa to lend him a strong detachment of cavalry, to call reinforcements from Satara ; while his two fleets—the Kolaba

50. Forrest, Home Series, Vol. II, p. 54.
51. S. P. D. III, 23.
52. *Ibid.*

and the Gheria Squadrons—would effect a junction and put an end to the blockade at Kolaba; and possibly would invade Bombay which would then be denuded of troops.[53]

Whatever Angria's ideas of fighting the combination might have been, the English occupation of Underi cramped his efforts for a time. For since the island passed into their possession Sekhoji ever remained in apprehension of an attack from Bombay or Underi and was unwilling to march his men to Rajpuri and send his fleet against Janjira.[54]

The rumoured formidable combination however did not materialise immediately. Angria's envoys returned to Kolaba reporting that the English ever desired to live in amity with their neighbours and bore no hostility to the Angria.[55] The main condition on which they would agree to a lasting and permanent peace was that their merchant shipping should have a free passage, and that Angria should surrender his rights over the western waters of giving pass-ports. Awaiting the results of the negotiations, it is worth while watching the progress of events in the southern sector.

The southern Maratha force was commanded by the Pratinidhi and had arrived at Mahad on 25th May,[56] that is, exactly a month after the Peshwa had sat down before Janjira. Its first spectacular success, the occupation of Raigarh, had been achieved without firing a shot on June 8th.[57] From Raigarh the Pratinidhi had been directed by the Maharajah to march against Anjanwel, the Sidi's stronghold in the south.[58] Any attempt against Anjanwel without first reducing Gowalkot left the rear of the investing force open to attack. Gowalkot, besides, had assumed special importance on account of its vicinity to the holy shrine of Parashuram, a place sanctified by its association with Brahmendra Swami, the Raja's religious pre-

53. S. P. D. III, 24.
54. S. P. D. III, 50-52, 62.
55. S. P. D. III, 34, 42.
56. Kavyetihas Sangraha, No. 22.
57. S. P. D. III, 7.
58. S. P. D. XXXIII, 28, 38.

ceptor. The southern army was expected to capture these two places, and once for all free Parashuram from the persecution and humiliation it had suffered from Sidi Saat, the Gowalkot Commandant. The Pratinidhi marched towards Chiplun (of which Gowalkot was the port) exhorting Angria's officers to co-operate with him.

In this region Angria had already a small force of about 1,500 operating under two very capable officers, his Diwan Raghunath Hari and Bakaji Naik Mahadik.[59] The Sidi's possessions comprised Mandangarh, Bankot, Gowalkot, commanding the trade of Chiplun and the strong fort of Anjanwel at the mouth of the Vashisti, hardly 25 miles from Gowalkot. As the Sidi's main force was hard pressed at Janjira by the Peshwa, the occupation of these isolated out-posts appeared a matter of comparative ease. Bankot and Mandangarh fell at the first onslaught and passed into Angria's hands before the end of May[60] and the conquest of the remaining places looked imminent. Vijaygarh on the northern bank of the Shastri river and facing Jaygarh, was invested on 24th May by Bawaji Mhaske. Mahadik with a picked force of about 500 had turned towards Gowal to protect the temple of Shree Bhargava at Parashuram from desecration ; beating back a party of the enemy that had ventured near the place he advanced near the fort to engage the enemy at close quarters. A hasty reconnaissance of the place however showed that without artillery the investment of the place was futile. Bakaji therefore called for heavy guns from Jaygarh to prosecute the siege with vigour. It was some time before the guns bombarding Vijaygarh could be removed to Gowal. Vijaygarh was stormed on 6th July[61] but before the besieging party could reinforce Mahadik's small force, the Sidi collecting together the remnants of the defeated garrisons of

59. Purandare, I, 104.

60. Br. Ch. app. 203 informs of the reduction of Bankot and Mandangarh ; also Purandare Daftar, I, 104, S. P. D. XXX, 95.

61. Rajwade III, 305 ; S. P. D. XXXIII, 66 gives the date as 30th June which is confusing.

Anjanwel, Vijay and Gowal, came down and attacked him on the 8th. The situation was critical ; Mahadik's detachment was heavily out-numbered and for a time it looked that the day was lost. A small party of the Pratinidhi that had previously joined Mahadik fell back in disorder. The brave Mahadik, however, rallied his men to another attack and drove back the enemy.[62] The Pratinidhi who had then arrived at the close of the day at Parashuram witnessed the fighting and hoped to win fresh laurels with the co-operation of Angria's force. On the next day Mahadik was joined by the reinforcements from Jaygarh and the fall of Gowalkot looked imminent.

Things had progressed satisfactorily so far. The Sidi's opposition was fast crumbling. The enemy now received aid from an unexpected quarter. The intrigues set on foot by the Peshwa vitiated the whole situation : the Pratinidhi's advance in the Anjanwel quarter was looked on with disfavour by Angria, who imagined that the former's success in that region would deprive him of a valuable part of the sea-board in the division of spoils. His views were encouraged by the Peshwa who was embittered by his failure against Janjira, and by the Pratinidhi's late conduct towards him, especially in stealing a march over him at Raigarh. A suggestion had been made to the Peshwa by the Admiral that he should detach a part of his force to co-operate with the Angrian troops in the attack of Anjanwel. The Peshwa had readily assented, but when later he found that the Pratinidhi had advanced in that quarter, he not only withheld his detachment, but advised Angria to instruct his southern force to defy the Pratinidhi's authority and refuse joint action with him. Angria had made himself subservient to the Peshwa's views and at once acquiesced in the suicidal policy. He instructed Mahadik and other officers to decline co-operation with the Pratinidhi, and to abandon the siege of Anjanwel if the latter should arrive at the place with his force. The instructions reached the Naik just at the moment when he had perfected his arrangements for an attack

62. S. P. D. XXXIII, 57, III, 15, 16.

on Gowal, and the Naik in spite of admonitions from the Rao withdrew,[63] leaving the Pratinidhi to carry on the siege single-handed. So far went the Peshwa's desire for revenge that he despatched secret agents to the Sidi Commandant encouraging him in his resistance against the Pratinidhi.[64]

Mahadik had been repeatedly advised to refuse any kind of assistance to the Pratinidhi and to withdraw from the scene of action, should the latter persist in seeking his collaboration. The Naik made plain his attitude and advised the Rao to proceed against Anjanwel and not hamper him at Gowal. The Pratinidhi, well aware of his own inability against the doughty enemy, set aside the Naik's plan and persisted in joint action against both places and occupying them in the name of the Maharajah. The Naik was bound by his instructions and had no other course left than to march back his men to Suvarnadurg.[65]

Shriniwas Rao Pratinidhi, who ever prided himself on his skill in diplomacy, invited the Sidi Commandant of Gowal, Sidi Saat, to a personal meeting (14 July) and advised him to accept of the Maharaja's service when he would be reinstated in his command.[66] Sidi Saat pretended himself anxious to take the Raja's service which he was prevented from doing by fear of the Angria, and desired that as the first preliminary the Angrian force should be withdrawn from its threatening position. The Naik had already prepared to abandon the siege; his march back was hastened by the Pratinidhi's anxiety to win the Sidi to his side. When the condition for surrender was thus automatically fulfilled Sidi Saat showed his fangs. He declined going to Satara to make his submission to the Raja, said he would deliver the place after four months thereby making it plain that he was biding his time.[67] The Rao at

63. S. P. D. III, 15, 19, 21, 36, XXXIII. 62, 69.
64. S. P. D. III, 21, 60, 61, Raj. VI, 86.
65. S. P. D. III, 10, 15, 19, 21 ; Raj. III, 330.
66. Rajwade III, 330.
67. S. P. D. III, 21, 25.

last realised he had been duped and prepared for laying siege to the place.

Reinforcements were called from Vishalgarh, the Rao's native fort, and arrived at Chiplun on 30th July and on the very day of their arrival successfully assaulted one of the Sidi's outposts. The news was carried to the Pratinidhi at Parashuram who ordered his entire force to attack the place from the northern side. His troops crossed the creek, and went right up to the ditch encircling the fort on the north. Here they were furiously counter-attacked by the Sidi's garrison and driven back Heavy rains swelled the creek and added to the miseries of the defeated force.[68] The Pratinidhi reported his plight to the Maharaja beseeching him to aid him with fresh troops and directly charging the Peshwa and the Angrian chiefs[69] for complicity with the enemy and attributing his failure to their intrigues.

The Rao's further progress being impeded for want of cruising vessels he approached Sambhaji Angria, the Admiral's brother, to aid him with his ships and called further reinforcements from the Raja.[70] While the Marathas were awaiting relief, the Sidi on 5th August once more led his men and delivered another surprise attack on the outpost stationed near the mouth of the creek. Tambat and Amolik and about twenty-five men were cut down, the rest retiring to the main camp with the loss of their colours and drums.[71]

The Pratinidhi now pressed forward his negotiations with Sambhaji Angria agreeing to whatever demands the latter chose to make. While the negotiations were yet under discussion the High Admiral died ; Sambhaji Angria abandoning the negotiations proceeded to Kolaba to take the command of the fleet. The Rao apprehending that Anjanwel would be the grave of his reputation, made a last desperate attempt to take the place. He threatened to lay waste Angria's territory near

68. S. P. D. III, 38, 45.
69. S. P. D. III, 39, 98.
70. S. P. D. III, 45.
71. S. P. D. III, 47, 54.

Suwarnadurg[72] if the Angrian force should still persist in its policy. On 23rd September the Rao scored a small success over the Sidi when the latter attempted another lightning raid on the Maratha lines. The point where the attack was delivered was held by Chavan's veteran troops. As the Sidi's infantry sallied forth crossing the moat they were overpowered by Maratha horse and beat a retreat to the castle.[73]

The final general attack on Gowalkot came on 5th October, Friday morning, early at dawn. Yesaji Gaikawad, Dhanaji Thorat, Sidoji Barge and the Huzarat troops crossed the north trench and marching to the left attacked the Sidi's first outpost. As they advanced, the fort opened a murderous fire on the party. Another party under the Rao's brother and Baburao Karhadkar advanced from the right. Before the two parties could join in an attack on the main gate, five ships of the Sidi landed a party of desperadoes at Kasi Bandar and the assaulting Maratha force was caught between two fires, defeated with heavy loss and forced to retire. The division under Himmat Bahadur and Yamaji Shivdeo that was to attack the place by descending from the Kalikesar hill on the west, never made its appearance, and another under the Pratinidhi that had been assigned the task of holding the landing place fled at the first appearance of the Sidi's galbats, thus enabling him to land reinforcements. The detachment under Gangadhar and Mahadaji Ghatge sent to surprise Anjanwel achieved no better results ; it simply marched and counter-marched.[74]

Thus ended ignominiously for the Pratinidhi his campaign in the Konkan. An army of three thousand had kept the field for nearly six months without one remarkable achievement to its credit. A small garrison had defied the efforts of an army six times its number by mobility, clever counter-strokes and diplomacy. By October 25th the siege was raised and the Pratinidhi was back in the capital.[75]

On other fronts affairs, though not so bad, were in a condi-

72. S. P. D. III, 55.
73. S. P. D. XXXIII, 105.
74. S. P. D. XXXIII, 115.
75. S. P. D. III, 102.

tion of stalemate. We had left Angria negotiating for the neutrality of the British. Convinced that the British would not directly support the enemy by attacking him in the rear and urged to activity by the frequent representations of the Peshwa to aid in his attack on Janjira from the sea Sekhoji prepared to sail south with his fleet. Before however the fleet could leave Kolaba and engage the enemy, the Admiral was in his death throes. The constant exertions and strain of the campaign told upon his frame and gave rise to high fever accompanied with bleeding from the nose. After a short illness of a week the Admiral Sekhoji expired on August 28th, 1733[76] and with his death faded all hopes of speedy victory over the Sidi. Consternation and gloom spread among Angria's garrisons and outstations. The detachment co-operating with the Peshwa at Rajpuri lost all heart for the fight and showed signs of weakening. The news quickly spread to enemy quarters, who heralded it by shelling of Angrian positions and destroying their outstation at Nanivali.[77]

Still more disastrous were the effects of the Admiral's death on the Peshwa's plan of campaign. All the while he had remained chafing at the inactivity enforced on him. He saw enemy vessels prowling in and out of the creek in the rainy weather and remonstrated with Angria for the inactivity of his fleet and the lack of spirit shown by him.[78] When in this state of suspense the Raja called from the Peshwa his views about the progress of the campaign, he reported back that unity of command was the first essential for success and that the presence of three different forces working independently of each other merely frittered away the national resources, instead of helping the joint result.[79]

While impressing upon the Satara authorities the need of a united command and of ample reinforcements he showed himself sceptical of Angria being able to hold his own against a

76. S. P. D. III, 70-78. 77. S. P. D. III, 83-87, 99.
78. S. P. D. XXXIII, 46, 49, 61.
79. S. P. D. XXXIII, 42, 43, 77, 79, III, 43.

combination of the English, the Portuguese and the Sidi, not to speak of taking the offensive. He advised the Maharaja to accept overtures of peace received through the Nizam if the Sidi, in addition to the conquests already in Maratha hands, was prepared to concede Anjanwel and Underi, contenting himself with the island forts of Janjira and Padmadurg.[80]

While affairs were in this state the news of Sekhoji's death reached him. It had been settled between the Peshwa and the Admiral that the long deferred attack on the rock island was to be delivered on the closing of the monsoon. This had to be now definitely abandoned on account of the impossibility of securing the support of the navy. The Angrian fleet lay idle at Kolaba awaiting the arrival of its new master, whose relations with the Peshwa were none too friendly. Between Sekhoji and his successor Sambhaji had existed a long standing feud[81] which the latter had not the wisdom not to introduce in politics. The only policy he understood and had followed so far was to range himself on the side of his brother's enemies. As the Peshwa had shown himself partial to his brother he was an object of particular execration to Sambhaji as were all his brother's loyal servants, Raghunath Hari and others. Without an efficient artillery to cannonade the castle's communications and a navy to enforce a complete blockade, the attack on Janjira could never succeed.

The Peshwa, of course, did not yield without a struggle. On learning of the death of Sekhoji his first steps were to convey assurances of sympathy and encouragement to the Admiral's garrisons and out-stations and to call to his presence his Diwan to hearten the Rajpuri detachment. Fresh batteries were opened against Janjira and messages were sent to the new Admiral inviting him to Rajpuri for a personal meeting.[82] Sambhaji shamelessly told the Peshwa's envoy "his brother

80. S. P. D. XXXIII, 79.
81. Sekhoji refers to this in S. P. D. XXXIII, 29, III, 68.
82. S. P. D. XXXIII, 106, III, 102.

was a friend of the Peshwa, not he !"[83] On the 21st the envoy wrote back to his master that Sambhaji declined visiting him just now, and frankly gave it as his opinion that hopes of securing the support of the navy were slender in view of the recent changes at the Admiralty.

To the Janjira that was to be blockaded and starved by the Marathas was brought succour by a strong complement of English ships under Capt. M'clean—a strange spectacle was this—the English for political reasons aiding their erstwhile enemy the Sidi, while the Angrian navy that was planning to join in the attack on the fort for three months never put in its appearance on account of the failure of the High Admiral to forget his personal animosity towards the Peshwa. A fitting commentary on Maratha Politics !

The Peshwa's despatch of 27th October[84] definitely marks the end of the offensive. Bajirao put it finally to Sambhaji to define his attitude to the struggle and asked him if there was any chance of the navy co-operating with him at Janjira. With the opening of the seas succour was pouring in Janjira from Surat, from the Portuguese and from the English. An English fleet took up a menacing position in the Rajpuri creek.* The Anjanwel and Gowalkot garrisons relieved of pressure, now prepared to embark for Janjira and the superiority in number and equipment passed to the enemy. Bajirao's pressing appeals drew from Sambhaji only formal replies.[85]

The Peshwa realising the hopelessness of the situation now gave a willing ear to the offers of the English for mediating in the dispute. The Satara Durbar was prepared for ending the war and asked the Peshwa to learn from the English the Sidis' terms, while it opened direct negotiations through its

83. S. P. D. XXX, 99, 100 84. S. P. D. III, 102.

* The Sidi signed a treaty of offensive and defensive alliance with the English in Dec. 1733 which however did not much affect the fortunes of the war. The treaty was mainly directed against Angria.

85. S. P. D. XXXIII, 117.

envoy Anand Rao Sumant. The envoy left Satara for Rajpuri on his mission of peace on November 4th.[86] Truce was declared and on December 1st Abdur Rahman, the Peshwa's nominee, was seated on the Janjira masnad. The preliminaries were settled, the Peshwa agreeing not to claim beyond what was then in actual possession of the invading force.[87]

The results of the first Offensive.

Thus ended the Peshwa's offensive against Janjira : as a result the Sidi was driven back to the sea ; with the exception of a small strip of territory the Marathas were masters of his land possessions ; Raigarh, the capital of the great Shivaji, was recovered ; Thal, Rewas, the Sidi's out-posts in Angrian districts from which had descended roving bands to plunder villages and towns fell in Angria's hands, as also Cheul, commanding the Rewdanda creek. The Sidi's possessions dwindled to his rock islands Janjira, Underi and Anjanwel and Gowalkot in the south. Abdur Rahman, the Maratha nominee, was recognised as the successor. The back of the enemy's resistance was broken and it was a question of mere time when he would be completely liquidated. The Sidi's strength had lain in his connection with the Mughal Govt. and in his island castles. The Mughal power having suffered a total eclipse in the south, could no longer aid their Sidi feudatory : it was his island retreats that saved the Sidi from total annihilation and it was round these forts that the struggle raged during the next three years.

86. S. P. D. III, 103.
87. S. P. D. XXXIII, 131 ; the Peshwa returned to the capital on 11th Dec. 1733 (S. P. D. XXX, p. 328).

CHAPTER V

JANJIRA CAMPAIGN, II.

The Siege of Gowalkot and Anjanwel.

(1734-35)

The Peshwa had marched away from Rajpuri before the conclusion of the treaty, the details of which were left to be worked out between the envoys of the Sidi and the Maratha Court.[1] "Some days afterwards Sidi Saat and Sidi Masud embarked a sufficient number of troops on board their fleet and laid siege to the port of Bancote about 5 leagues to the southward of Rajapore, garrisoned by Angria's force, which being attacked by the Sidi's fleet and some batteries from the shore Angria's people in the night deserted it and made their escape to Suwarnadurg : the Sidis having put a sufficient garrison therein they proceeded up the river to Mahad formerly belonging to them, but taken by Shahu Raja's troops who were then in garrison. This fort they took without much opposition and some others of less consequence in that neighbourhood.

"Flushed with success they sent a detachment to besiege Raigarh which had been likewise taken by Shahu Raja's troops.

"On the news of the Sidi's success against Bankot and Mahad reaching the Raja's Court the Peshwa was severely censured for his hasty retreat out of the Sidi's territory and he was ordered to march back with his army."

"On this Bajirao wrote the President a letter complaining of the Sidi's impatience and rashness in the enterprise while he was endeavouring to bring the Rajah to consent to an accommodation and he desired the President to prevail with the Sidis to lay aside the thought of besieging the fortress."[2] But

1. S. P. D. XXXIII, 131.
2. Bombay Letter to Court of Directors, dated 1 Feb. 1734 (Mss.).

before the letter could reach Sidi Saat, the Maharaja roused to activity by the threat to Raigarh had ordered a strong force of the Huzarat troops (3000) to march to the relief of the beleagured fort.[3] The force, supported by the levies of Pawar the Sarlashkar, Hindurao and others of smaller note, marched down in Konkan in early January ; near Pachad it was joined by the Peshwa's contingent of 500 troops under Baji Bhivrao. Against this strong column the Sidi detachment besieging Raigarh was no match. It was surrounded, attacked on 10th Jan. (1734) and completely destroyed. Its leader Sidi Ambar Afwani was slain and the rest fled in the direction of Mahad. Raigarh was relieved.[4] So highly was the possession of Raigarh prized by the Raja that he directed the place to be garrisoned by trusty Maratha soldiery, relatives of Deshmukhs in Satara and Poona districts.[5]

After the relief of Raigarh the Maratha force halted at Pachad for about a week and then descended the ghaut towards Mahad. On arriving near Mahad, it found the enemy strongly entrenched and remembered the guns left behind at Pachad. On a representation to the Raja orders were issued to move five pieces of artillery from Pachad to support the attack on the enemy's position.[6]

While this attack on Mahad was developing, information reached Sidi Saat of another Maratha force preparing at Satara to strike against his stronghold of Anjanwel, where it was expected to be joined by Sambhaji Angria.[7] The communication between Mahad and Anjanwel now became unsafe and uncertain owing to the surrounding country being overrun by Maratha horse and Sidi Saat wisely fell back on the latter place by way of Bankot without offering battle or suffering

3. S. P. D. XXXIII, 149, 152.
4. S. P. D. XXXIII, 149, 150, 152, 161.
5. S. P. D. XXXIII, 157, 164.
6. S. P. D. III, 173 and XXXIII, 158, 160, also Rajadnya's letter in Br. Ch. pp. 54-56.
7. Br. Ch. pp. 56-7, S. P. D. XXXIII, 163.

loss. By February 24 Mahad passed in the possession of Marathas[8] who followed the retiring enemy to Bankot. The latter place was carried by assault on 8th March[9] and was put in command of Baji Bhivrao of the Peshwa's contingent. Men and material were sent down from Satara to repair the defences and put the place in a position to hold against surprise.[10]

Having cleared Raigarh, Mahad and Bankot of the enemy, Maratha forces now converged on Gowalkot and Anjanwel, the strongholds of Sidi Saat. The Huzarat troops under Rajadnya and Pawar pushed on from Mahad towards Gowalkot while Jiwba Chitnis led the second force against Anjanwel.[11] The interval of four months since the Pratinidhi's retirement in October of last year had been taken advantage of by the enemy to increase the natural strength of the defences of the two places, throw in provisions and make them almost impregnable. He also secured material aid from the English and the Portuguese who now patrolled the sea near Gheria and prevented the Angrian fleet from putting out to sea.[12] Its water communications open, Anjanwel laughed at Maratha attempts to blockade and surround it. It was against these places that the Huzarat troops, ill-equipped for siege operations, were to match themselves. Cavalry was expected to hurl itself against a foe entrenched behind strong walls and overawe it with numbers. The contest was on unequal terms : superiority in numbers instead of adding to the strength of the besiegers, increased their difficulties of securing provisions in the barren tract round Gowal and Anjanwel.

8. Purandare Daftar I, 100 ; the correct date of the paper is 24 Feb. 1734.

9. S. P. D. XXXIII, 256.

10. S. P. D. XXXIII, 173, 185, 175.

11. Chitnis reports his operations in S. P. D. XXXIII, Nos. 182, 184, 189, 202 ; No. 188 speaks of Baburao of the Huzarat troops having left for Gowalkot from Mahad ; also see III, 9.

12. Sambhaji Angria's letter in Br. Ch. pp. 56-7 and Pub. Dept. Diary, Vol. VII.

The 1734 expedition repeated the mistakes of the last year. The Raja persisted in retaining the direction of the expedition in his own hands ; while he remained in the capital, the forces sent into Konkan, made up of small contingents of several feudatory chiefs, owed allegiance to no one common commander. The Sarlashkar's troops fought under Anand Rao Somvamshi, Hindu Rao's under Appaji Somvamshi, the Peshwa's under Baji Bhivrao and Mankar, while the Huzarat troops were commanded by as many as four captains, Hari Moreshwar Rajadnya, Shaikh Mira, Lingoji Hawaldar, and Deorao Meghashyam—the Daroga of the artillery. These gentlemen were mere courtiers—carpet knights—none possessing qualities of leadership. Udaji Pawar broken in spirit and health accompanied the force to retrieve his fortune. A strange group marched against a doughty enemy who had only four months back worsted the Pratinidhi and obliged him to retire in disgrace. Not one understood the difficult nature of the enterprize he had been sent upon and none had the sense to trust in the superior wisdom of another. The expedition was doomed to failure as was proved by results.[13]

Batteries were erected and the first assault on Gowalkot was delivered on 31st March, but not being supported by heavy fire, was easily repulsed by the Sidi.[14] Artillery was called from Satara and Bankot. The Raja sent five pieces, issued orders that one piece from every fort should be supplied to the besieging force and interested himself in the casting of guns.[15]

Sidi Saat now began using the old tactics that had worn out the Pratinidhi's strength and forced him to abandon the siege. On 9th April under cover of the fire of his guns he sallied and attacked Maratha batteries. He however met with

13. S. P. D. XXXIII, 158, 160, 163.

14. S. P. D. III, 9 ; XXXIII, 167. The correct date of the letter is 1st April 1734. No. 9 of Vol. III is also written a day or two after 1st April.

15. Idem ; and S. P. D. XXXIII, 205.

stiff resistance, the Angrian division, Bhapkar and the Huzarat troops counter-attacked and forced him to retire to the walls.[16] He proved more successful in the second sally made by him in May. The besiegers had been reinforced by Dabhade's troops and the superiority in number gave them a false sense of security.[17] Emerging in the dusky light of evening he fiercely attacked Maratha lines, killing Baburao Joshi and other officers of note and wounding many.[18] The besiegers were thrown in confusion and became too dispirited to continue operations any longer. By 15th May Hari Moreshwar realised full well how very difficult was the enterprise set before him and his own incapacity to execute it. He retired to Satara[19] and his return was a signal to the troops to disperse. When the Rajah became aware of the slow fading away of the investing force he issued orders asking the commanders not to return, but remain in cantonment at Chiplun ready to commence operations at the next favourable season. In response a remnant of the force lingered on at Chiplun, powerless to engage the enemy at close quarters or succeed in blockading the place.[20]

Things at Anjanwel too had not prospered according to plan. The second force under Jiwaji Chitnis arrived before the place on 1st April and was joined by a strong Angrian detachment.[21] Taking a position on the Veldur side it opened batteries and began shelling the walls. The Angrian fleet which was to aid in the attack gave a slip to the patrolling ships of the enemy and sailed upto Anjanwel and opened fire against the castle. But as ill luck would have it, a violent storm blew on the next day and obliged it to seek the shelter of Gheria.[22] The possibility of developing a simultaneous attack from land and water was lost, the vessels being no longer able to take to

16. S. P. D. XXXIII, 183.
17. *Ibid.* 193.
18. Idem. also Nos. 203-4.
19. S. P. D. XXXIII, 202.
20. *Ibid* No. 205, 206, 163.
21. S. P. D. XXXIII, 182, 184.
22. S. P. D. XXXIII, 189.

sea on account of the violent gales that now set in. The Angrian force under Mhaske and Mirza Yar Beg vainly opened a cannonade against two important bastions, Halkeshwar and Haldi, commanding the water-front :[23] the enemy secure within the walls replied to the Maratha guns with superior artillery lent by the English. Chitnis called fresh reinforcements from Satara in the hope of assaulting the place, but the reinforcements never came.[24] May with its long and weary hot days came and the chances of Maratha victory were as remote as on the first day. Raising the siege Chitnis retired to the Capital in June.[25]

Operations against Gowalkot and Anjanwel in the next season (1734 Nov.—1734 May) were delayed and hampered by a civil war that broke out in the Angrian house. In Dec. 1734 Manaji Angria who was at Kolaba, suddenly fled to Rewdanda and raised the standard of revolt against his brother. Angria's hereditary enemies, the English and the Portuguese, welcomed the opportunity of weakening their rival, and immediately took up Manaji's cause. The Portuguese soon retired from the contest, but Manaji called in the Peshwa to his aid and forced his brother to agree to a humiliating treaty by which Sambhaji was driven out from the vicinity of Bombay to remain content with his southern possessions, which were altogether inadequate to support him and maintain his supremacy at sea.[26] With his attention thus distracted, Sambhaji was in no mood to take part in the operations against Gowalkot.

The Raja's hopes of succeeding in the operations however, lay in conciliating Sambhaji and securing his co-operation—especially the support of his artillery.[27] He renewed his representations and persuaded Sambhaji to aid the besieg-

23. Idem. 24. S. P. D. XXXIII, 189.

25. S. P. D. XXXIII, 204, 214.

26. For the civil war in the Angria family see Kavyetihas Samgraha Patren Yadi no. 23 (1930 ed.). S. P. D. III, 112 ; XXX, 113 and XXXIII, 147, 159, 165, 245, 264, 274, 437. Also Public Dept. Diary, VII, consultation dated 22 Nov. 1734.

27. S. P. D. XXXIII, 238, 259.

ing force at Gowalkot. Sambhaji yielded so far as to order Bawaji Mhaske Killadar of Jaygarh to support the operations against Gowalkot. Mhaske arrived at the Kalusta hill (to the north of Gowal) on 14th April (1735) and started about his job in right earnest. Guns were laboriously drawn up the Kalusta heights and began pounding the walls. So well directed was the fire that some of the shells landed inside the castle and set on fire a few houses. But Mhaske's strategy required that the cannonading should be carried on simultaneously from the three heights that closed on Gowalkot so that the enemy should not be able to take cover in any direction. This point was altogether missed; the Huzarat troops remained inactive at Dhamni and failed to support the attack. The men were ill supplied with provisions and military stores and the attack petered out. The heavy monsoon that set in, in June put a stop to all military activities and caused a general sickness among the besiegers. The enemy's communications with the outside world remained intact from the Dhamni side, from which he threatened the Maratha rear as far as the Kumbharli pass. One after another the chiefs abandoned their advanced positions and went into cantonments at Chiplun.[28]

CHAPTER VI

THE JANJIRA CAMPAIGN, III.

The Last Phase.

(October 1735—February 1737.)

The Angrian detachment under Mhaske had taken post at Kalusta and had lingered there for over six months. It commanded but one of the channels leading inside the fort of Gowal: the other passage required to be similarly watched. It was however weakly held by the Huzarat party and re-

28. Operations of 1735 are reported in S. P. D. III, 116-17, XXXIII, 53, 190, 259, 389.

mained open enabling the enemy to provision the garrison. Despite protracted operations the enemy showed no signs of weakening. The stubborn resistance of the inmates wearied the patience of the besiegers. In the interim, the neighbours of Angria, the Kolhapur Raja and Bhagwant Rao Ramchandra of Bawda began creating disturbances in his territory which had been denuded of troops. Disgusted with his colleagues' incapacity, lack of understanding of military strategy, want of spirit and the languid manner in which the siege was carried on by the Huzarat commanders, Mhaske took advantage of an alarm raised by the approach of the enemy, destroyed his batteries and broke up his camp. (Oct. 1735).[1]

The Huzarat commanders expostulated in vain with him. At Satara there were heated discussions about rushing reinforcements to the place.[2] A small force of 500 marched under Yamaji Shivdeo to sustain the fading spirits of the besiegers. Govindrao Chitnis and Bhaskar Waidya were deputed to remonstrate with Angria for the indiscreet conduct of his detachment and persuade it to resume the operations. As his reward the promises of redressing the wrongs he had suffered from his brother and restoring Kolaba to him were renewed.[3]

But there was a serious reason for Angria's disquiet and for recalling his detachment. Sidi Saat being now in the lowest extremity represented to the English that he would be obliged to surrender to his enemy if they denied him material aid. The English apprehending such a development now came forward to mediate in the dispute, at the same time sending a powerful fleet to demonstrate against the Angrian coast line. Their ships were joined by Portuguese vessels ; the appearance of the squadron cruising off Anjanwel and threatening his defences (Suwarnadurg, Vijaydrug, and Jaygarh) so alarmed Sambhaji as to oblige him call back his troops. Ba-

1. S. P. D. III, 123, 165.
2. S. P. D. III, 123, 165, 124 ; XXXIII, 326, 333.
3. S. P. D. III, 123, 167 ; also XXXIII, 313, 327, etc.

waji Mhaske in spite of all the protests and promises to the envoys withdrew to Jaygarh.[4]

The withdrawal of Mhaske had an immediate effect on the Huzarat troops. The commanders losing heart, fell back on Chiplun and requested the Rajah to allow them to evacuate the place and return home. On November 9th Sidi Saat arrived at the place carrying strong reinforcements and marked the occasion with discharge of guns.[5]

In the wake of the abandonment of the siege by Maratha troops ominous reports began to reach the Darbar. Sidi Saat who had so far contented himself with defending his positions, now began to act on the offensive. Riding boldly from Anjanwel he descended on coastal hamlets belonging to Angria, burning and pillaging them as he went.[6] Sambhaji Angria had all along felt that his interests had been neglected, that he had been outwitted by the Peshwa and ill used by the court. Chafing at the shabby treatment meted out to him and alarmed at the enemy's gathering strength he openly came out with offers of peace which the Sidi welcomed. Sambhaji offered to restore to the latter the places taken from him on condition of securing his co-operation in an attempt on Kolaba.[7]

The Angrian opposition having been liquidated, Sidi Saat became free to hurl himself against other vital Maratha positions. He chose Bankot for his attack. Turning back, on 2nd December 1735 the Sidi landed near Kelshi and made a feint against Mandangarh. With Sambhaji Angria unfriendly and the enemy operating at no great distance, the Bankot garrison was a lonely post ; fearing to be surprised it sent out urgent appeals for aid. Before however any relief could reach the place, the joint fleets of the English and the Sidi pounded it from the sea ; the Sidi soldiers stormed it and occupied it on

4. S. P. D. XXXIII, 327.
5. S. P. D. XXXIII, 334 ; III, 126.
6. S. P. D. III, 169, XXXIII, 336-7, 380.
7. Idem ; also III, 134 and XXXIII, 350 ; Pub. Dept. Diary XIV, pp. 196-197.

5th December. The Maratha Commander Hari Ganesh and a few of his men were killed, the remnant fled to Mahad. The enemy began moving up the creek and reached Ambet.[8]

The port of Bankot since its capture by the Marathas in March 1734 had been held by the Peshwa's troops while Mahad on the upper reaches of the same river, and Raigarh were held directly of the King by the Huzarat troops. The loss of the important out-station roused both the Poona camp and the Satara Darbar into frenzied action. Reinforcements were rushed to Mahad in time to beat back the Sidi who was sailing up the Bankot river.[9] Pilaji Jadhav who soon afterwards arrived at Mahad drove the advantage home. Following in the wake of the retiring foe the Marathas once more appeared before Bankot. The Sidi realising that the place offered no advantages for defence removed the stores and provisions to his ships and under cover of night withdrew his men and sailed away abandoning the place.[10]

Instead of following their success and closing with the Sidi the large force that concentrated on Mahad now dispersed to its several stations, the Raja's suspicions and shifting orders being mainly responsible for the dispersal and for the loss of an opportunity of closely grappling with the enemy.[11]

Plans for reducing Gowalkot were again mooted. The task was this time assigned to Pilaji Jadhav Rao, commanding the Peshwa's troops, the Huzarat captains having twice failed before the place. Sambhaji Angria, after a good deal of persuasion and an appeal to his sense of honour agreed to cooperate with a small force. At last on 7th April 1736 marched from Satara a fresh army led by the Peshwa's most

8. S. P. D. III, 135-40, 145, 151 ; details of the Sidi's attack are obtained from III, 128 which is written a day after 14th Dec. and not on 4th Dec. Also S. P. D. XXXIII, 340-44.

9. S. P. D. III, 128, 152-153, 162, 169, and XXXIII, 341, 361,

10. S. P. D. III, 166 ; XXXIII, 350, 355.

11. S. P. D. III, 138. Chimaji refutes charges of disloyalty in 128.

trusted General to try its fortunes against the enemy's citadel that had defied Maratha arms for over three years.[12]

Pilaji's march was marked by his usual celerity : reaching in the vicinity of the place on 15th April he reconnoitred the ground and immediately decided on his plan of operations which was not dissimilar from the old one adopted partially by his predecessors.[13] Entrenching himself at the Dhamni point he advised the Raja to direct the Huzarat force that had been appointed for the siege to take its station near the Kalusta village and mount batteries at that point. The dominating positions of the two Maratha batteries would cover the communications of the fort with Anjanwel and the outside world and would completely stop the passage of vessels carrying provisions or succour to the besieged. The inmates trapped in their narrow shell, with no hope of aid reaching them from outside and driven to desperation by hunger would, Jadhav surmised, either come out and offer battle in the open when the advantage of numbers would be on his side ; or lay down their arms and surrender. The success of the scheme, however, depended on the rapidity with which it was executed ; once the enemy secured provisions sufficient to last a long time he would refuse to show himself outside and the investment would be a protracted affair requiring the cantoning of a large Maratha army in the infernal monsoon weather of Konkan. The country round Gowalkot was a desolate waste in the hot summer months of April and May without verdure or vegetation, food or forage for men and cattle. For feeding the men in the field it was necessary to organize a commissariat service as well as to keep open the lines of communication between Gowal and Satara intersected by deep ravines of three small rivers upto the Tiwra pass. Jadhav knew that an army marched on its belly and pressed the Satara authorities not only to send him ample supplies of military stores, but provisions as well. He remarked in one of his despatch-

12. S. P. D. III, 174, 175.
13. S. P. D. XXXIII, 392.

es, "I can hold the ground so long as I am well supplied with shot for cannon and food for men. No provision can be procured in this God forsaken country."[14]

But the scheme remained on paper. The Huzarat division did not make its appearance in the field till a fortnight later (26th April)[15] and the element of surprise was lost. The enemy, though no longer able to use the Dhamni channel, continued to communicate by the Kalusta water course, and hastily threw in provisions. The force Jadhav was commanding, consisting of 750 infantry and about 400[16] cavalry, was not large enough to spare troops to take a position at Kalusta. All that Pilaji could do was to call up reinforcements from Satara and Poona.[17]

Events in other quarters however prevented Appa from reinforcing Jadhav for some time. Sidi Saat was a skilful soldier full of resources. Availing himself of dissensions in Angria's house he now thought of recovering Rewas, Thal and other places captured by the Marathas in 1733. Taking his fleet in Bombay waters, he suddenly pounced upon Rewas, carrying the place by assault put to sword the entire garrison. Angria's stronghold of Kolaba lay hardly within thirteen miles of Rewas in the straight line and in this direction the Sidi began to march brushing aside the columns sent by Manaji to oppose his advance. Manaji appealed for help to his patron and ally, Chimaji Appa. Chimaji at once realised how dangerous would be the developments if the enemy were allowed to reach Kolaba. There were rumours that the Sidi was not acting alone in his new offensive, but was being supported by the disgruntled Sambhaji.[18] The return of Sambhaji to Kolaba and the reversion of the Angrian power would lead to serious consequences which the Peshwa and his brother were determined to prevent at any cost. The situation was too

14. S. P. D. XXXIII, 392, 396, 411 ; III, 180, 181.
15. S. P. D. III, 189. 16. *Ibid* 181.
17. Idem. Also III, 186, 188, 195.
18. S. P. D. III, 192.

critical to be left to the control of a subordinate. Mustering to his standard as many troops as he could,[19] Appa left Satara on the 13th and with a tearing speed rushed to the front arriving near Charhai Kamarle on the 18th April. So sudden was Appa's march that to the last the Sidi remained ignorant of it. He was camping at Charhai and when intelligence was brought to him of a Maratha force being near by, he took it for one of Manaji's defeated columns and immediately advanced to attack it. (19 April) Unapprized who his opponent was, Sidi Saat threw to the winds his usual caution, moved back his artillery and with a grim determination to destroy what he supposed to be the Angrian force, closed with his opponent.[20] This was his undoing; his infatuation trapped him, his small infantry force was opposing Maratha horse three times its number. As his men advanced and began firing the Maratha horse reeled and wavered for a time. But Appa's presence and the timely junction effected by Manaji's detachment rallied the men and saved the day. With a wild yell the Maratha horse rushed headlong into the enemy columns, broke their lines and swept everything before it. The small Sidi force was outnumbered and outflanked.[21] In the end the entire Sidi force was annihilated only a handful escaping to the sea in boats. The dauntless Sidi Saat and his brave captains Sidi Yakub, Subhanji Ghatge were slain and his camp plundered. It was no defeat or rout of the Sidi; it was the total destruction of an enemy who had harassed the Marathas for over ten years.[22] The final end of such a stubborn foe was acclaimed as a national victory and salvoes of guns and beating of drums announced the event to the populace of the capital.[23] The messengers from Appa and

19. According to 183 III his force consisted of 2500 infantry and 800 cavalry.

20. S. P. D. XXII, 320, 322.

21. According to III 192 the Sidi's force numbered 1500, while Chimaji led a much larger force.

22. S. P. D. III, 192. This is a report of the action by Appa himself. Also III, 177, 179, 181-4, 187, 191, 192, 196-9; XXXIII, 397, 402.

23. S. P. D. III, 182.

6

Manaji Angria carrying the glad tidings were rewarded with gold and silver bracelets respectively ; the two Chiefs were the recipients of the most distinguished marks of royal favour, robes of honour, a sword, a medallion and the shawl the Raja was wearing.[24]

This was the greatest success Maratha arms had achieved since the beginning of the campaign in 1733. The Sidi lord of Anjanwel who had desecrated the holy shrine of Parashuram, who had arrogantly refused to come to terms and defied several armies sent against him, was laid low in the dust. The fall of his strongholds, Anjanwel and Gowalkot, now looked so easy. The Satara Darbar discussed plans of overwhelming the garrison and talked of furnishing another army for invigorating the languishing siege operations.[25] Even Chimaji Appa thought that the isolated garrison of Gowalkot, in the hour of defeat and despair would be in no mood to resist Maratha arms and proposed to take advantage of the tide of success by moving down with the force he was commanding and hurling it against the place. He asked Pilaji if his victorious force was not adequate for such an attempt.[26]

But Jadhav had seen for himself how strong the place was by nature and how its defences had been strengthened by human skill. He knew it was foolhardiness hurling men against rocky scarps surrounded by deep water channels.[27] He pinned his faith on the strategy of blockade.

To constitute a blockade the investing force must be able to close every point of practicable access so as to render it dangerous either to enter the place or leave it. It was essential to command the communications of the place, to mount batteries at vital points, and prevent ingress or egress or the reception of supplies. The situation at Gowalkot was the reverse of this. Jadhav's small force was occupying the ground

24. S. P. D. III, 182, and S. P. D. XXXIII, 402, 406.
25. S. P. D. III, 182. 26. *Ibid* 183.
27. S. P. D. III, 183.

at Ambdas near the Dhamni heights; the other side was commanded by the Huzarat troops lying encamped at Kalusta. Both were deficient in firearms which deficiency they expected to make up with supplies from the Satara Darbar and Sambhaji Angria. Sambhaji who had so far assisted the operations in a half-hearted manner, had now turned definitely hostile to the Maratha cause. He was in collusion with the Sidi who had promised him aid in recovering Kolaba. With his characteristic impudence he told the Raja's messenger that the Konkan belonged to him and the Sidi and it was none of the Raja's business to meddle, and had the further effrontery to add that he was a pirate and owed allegiance to nobody.[28]

To this man Jadhav addressed his appeals for co-operation and met him at Jaygarh about June 7th.[29] The defeat of Sidi Saat in the interval brought a change in the tone of Angria but could bring in little aid.[30] The Huzarat troops (commanded by Dhumal, Fadtare, Yesaji Anant and Bhoite) lay inactive in their cantonment and neglected erecting batteries. The poor Raja bustled at Satara, made proposals and suggested methods to enforce the blockade, but nothing came out of his suggestions.[31] During this while the month of May had slipped by and the western monsoons had set in. Jadhav realized how very worthless were his allies. In utter despondency he admitted to the Peshwa his defeat.[32]

Sickness raged in the small force already depleted by desertion; the Peshwa continued to reinforce it with small batches of men and military stores.[33] But as luck would have it Jadhav himself fell ill and his life was despaired of. The gallant soldier however thought it a disgrace to abandon the task for which the Raja had chosen him and spoke not a word of his illness. His men apprehending for his life com-

28. S. P. D. XXXIII, 401. 29. S. P. D. XXXIII, 428.

30. S. P. D. XXXIII, 411, 413; Sambhaji Angria's letter of 11th July (Br. Ch. p. 70) brings out this change markedly.

31. S. P. D. XXXIII, 420. 32. S. P. D. XXXIII, 429.

33. S. P. D. III, 207-9.

municated the precarious state of his health to the Satara Darbar and pressed the Peshwa to recall him.[34] Jadhav was recalled[35] and a treaty was concluded on the basis of the terms suggested by the Peshwa in 1733.

The agreement of September 25th, 1736 brought peace to the harried land establishing double government in the eleven mahals of the Sidi's territory. The five mahals contiguous to Janjira—Nandgaon, Murud, Shriwardhan, Diwa, Mhasle, Mandle and the half of Gowal—were to be administered directly by the Sidi's officials, while Maratha rule was established in the inland districts of Tala, Ghosala, Nizampur, Birwadi, Goregoan and the remaining half of Gowal. The revenues of the eleven Mahals were however to be jointly enjoyed by the two powers and for this purpose agent or agents were to be appointed by them in the mahals administered by the other party. The port of Rajpuri was to remain under the sole control of the Sidi : Roha was to remain exclusively in Maratha hands.

The treaty was a complete triumph for Maratha diplomacy. The establishment of double Government in the eleven mahals was an arrangement which worked obviously to the advantage of the stronger power enabling it to infiltrate its influence in the Sidi's country. Only his island forts of Janjira, Kansa and Underi remained outside Maratha influence. His frontier on the land side open to Maratha attack, his resources greatly reduced and Maratha revenue collectors entrenched in his territory the Sidi could no longer pursue a policy hostile to his Maratha neighbour. A part of his fleet lost to the enemy in the early stages of the war was another serious blow suffered by him. His power on the sea declined and the Sidi became in all but name a tributary of the Maratha state. Only the narrow strip of water dividing his island castle from the mainland, saved him from total extinction.[36]

34. S. P. D. XXXIII, 431.

35. Jadhav arrived back at Poona on 30 July 1736. (Peshwa—Daftar Mss.)

36. For the text of the treaty see Treaties, Agreements and

The operations against Gowalkot continued in a languid manner under Tubaji Anant till February 1737, but the fort remained unbeaten for another nine years till it was finally reduced by Tulaji Angria in 1745 January.[37]

CHAPTER VII

MARATHA EXPANSION IN THE NORTH

I

(*Conquest of Malwa, 1700-1730*)

The eighteenth century witnessed a change of the first magnitude in the political aspect of India—the transfer of supreme authority from the Mughal rulers to the Marathas. Aurangzeb's Deccan wars (1681-1707) proved a colossal failure. His enemies the Marathas ill-equipped to fight the Mughals in their way, resorted to guerilla warfare which demoralised the splendid armies of the Emperor, broke their spell of invincibility and wore them out. The magnificent fabric of order and civil administration built up by the great Akbar and his successors was dissolved and Mughal authority lost the reverence

Sanads, pp. 107-113. Jervis in his 'Konkan' prints a translation of this in English with a wrong date. The month and dates given by him are the same, but the year is different, '*Salas*' (three) being a misreading for '*Saba*' (seven). The low state to which his power was reduced is acknowledged by the Sidi himself in his interview with the English envoy S. Walker. (Pub. Dept. Diary XIV, p. 266.)

37. The final operations of Tubaji Anant against Gowalkot are reported in S. P. D. XXXIII, 249, 247, 262-72, 276-78, 280, 283, 285, 286. These papers are wrongly dated 1734 Dec. or 1735 Jan. They all belong to the Year Saba or 1736 Dec. to 1737 Feb. From a letter in Br. Ch. p. 69 and S. P. D. XXX, p. 332 it is obvious that Tubaji was at Chaul in 1735 January. Besides there are a number of entries in Peshwa Rozkird for the year Saba (Shaban, Ramzan, Shawal) showing sums of money sent to Tubaji Anant at Gowalkot

with which it had been looked up to by the millions of India.[1] The aged Emperor Aurangzeb in his last years attempted to come to an understanding with the Marathas, to seek peace with honour,[2] but before a settlement could be effected the Emperor sank into the grave (Feb. 1707), with the Marathas hovering round his camp, plundering his armies and ravaging his distant provinces. The Emperor's son Azam now anxious to secure his succession, desired respite from these attacks and came to an understanding with the captive Shahu : he recognised him as the head of the Maratha state, and promising him grant of Sardeshmukhi released him.[3] Azam was defeated by his brother Shah Alam (Muazzam) at Jajau (June 1707), but the pact made with Raja Shahu continued in operation. The Mughal Government was no longer in a position to refuse the victorious Marathas the Chauth and Sardeshmukhi of the six subahs of the Deccan, but left the issue undecided whether to pay it to Shahu or Tarabai, merely to gain time.[4] This payment of Chauth was an acknowledgment by the Mughals of their defeat, of their inability to hold their own against the Marathas ; the victor always exacts a price for his victory. It is misleading to speak of these grants as concessions made to the Maratha marauders by their Mughal overlords. The Marathas had broken the loins of the Mughal enemy and de-

1. Even contemporary writers like Khafi Khan and Manucci recognised this decay. See Khafi Khan, p. 387 and, Manucci III, 249, IV, 100, Prince Akbar's letter to Aurangzeb in Manucci IV, pp. 175-6 ; Sarkar's Aurangzeb, V, Chapter LXII.

2. Khafi Khan, p. 376 ; Dilkash II, 154-55 ; Manucci IV, 245-46.

3. Khafi Khan in Elliot and Dowson, Vol. VII, p. 396 ; the conclusion of Dr. Raghubir Sinh drawn from an akhbar that Shahu ran away from Azam's camp, goes against facts. If Shahu had fled the Mughal camp, Azam could have easily secured his person as Shahu's escort was slender consisting of about fifty horsemen, and could have withdrawn the terms offered to him. It is likely Shahu left the Mughal camp before negotiations were completed.

4. Khafi Khan, pp. 408-9.

manded tribute which it suited their genius to take in the form of Chauth or one fourth revenue of the countries of the Deccan.

The Marathas entered the northern provinces of the empire in the first decade of the 18th century : a measure adopted in the early stages of the struggle as a counterpoise against the Mughal attacks on their bases, this northward drive gained in momentum as the century advanced. In Peshwa Bajirao the policy of northward expansion found its most fearless champion : he realized full well the weakness of the empire, the levity of its rulers, the incompetence and corruption of its officers, and made a bid for the overlordship of Hindustan. If Shivaji secured the freedom of his people and united them into an independent state, the Peshwa would carry forward his policy ; would establish Maratha hegemony throughout India and would hoist the ochre-coloured flag on the heights of the Himalayas. How far he achieved these aims would be unfolded in these pages.

Malwa : its geographical situation & importance.

The Mughal province of Malwa which is now merged in Central India was the connecting link between the Deccan and Hindustan proper. The river Narmada formed its southern boundary. The forests of Gondwan and Bundelkhand skirted it on the eastern side. Its western boundary merged in the Rajputana desert and north east Gujarat, while to the north lay the province of Agra. On account of its central situation, the province was looked on as an important charge. The highways of commerce and military routes to the Deccan and Gujarat passed through it and armies based on Malwa could strike at Rajputana or Gujarat and move into the Deccan or Bundelkhand with the greatest ease. The province produced a number of the higher crops and boasted a flourishing cloth weaving industry.[5] First conquered by Humayun and later reduced by Akbar the subah of Malwa had enjoyed peace for over a century from

5. Jarret's Ain, II, pp. 195-208 ; India of Aurangzeb, pp. 168-71 and Malwa in Transition, pp. 2-12.

which it was rudely shaken by the advent of the Marathas from the south.

The first incursion of the Marathas in Malwa occurred in 1699 when Krishna Sawant crossed the Narmada with 15000 cavalry, ravaged places near Dhamuni and retired.[6] Rajaram died in March 1700 ; the Emperor imagining he could now not merely subvert Maratha power but obliterate the existence of their headless state, opened his last offensive against them. The Marathas replied by a counter offensive which was daring in conception and brilliant in execution. The Mughal attempt to reduce their important fortresses and thus seize the nerve-centres of their activities, the Marathas answered by harassing the enemy's lines of communications and by raiding the provinces of the empire from which his armies were drawing their sustenance.[7] In pursuance of this plan while the Emperor was besieging Kondana in January 1703 the Marathas crossed the Narmada and caused disturbances upto the environs of Ujjain.[8] Some months later another band overran Khargon and a part of the province. In October of that year Nemaji Sindhia defeated Rustam Khan (the Governor of Berar) and fording the Narmada burst into Malwa and raided upto the neighbourhood of Sironj. Here he was overtaken by the pursuing Firuz Jang and defeated, (Nov. 1703). Firuz Jang followed him into Bundelkhand and surprised his force near Dhamuni in February 1704. Firuz Jang's activities opened the roads that had been blocked up and the Emperor was able to receive treasure, baskets of fruit and letters from the capital that had been held up by the fear of the Marathas.[9] The de-

6. Aurangzeb, V, p. 382. Sir Jadunath Sarkar makes this statement basing it on Bhimsen's Nushka-i-Dilkasha. Malcolm in his memoirs mentions raids on Dharampuri as early as 1690, but is not reliable so far as chronological sequence is concerned.

7. Khafi Khan, pp. 374-75.

8. Aurangzeb, V, pp. 382-3, Gadadhar Pralhad Shakavali in Shiva Charitra Pradeep, pp. 67-68 ; Manucci, III, 426.

9. Sarkar's Aurangzeb V, pp. 383-4, Shiva Charitra Pradeep, p. 68 (J.S.)

vastation caused by the Maratha raid was great. Khandesh was wholly ruined and the half of Malwa adjacent to Khandesh was desolate.[10]

In October 1704 there were reports of Nemaji Sindhia repeating his exploits of the last year, but the invasion did not materialise. Though no irruptions occurred in Malwa for the next few years the local officials continued to report about the desolate condition of villages caused by the infidels and the general ruin of the province. "The path once opened," remarks Sir Jadunath Sarkar, "never again closed till at last in the middle of the 18th century Malwa passed into regular Maratha possession."[11]

Probably on account of strong imperial forces that were operating in the Deccan against Kam Bakhsh in 1709 the Marathas lay quiescent and did not disturb Malwa. From 1710 onwards they again made their appearance in the province. In October 1710 one Gangaram[12] who was serving the Subahdar of Gujarat with 10,000 Marathas lost his employment by the death of his patron, and thought of taking to a career of pillage. He attempted to force a passage into Malwa but was forced back by the Deputy Governor. Another body commanded by Khanderao Dabhade plundered Sultanpur in Nandurbar district (11 March 1711). Gangaram, who had since taken service with Daud Khan abandoned it, collected a large force, was joined by Kanhoji Bhonsle and Chimnaji Damodar and marched on to Amjhera. After exacting a fine of 25,000 rupees from that place the army moved to Nolai Badnagar. At this place they destroyed a small force sent against them by Sher Afghan (30 March 1711), advanced

10. Malwa in transition, p. 65.

11. Aurangzeb, V, p. 382.

12. This Gangaram cannot be identified. The account of Maratha activities in Malwa from 1710-17 is constructed from Akhbarat, copies of which are in the possession of Dr. Raghubir Sinh of Sitamau. I have used for my work a copy (in English translation) given by him. Dr. Raghubir Sinh has detailed these activities in his article in the Sardesai memorial volume.

on Ujjain, but dispersed as soon as they learned that imperial troops were moving against them from Bundelkhand and the Deccan.

Small bands continued to rove in the Narmada basin and take advantage of local disturbances. In the early months of 1713 occurred an irruption on a large scale when Gangaram and Kanhoji Bhonsle at the head of 30,000 horse crossed into Malwa, entered the pargana of Ashta and marched towards Ujjain devastating the country round. The Subahdar Nijabat Ali Khan and Nizam-ul-mulk who was then going south to take up his new appointment, moved promptly in the direction of the invaders. Gangaram and Kanhoji did not offer opposition, but retired in May (1713).

The Maratha attempt to overrun Malwa in the next cold season was foiled by the vigilance and care of Sawai Jai Singh, the successor of Nijabat Ali Khan, and Chatrasal Bundela. In 1715 a Maratha force was reported operating near Khargon ; it collected Chauth from Barwani and Dharampuri ; engaged the Nizam near Burhanpur ; joined as the season advanced by Dabhade and Kanhoji Bhonsle it then swept on towards Malwa; laying Mandu and Maheshwar under contribution the Marathas pressed in the direction of the capital. This horde was followed by another 12,000 strong, which forced the passage over the Narmada at Barwah. For full one month the Marathas went on collecting their dues in the south western region. When at last Jai Singh, the Subahdar, advanced against them in May they retired but not before they had been engaged by him. He came up with them on May 10th at Pilsud and engaged them at close quarters. The light Maratha troops were in no position to face their opponents ; they were worsted and dispersed under cover of darkness abandoning their booty and camp equipage. Jai Singh's victory was complete and for a time he had rid the province of the intruders.

Early next year the Marathas under Santaji Bhonsle entered the province further east and engaged the Zamindar of Chaukigarh and from there advanced to Sihora and Duraha

(May 1716). Yet another force forded the Narmada at the Donkalia ferry and moved northward plundering and ravaging. The Marathas were here, there and everywhere and the Deputy of the Governor, Rupram Dabhai, merely contented himself with looking to the defence of the capital. The Marathas were slowly establishing outposts on the Narmada—vantage points from which to emerge as the campaigning season opened.

In October 1716 there were rumours of the Marathas preparing to invade Malwa and the local officers were instructed to keep the passes well guarded and not allow the Marathas to cross. But the petty officials were helpless and unable to check the enemy's advance. In April 1717 Khanderao Dabhade and others burst into Malwa and laid Ashta, Deogarh, Sehore and several other parganas under contribution. Dabhade was joined by Santaji Bhonsle and they inflicted a severe defeat on the imperial troops that had advanced against them, capturing two prominent officers of the Governor. Without wasting time to reduce the capital which had been prepared for a siege, they moved northward. Their march was unopposed as the Governor, Sawai Jai Singh, was absent elsewhere conducting operations against the Jats. On their way back they had a brush with Dost Muhammed Khan Rohilla and levied tribute from Bhilsa.

Jai Singh soon made way for Muhammed Amin Khan. Muhammad Amin's Governorship was not very eventful. Sayyid Husen Ali the Subahdar of the Deccan and the brother of the Vazir, was negotiating a peaceful settlement with the Marathas and to help forward the negotiations they, for a time, ceased harassing the Malwa region.[13]

The situation at Delhi was all this while fast deteriorating. The empire of the Mughal had lost its vital energy and was crumbling rapidly. The successors of Aurangzeb were feeble minded persons unworthy to rule over his far flung empire and unfit to hold sceptre over a continent. Given to wine,

13. Jaipur Akhbarat, mss.

opium and debauchery they left the affairs of the state to be managed by their ministers. A scramble for power naturally ensued among the nobility, each party and each chief fighting for his own selfish interests. Bahadur Shah died on 18th Feb. 1712 and was succeeded by the idiotic Jahandar Shah who left the entire management to Zulfiqar Khan Amir-ul-umra. Within nine months of his enthronement he was defeated in the battle of Agra on 10th January 1713 and was despatched in the most cruel manner. His successor Farrukh Siyar "was strong neither for evil, nor for good." He owed his throne to the Sayyid brothers who assumed complete control of the state and left him not a vestige of authority. Farrukh Siyar resented the tyranny and thraldom under which he was held by his former benefactors, secretly intrigued for their destruction, but lacked the resolution to act at the right moment ; the distrust between the master and ministers grew into an open rupture till at last the Sayyids in self-defence, seized the person of the Emperor, blinded him (Feb. 1719) and raised another person in the Emperor's place.[14]

The rivalries of the nobility, the plots and counter-plots, murders and bloody contests portended an early break-up of the empire. Distracted by intrigues, divided by parties, the Mughal Government fell into complete neglect ; the defence of distant provinces was abandoned ; the army lost its discipline and descended into a mere rabble and the civil administration fell into utter disorder.

The success of the Sayyid brothers against Farrukh Siyar proved of short duration. The new emperor Muhammad Shah[15] and his mother cleverly plotted their ruin and within a year

14. Khafi Khan, in Elliot and Dowson Vol. VII, pp. 390-485 is the best contemporary account of the period. Siyar-ul-mutakherin prepared late in the 18th century is another history for the same period. These two and many other Persian histories have been used by Irvine in his 'Later Mughals', I and II. Irvine is rather defective in his treatment of Maratha affairs.

15. Enthroned 18 September 1719, Khafi Khan, p. 485.

and a half had themselves liberated from their controlling authority. Husen Ali was murdered at Tora Bhim on 28th Sept. 1720, his brother Sayyid Abdulla was defeated at Hasanpur (4 November 1720) and thrown into prison. The Turani party was now called to manage affairs of the state, but had neither influence with the Padishah, nor his confidence.

While the Mughal affairs were thus in a state of turmoil and utmost confusion, there appeared on the Maratha side a soldier and a statesman of rare insight, enterprise and courage, Bajirao, son of Balaji Vishwanath, who had been called to the premiership in April 1720. With a prophetic vision the young Peshwa saw that the empire against which his people had been buffeting for half a century was tottering to its foundations and the moment had arrived to give it its final blow. The race of the Mughals had run out and the Marathas would grasp supreme power from their palsied hands and dominate the empire. His state appeared weak and disorganised, but the nation or the people were strong and full of the confidence born of success. The struggle with Alamgir had transformed the nation into a vast military camp. To the energies of his people that were being wasted in civil war and internecine struggle, he would find new outlets and direct them towards foreign conquests. The path had been shown by the father and the son would now traverse it. In an eloquent speech he urged his views on the Maharajah ; "The Mughal power is lying prostrate ; it is nearing its end ; it is torn by factions and internecine feuds ; the Padishah desires to bolster up his throne with our support. You speak of the Nizam breaking the treaty and commencing hostilities. But he is of no account. Aurangzeb when a prince reduced the subah of Aurangabad and resided there. Undeterred by his presence in the Deccan the great Shivaji attacked the Adil Shahi and Qutb Shahi kingdoms and laid them under tribute. After him Sambhaji lost everything, his forts, his kingdom and, his life. The Padishah remained in the Deccan with a formidable army to round off his conquests. Undaunted Rajaram carried on the struggle from Jinji. After a time even that citadel was lost to the enemy and the Padishah was still here with his innumerable hordes. Despite these heavy odds Rajaram marched on Aurangabad, ravaged the enemy's country, wrested his forts and recovered the entire kingdom from the Mughal. (Now the situation has changed in our favour). You (a monarch of great qualities) occupy the throne and are assisted by able counsellors. Our aid is sought by the Mughal and by its means Kings are made and unmade. Is not this the moment when we should attempt to seize supreme political power? I undertake to hold the Nizam in check as well as effect a northward drive. You speak of reducing (South) Karnatak as more urgent, but hardly any opposition is to be countered in that quarter. The old Adil Shahi and Qutb Shahi no longer exist. The reduction of Karnatak is as good as a domestic affair and can be easily effected by the Huzarat troops. The Pratinidhi will manage it. The Great Shivaji's dream of a Hindu domination has remained unfulfilled to this date. Balaji Pant Nana has prepared the ground work establishing friendly relations with the Hindu Rajas. This is the time to strike the blow."[16]

The Peshwa had moved about with his father while yet in his teens: he had accompanied him to Delhi in 1719 and had become well acquainted with the political situation at that court. Aurangzeb's bigotry and policy of religious persecution had undone the work of his predecessors, alienated from him the sympathies of the millions of the Hindus over whom he ruled.[17] This policy of degrading the majority community

16. Shahu Charitra by Chitnis, pp. 60-61. This contains the best reply by the Peshwa himself to the controversy among modern historians in Maharashtra whether the expansion of Maratha power to the north before the conquest of the south was not a grave political mistake.

17. For a succinct account of Aurangzeb's religious policy towards Hindus see Cambridge History of India, Vol. IV, Chapter on Aurangzeb, by Sir Jadunath, esp. pp. 240-43. This is based on his Aurangzeb, III, Chapter, 34 and V, pp. 485-86. In this connection

combined with his treatment of the young Marwar prince Ajit Singh, estranged for ever the brave Rajputs who had shed their blood in the service of the empire in the four corners of India.[18] Maratha resistance in the south had encouraged the Jats, the Bundelas and the Sikhs to resist Mughal authority with impunity whenever and wherever they could do it. Malwa, mainly populated by Hindus and dominated by an unfriendly Rajput nobility, was no exception. Without adequate support from the court or the adjoining provinces and active co-operation of the indigenous populace, the defence of the province offered insuperable difficulties and this the succeeding Malwa Governors were to find to their cost.

It was no mere coincidence, but a stroke of deliberate policy that in the apportioning of spheres of influence following the imperial grants of Chauth and Sardeshmukhi, in 1719 Khandesh and the province of Malwa bordering on it were assigned to the Peshwa for making collections.[19] Maratha influence had penetrated the province for some time and for this they were anxious to secure legal recognition in the grants. The demand (for chauth from Malwa) was turned down by the Emperor, and the Peshwa therefore directed his efforts to wresting by arms what his father could not achieve by diplomacy. The early months of 1721 saw him active in the Khandesh Baizapur region[20] collecting chauth and acquainting himself with the country his forces were to traverse later. Khandesh is contiguous to Malwa and into Malwa two years later burst the Peshwa.

Shivaji's letter to Aurangzeb on the imposition of the Jaziya may be read with interest. The Factory records on a number of occasions sound a note of warning about the intolerant attitude of the Emperor towards his Hindu subjects, English Factories, Vol. 12, p. 284, Vol. 13, p. 205.

18. Cambridge History of India, IV, pp. 247-52.

19. Chitnis, p. 71, Duff. I, p. 373.

20. Balaji Bajirao Roznishi, (Bajirao's itinerary, p. 221). The P. D. (MSS.) contains orders issued by him to the officers in this region to pay him chauth.

Bajirao left Satara in November 1722 and advancing by way of Poona and through the basin of the Godavary, came upto Burhanpur. The Pawars who were active in southern Malwa were invited by the Peshwa to co-operate with him.[21] On 1st February 1723 he forded the Narmada near Handia and entering Nemar the southern division of Malwa, moved on to Dhar.[22] On 13th February he had a meeting with the Vazir, Nizam-ul-mulk, at Badaksha (Bolasha?) near Jhabua. The Vazir was then marching towards Gujarat to punish the rebellious Haidar Quli Khan. For six days the Peshwa remained in conference[23] with him, and promises of satisfying his claims appear to have been held out to him. If this was not so, why should the Vazir seek a meeting with an intruder and remain closeted with him? The Nizam's position at the court was not very happy; he was looking out for possible allies and fancied he could use the young Peshwa for forwarding his ends. Bajirao returned to Khandesh by way of Amjhera and Dhar recrossing the Narmada at the Akbarpur ferry. He remained in Khandesh collecting Chauth for some time, settled disputed points with Iwaz Khan and then again moved into the Handia district. He remained there for some time and despatched his troops to co-operate with the Nizam in reducing Dost Muhammad Rohilla and finally quitted the country in the first week of April 1723. During this period he collected Chauth from a number of places in southern Malwa.[24]

In 1724 the Peshwa once again visited the province. Leaving Satara on 27 January he marched into Khandesh;[25] on 14th March carried by assault the stronghold of Lambkani,[26]

21. The History of the Pawars of Dhar, Letter dated 3 Dec. 1722 at pp. 10-11.

22. Balaji Bajirao Roznishi, p. 223.

23. S. P. D. XXII, 4; S. P. D. XIII, 3.

24. Balaji Bajirao Roznishi, pp. 223-4, S. P. D. XIII, 3, S. P. D. XXX, 310.

25. B. B. Roznishi p. 224.

26. Shahu Roznishi, p. 94, S. P. D. XXX, p. 269.

and on May 8th crossed the Narmada at Akbarpur.[27] On the 18th of that month at Nalcha there was another meeting of momentous importance between him and the Nizam.[28] The Nizam had thrown up his premiership in disgust and was retiring to the Deccan to resume the viceroyalty. He was expecting trouble in the resumption of office. His deputy, Mubariz Khan, and other Deccan and Gujarat officials had been secretly instigated by the court to oppose him and destroy him, if possible. In this predicament it was to the advantage of the Nizam to secure allies and in his conference with the Peshwa he made him profuse promises. He agreed not to oppose the collection of Chauth and Sardeshmukhi in the six Subhas of the Deccan, reissued the grants under his signature[29] and may have encouraged the Peshwa's pretensions to Malwa. In the battle of Fatehkharda on October 1st, 1724 the Peshwa's force fought on the side of the Nizam and contributed materially to his victory.[30]

The next four years kept the Peshwa busy in other sectors, but he was not a man who would allow his grip on Malwa to relax. He knew the value of continuous hammering. A strong force under his trusted lieutenants Baji Bhivrao, Udaji Pawar and his Diwan Ambaji Purandare marched into Gujarat in February 1725, took a decisive part in defeating Rustam Ali at Basu,[31] and by way of Sunth, Jhalod, Jhabua, entered Malwa in April of that year.[32] Anup Singh of Jhabua paid one lakh in tribute and the districts of Amjhera and Shajahanpur were laid under contribution.[33]

The incursions of the Marathas since 1720 were headed by the Peshwa in person and deserved to be closely watched

27. B. B. Roznishi, p. 224.
28. S. P. D. p. 269, XXX.
29. Dr. Pawar's paper at the Ind. Hist. Records Commission, 1940 session, Vol. XVII, pp. 204-5.
30. S. P. D. XXX, p. 270; also No. 34. See chapter II.
31. For details see chapter 'Marathas in Gujarat.'
32. S. P. D. XXX, p. 272.
33. Malwa in transition, p. 155.

and stoutly opposed. The appointments of regular Maratha officials like Keso Mahadeo, Keso Vishwanath, Godaji Deokate, Udaji Pawar to levy chauth from the south districts of Malwa afforded evidence of their growing influence[34] and presaged the loss of the province to the empire.

The appointment of Giridhar Bahadur to Malwa in June 1725 prevented for a time the slide-down. Giridhar Bahadur came of a notable family of Nagar Brahmins and had held before several important charges. He was Governor of Malwa for a short period from August 1722 to May 1723 and was again sent down to the province in 1725 to hold it against the wiles of the Nizam and the increasing pressure of the Marathas. He was an officer of character and refused to compromise with the enemies of the empire. His policy of no compromise was soon to cost him his command and his life.[35]

The regime of the new Governor began with friction with the Maratha Kamavishdars. He turned them out and stopped their collections. They complained to Shahu Raja of the unexpected resistance they were meeting with from the Subahdar in levying chauth, on which representations were addressed to him not to disturb the collections.[36] The representations fell on deaf ears. Daya Bahadur, the commander of the Subahdar's troops and his cousin, moved about the province and showed great activity in watching the movements of Santaji Bhonsle, Krishnaji Hari, Keso Mahadeo and several other Maratha captains, prevented their junction with Ambaji Purandare's troops, and followed them till they were out of the province.[37]

Udaji Pawar and Baji Bhivrao were appointed by the Peshwa to make collections for the year 1726-27.[38] They did not fare better than their predecessors. All that their officials

34. S. P. D. XXX, pp. 272-73.

35. For the early history of Giridhar Bahadur see Irvine II, pp. 6-16.

36. S. P. D. XIII, 5.

37. S. P. D. XIII, 6-9.

38. Dharcha Itihas, pp. 17-18.

could collect amounted to 20,000 rupees.[39] Daya Bahadur was most zealous in his duties and would not suffer the country to be ravaged. He kept his troops moving and pushed the Maratha forces to the Narmada.[40] Giridhar Bahadur appeared to have stemmed the Maratha advance.

The Peshwa had gone south to assist Fatehsingh Bhonsle to establish his claims in the Karnatak (1725-26, 26-27) and later the struggle with the Nizam near home diverted his attention from the Malwa venture. In 1728 February the great Nizam-ul-mulk was brought to bay at Palkhed and obliged to submit to the terms dictated to him by the victor. The Peshwa's success not only overawed the Nizam and his own domestic enemies but gave him a dominating voice in the royal counsels and he chose this moment to hurl his hordes northward against Malwa and fix his hold on that province. The absence of his troops in that quarter had encouraged his rivals Dabhade and Bande to encroach on his field[41] and an alliance between these two chiefs and the Subahdar of Malwa would further imperil the position already weakened by withdrawal of large forces southward. The campaign against the Nizam having closed in March 1728 the season was too far advanced to invade Malwa immediately; the Peshwa contented himself with issuing letters to the local Malwa officials asking them to pay chauth to his Deputy, Udaji Pawar.[42]

The Peshwa knew that his wishes in order to be respected must be backed by the power of the sword. On the conclusion of the Dashera of that year a formidable force[43] composed of veteran chiefs, Udaji Pawar, Ranoji Sindhia, Malhar Rao Holkar and the flower of Maratha Shiladars, was called to arms and under the command of Chimaji Appa, the brother

39. S. P. D. XXX, p. 281.
40. Siyar-ul-Mutakherin, p. 235.
41. Shahu Roznishi, 214.
42. Dharcha Itihas, pp. 27-9.
43. S. P. D. XIII, 22, and 23 give the strength of the Maratha armies operating in Malwa and Bundelkhand at 25,000 each; Jaipur Akhbar places it at 22,000.

of the Peshwa, commenced moving north on 24th October. The young general marched with incredible rapidity. On 21st November he reached the Satpura hills, on the 22nd the Karwand Bari pass was negotiated ; on the 25th the Narmada was forded ; on the next day the Mandu Ghat was ascended and on the 27th the Marathas lay encamped at Nalcha.[44] Raja Giridhar Bahadur having just then followed Kanthaji Kadam to the frontier of Malwa and driven him out, lay encamped on the border town of Amjhera. Chimaji Appa, leaving a detachment at Dhar to hang on the Mandu fort and prevent the Killadar Muhammad Umar Khan effecting junction with the main army, closed upon the enemy on the 29th.[45] Completely surprised and fearing to be cut off from his rear, Giridhar Bahadur swerved round and attacked the enemy's advancing columns. Bahadur's troops fought with the courage of despair, but they were outnumbered and outmanoeuvred. After six hours of close fighting the Mughal force was annihilated, its commanders with a number of chiefs were slain : its colours and all camp equipage were captured by the Marathas.[46] It was a complete victory for Chimaji and congratulations showered on him from all quarters.[47]

Resting his troops at Amjhera for a couple of days Chimaji pressed on towards the capital of the province (3rd December), by way of Ahu and Jepalpur.[48] He hoped to surprise Ujjain as he had surprised the enemy at Amjhera. But the son of the late Governor, Bhawani Ram, had assumed control and prepared the city for a siege. Earth works were put up, fresh recruits were raised and by the time the Marathas were near, the city was ready to receive them with confidence. The emperor wrote to Bhawani Ram condoling with him on his bereavement and asking him to carry on the

44. Chimna Appa's itinerary given in S. P. D. XXX, pp. 283-84.

45. Jaipur Akhbarat. (MSS).

46. S. P. D. XIII, 15, 17, 23, 26, 27 and Jaipur Akhbars.

47. S. P. D. XIII, 16, 25, 26-28, 31, 32, 35, 38 and 43.

48. S. P. D. XXX, p. 284.

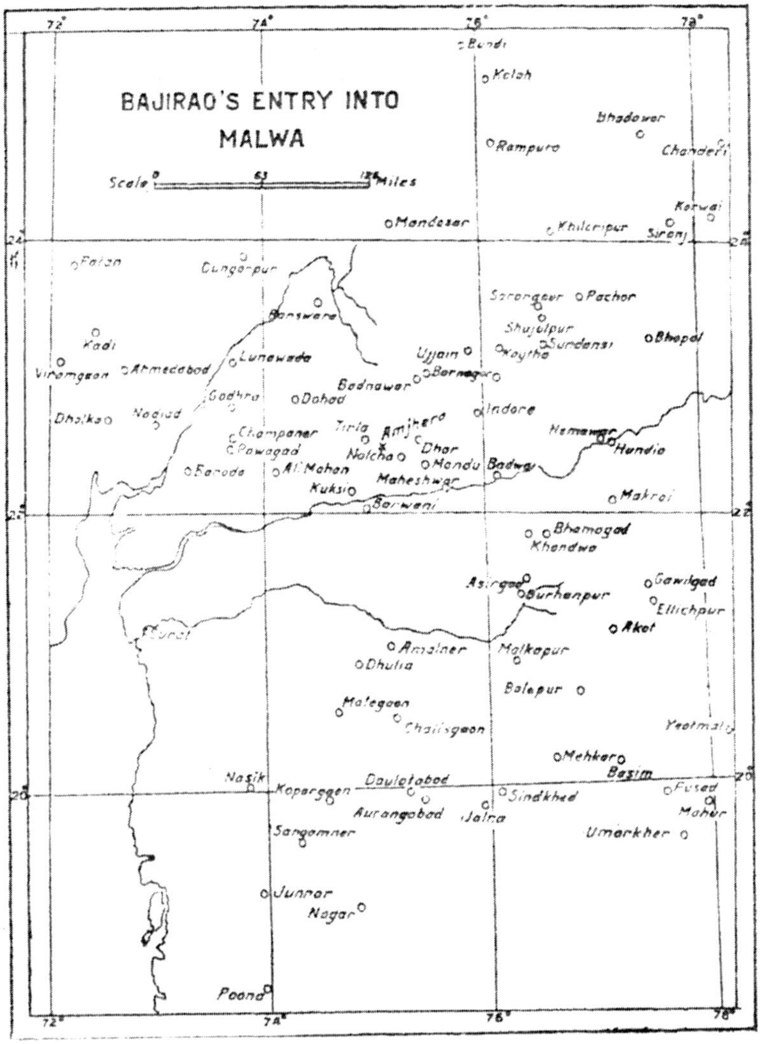
BAJIRAO'S ENTRY INTO MALWA
Scale 0 63 126 Miles
72°
74°
76°
78°
24°
22°
20°
Bundi
Kotah
Bhadawar
Rampura
Chanderi
Korwai
Mandesar
Khilchipur
Sironj
Patan
Dungarpur
Sarangpur
Pachor
Banswara
Shujalpur
Sundarsi
Bhopal
Kadi
Ujjain
Kaytha
Viramgaon
Ahmedabad
Lunawada
Barnagar
Badnawar
Godhra
Dahod
Indore
Dholka
Nadiad
Champaner
Tirla
Amjhera
Nemawar
Handia
Pawagad
Nalcha
Dhar
Baroda
Ali Mohan
Mandu
Badwai
Maheshwar
Kuksi
Makrai
Barwani
Bhamagad
Khandwa
Asirgad
Burhanpur
Gawilgad
Ellichpur
Akot
Surat
Amalner
Malkapur
Dhulia
Balapur
Malegaon
Chalisgaon
Yeotmal
Mehkar
Basim
Nasik
Kopargaon
Daulatabad
Sindkhed
Pusad
Aurangabad
Jalna
Mahur
Sangamner
Umarkhed
Junnar
Nagar
Poona

struggle. Money to the amount of two lacs was sent and Sayyid Najmuddin Ali Khan, Durjan Sal Hada, and Muhammad Umar Khan who commanded considerable troops in the province, were ordered to assist Bhawani Ram.[49]

The Maratha army lacked the means to press siege operations and was consequently held up at the capital of Malwa. On the 13th January 1729 a sally was made by the inmates when there was some close fighting. Chimaji was now advised by his brother not to remain tied to one spot, but move out into the open country and make collections of Chauth.[50] The siege was therefore abandoned and Maratha troops spread everywhere demanding their dues. Kayeth, Sundarsi, Shahjahanpur, Sarangpur, Nowlai, Badnawar, Dhar and a number of important places submitted.[51] The Kotwal of Ujjain paid Rs. 5,000. The open country denuded of its troops could offer little opposition. Chimaji moved to Sarangpur, then changed his course and headed towards Bundi, Kotah (Feb. 5).[52] Rajgarh, Bhanpura, Rampura, and Jawad were laid under contribution ; then retiring into Gujarat by way of Jhalod and Dohad, he returned to Poona on 4th May 1729.[53]

The campaign opened on 24th October 1728 and came to an end in May 1729. One major battle and a number of minor engagements had been fought. At Amjhera the enemy's force was not merely defeated, but completely destroyed. A few strong places like Ujjain and Sironj held out, but the remaining country was overrun by the Maratha troops. The decisive victory bringing the Marathas within striking distance of the imperial capital secured them a base from which to threaten the heart of the empire. The strategic passes of the Vindhyas passed into their possession : the flood gates were

49. Irvine II, pp. 244-45.
50. S. P. D. XIII, 30.
51. Peshwa Rozkird. There are several amounts credited to Chimaji's account during this month.
52. S. P. D. XXX, p. 284.
53. S. P. D. XXX, pp. 285-7.

thrown back and the tidal waters now rushed in. Within a decade of their victory they were complete masters of the province.

There was utter confusion in the imperial ranks in Malwa. The breakdown of Mughal administration in the province was well illustrated by the growing difficulties of the succeeding Governors. No money or reinforcements could be obtained from the emperor. The troops clamoured for their arrears. Sayyid Najmuddin Ali Khan who had been ordered to support Bhawani Ram, preferred to look on himself as the Subahdar and called on the latter to account for the revenues of the province. The two fell out and hostilities were averted only by the strong attitude taken up by Bhawani Ram. The defeat of the Subahdar's troops and the subsequent squabbles of the generals encouraged the peasantry and local zamindars to withhold revenues ; all the efforts of Bhawani Ram who had now been appointed to succeed his father, failed to hold up the avalanche.[54]

The Peshwa appointed officers to make collections. Malhar Rao Holkar and Udaji Pawar who had been assigned a number of districts last year were confirmed in the grant on 16th September 1729.[55] They assembled troops at Chikhalda and awaited the break up of the monsoon to commence operations. Kanthaji Kadam had in the meanwhile invested Khargon and levied 50,000 rupees from it. Bhawani Ram could no longer raise money to pay his troops, the jagirs granted to his father were confiscated and the aid he was led to expect from Jai Singh never came ; at last in October 1729 he was informed that Malwa was too important a charge to be left in his hands on account of the growing menace of the Marathas and that Sawai Jai Singh had been appointed to the province.[56]

Jai Singh's tenure of office though it lasted only for a year, witnessed the initiation of a new policy. The growing power

54. Sir Jadunath Sarkar in the History of Jaipur (Mss.) p. 208.

55. S. P. D. XXX, pp. 293-94.

56. History of Jaipur by Sir Jadunath Sarkar (Mss.) and Irvine II, p. 246.

of the Marathas and the convulsions in Malwa made a deep impression on his mind. He perceived that the only practicable policy that could succeed in the circumstances was the policy of appeasement which his sympathies for Maratha aspirations eminently suited him to pursue.[57] The immunity of Malwa was to be secured by granting to Raja Shahu a jagir in Malwa worth ten lakhs of rupees a year ; by thus meeting the Raja's demand of Chauth from the province it was expected " he would keep his Generals in check and would prevent the raids of his chiefs " in that province. To ensure the execution of the arrangement a Maratha general was to serve under imperial banners.[58] Written undertakings were exchanged with Dado Bhimsen, Shahu Raja's envoy, and Deepsingh, an eminent Rajput, was deputed (Oct. 1730) to the Maratha Court to bring about a lasting settlement, and an enduring peace.[59] To create a friendly atmosphere the Raja in the meanwhile had surrendered in March (1730)[60] the important fortress of Mandogarh captured by Holkar and Pawar four months back, and had asked the several Maratha chieftains to cease military operations. However before the negotiations could be completed, a change took place in the imperial counsels and it was once more resolved to offer resistance to Maratha demands. Jai Singh was transferred and Muhammad Khan Bangash was sent to Malwa to stop the onrush of the southerners.

CHAPTER VIII

MARATHA ADVANCE IN BUNDELKHAND.

While the Malwa operations were progressing satisfactorily (1728-29), the Peshwa embarked on another bold enterprise. The annual expeditions into Malwa, Khandesh, and Gujarat

57. S. P. D. XIII, 10.
58. Jaipur letter, dated Feb. 1730.
59. Deep Singh arrived in the Deccan in October after Jai Singh had been removed. S. P. D. X, 66.
60. Shahu Rozkird, 198.

necessitated putting in the field vast hordes, and these could not be raised without money. The recent campaign against the Nizam though it had been concluded to the advantage of the Marathas, was financially not quite a success. It had added to the huge debt the Peshwa had already contracted ; as a number of Siledar horse operated on the Raja's behalf, a part of the burden fell on the royal exchequer, and the Maharaja importunated the Peshwa to rid him of his debtors. The ambitious policy of expansion, of seizing imperial power could be pursued only by bringing into the field vastly superior forces that would immobilise the Mughal armies. All these added to the financial liabilities of the Peshwa which were accumulating and for lightening which he was anxious to find new fields for conquest.[1] In the search for new fields the Peshwa determined to lead his forces into Bundelkhand where the Bundela chief Chhatrasal had invoked his aid to repel the aggressions of the Mughal Governor, Muhammad Khan Bangash.[2]

Chhatrasal had a past as romantic and turbulent as that of the Maratha hero Shivaji himself. The Bundelas, a clan of the Rajputs, conquered the hilly country east of Malwa between the Jamuna and the Narmada in the 13th and 14th centuries. Birsing Bundela murdered Akbar's favourite minister, Abul Fazal, and was favoured by Jehangir. In consequence the Bundelas rose in prominence and for a time basked in the sunshine of imperial favour. On Jehangir's death however, Jhujhar Singh, the son of the deceased Bir Singh fled the Mughal court, but was hunted down to the wild forests of Gondwan in 1635 and there killed by the Gonds. His feudatory Champat Rai heroically struggled against the might of the empire for another two decades and was likewise destroyed in 1661. Champat's son Chhatrasal, left an orphan at the age of twelve, then sought service in the Mughal army, became dissatisfied, visited the great Shivaji in the south and was advised by him to raise the standard of revolt against the idol breakers. Chha-

1. S. P. D. XIII, 14, 15, 18, etc.
2. S. P. D. XIII, 10, and Br. Ch. Appendix, No. 43.

trasal returned to his homeland and kept up the contest against the Mughals with varying fortune. Aurangzeb's distraction in the south and the civil wars of his successors gave Chhatrasal a free hand and enabled him to extend his conquests till he became master of the eastern half of Bundelkhand.[3]

With the appointment in 1720 of Muhammad Khan Bangash to the subah of Allahabad there came a turn in the tide of the Bundela fortunes. Bangash was a renowned Pathan chief and worthy of the title. "Ghazanfar" i.e., Ali conferred on him by Farrukh Siyar. As soon as the menace of the Nizam was laid at rest, he directed his arms to the reduction of Bundelkhand which was included in his government of Allahabad and wherein he had a personal interest as the revenue of certain parganas had been assigned to him in 1713. In the beginning of 1727 Muhammad Khan Bangash took command of the operations and pressing the Bundelas hard, occupied parganas Bhind, Mauda, Pailani, Agwasi and Simani ; at Ijoli in pargana Mahoba he stormed the well prepared lines of the enemy and forced them to retire to the forest of Salhat near Jaitpur. Here the Pathan Chief pursued the fugitives and scattered them. Chhatrasal took shelter in the fort of Mahoba. The forts of Barigad, Lauri, Jhumar, Mahoba, Kulpahar were all reduced one by one and, at last about June 1728 Bangash laid siege to Jaitpur, the last stronghold of the Bundela chief. Throughout the rains the investment continued with relentless pressure. Chhatrasal sent out appeals for help in vain, and at last in December 1728 surrendered the place to the enemy.

It looked as if Bundela resistance was completely crushed. All their strongholds had been reduced by the Mughal Subahdar and the aged Chatrasal delivering himself with his family into the hands of the enemy waited to be taken to Delhi as prisoner. The imperial Court as usual, jealous of the successes of its Subahdar, began to entertain suspicions of his designs.

---

3. For a detailed account of the Bundela chiefs see Pogson's "Bundelas" and Irvine, II, 216-30.

Chhatrasal came to know from his agents at Delhi what powerful enemies the Subahdar had at the Court and resolved to renew the struggle. As the Marathas were everywhere challenging Mughal authority, he turned to them for aid. The Bundela overtures were accepted and Bajirao prepared to march to their support.[4]

The Peshwa opened the campaign in November 1728. Taking farewell of the Maharaja on 27th November the Peshwa, with the Sarlashkar, at the head of 25,000 horse[5] advanced through the Godavari basin by way of Beer and Pathri. These districts had been assigned to the Sarlashkar for making collections of Chauth which the hostilities with the Nizam had prevented from being raised for the previous two years. No opposition was met with ; the Peshwa's army marched into the Gangathari districts, resumed the collections and then headed towards Deogarh through Berar. At the request of Aiwaz Khan of Berar to spare his districts the Peshwa took a more southernly route by way of Mahur.[6] On the 13th January (1729) Bari, the first stronghold of the Deogarh Raja, was assaulted. On the 23rd an agreement was concluded by which the Raja promised to pay the Marathas an annual tribute of Rs. 65,000 and thus secured his territory from molestation. On the 4th of February the Peshwa pushed on towards Bundelkhand.[7] Moving through the wilderness by unfrequented routes a month later he established contact with the Bundela chiefs ; on 10th March he was received by Bharati Singh, son of Chatrasal. On the 13th the aged Chhatrasal welcomed his deliverer and entertained him.[8] Other Bundela chiefs now hastened to join the Peshwa's standard and the joint army swelled to 70,000 men.[9] From Mahoba it advanced on the 19th March to where Muhammad Khan Bangash was lying encamped.

4. S. P. D. XIII, 10, 22, 23, 30.
5. S. P. D. XIII, 14, 22, 23.
6. S. P. D. XIII, 34.
7. S. P. D. XXX, p. 288 ; and Peshwa Rozkird.
8. Idem.
9. Irvine II, p. 238.

Muhammad Khan Bangash was all this while resting in false security. All the enemy forts had passed into his hands; the Bundela forces had been beaten in the field, overpowered and scattered. The Chiefs had made their submission and were in his camp. Bangash sent back the major part of his force and lay encamped near Jaitpur with hardly 15000 men. He allowed the Bundela chiefs to remove to a distance from his camp on the pretext of celebrating the Holi.* Not before the enemy was within twenty miles of his encampment was he aware of their presence. Hastily he called together detachments scattered on garrison duties, dug entrenchments and prepared to resist. At the same time he despatched letters to the Court reporting his serious plight and calling for reinforcements.[10]

In the absence of heavy artillery the allied armies could not carry the enemy's position by assault and therefore surrounded it on all sides; the investment commenced on 27th March; not a grain of food or blade of grass could be secured from outside. Bangash made a sortie one day but was unable to pierce the besiegers' defences.[11] The son of the Subahdar, Qaim Khan, who was then at Taharwan, learned of the straits to which his father had been reduced and hastened to his relief with supplies and reinforcements. He was allowed to approach Supa, within 12 miles of Jaitpur, when his force was attacked and decimated. Qaim Khan succeeded in making his escape, but lost his baggage and military stores which all fell into the hands of the Marathas who besides other things secured 3000 horse and 13 elephants.[12]

Taking advantage of the diversion Muhammad Khan in the meanwhile had abandoned his encampment and escaped to

---

* The Holi that year fell on 4th March.

10. J. A. S. B. 1878 IV, pp. 297-8.

11. S. P. D. XIII, 45; According to Pilaji Jadhav the strength of the enemy (Bangash) was 20,000. Irvine gives it as 10,000 horses and the same number of foot. See Prof. Potdar's article on the Bundela episode.

12. Rajwade III, 14.

the shelter of the Jaitpur fort. The enemy returned and invested the fort and the town closely, resolved to starve the garrison into surrendering. The only food that could be obtained was the flesh of the gun bullocks and of troopers' horses. Many soldiers died of starvation and still more deserted.[13]

With the allied armies tightly closing round him, the Pathan's submission was a mere question of time. If he hoped to be relieved by imperial troops he was merely deluding himself. None at the court had the desire or the energy to extricate the luckless Governor from the miserable straits to which he had been reduced. But the season was too far advanced for the Marathas to remain in the north any longer. Leaving the Bundelas to complete the operations, the Peshwa left Jaitpur on 23rd May and hastened back by way of Garha, Ketughan, Burhanpur, Makrai and reached Poona on 16th July.[14] The investment of Jaitpur continued for another three months till at last despairing of ever being succoured, Muhammad Khan Bangash signed an agreement with the Bundelas "not to attack them again, but to content himself with the tribute they formerly paid." From that time Muhammad Khan never re-entered Bundelkhand.[15]

The year 1728-1729 marks a turning point in Maratha history. Chimaji's victory over Giridhar Bahadur established Maratha power in Malwa, while the help rushed to the Bundelas in their hour of peril won for the Maratha cause the sword arm of a grateful and heroic people. Chhatrasal came to look on the Peshwa as his son and left him a part of his kingdom in Jagir. The Marathas thus secured another foothold in a friendly country from which to direct a blow at the heart of the Empire.

---

13. J. A. S. B. 1878 IV, P. 300.
14. S. P. D. XXX, p. 289 : and Peshwa Rozkird.
15. Rustam Ali in Elliot VIII, p. 48 ; J. A. S. B. p. 301 of Part IV of 1878. Siyarui-Mutakherin speaks of Qaim Khan as having defeated the Bundelas and saved his father. The Author's information is obviously wrong.

CHAPTER IX

MARATHA PROGRESS IN MALWA.

(1730—1735)

The appointment of Muhammad Khan Bangash to the province of Malwa came at the same time as important changes in the Maratha command. Udaji Pawar who had been so far active in Malwa and had figured so prominently in recent operations fell out with the Peshwa. He felt he was not being rewarded according to his merit and demanded half the collections from the province. His demand met with a refusal from the Peshwa and on 3rd October 1730, Malhar Rao Holkar was appointed to the supreme command in Malwa ;[1] next year (20th October 1731) Ranoji Sindhia was associated with him and they were empowered to make settlements with the chiefs and local Zamindars.[2]

Sindhia and Holkar were not new figures. Both had begun their careers as common troopers and had risen to the command of considerable Pagas by their sheer ability. Ranoji was in personal attendance on the Peshwa's father and had seen service with him in several fields. He had distinguished himself in many important actions, the battle of Balapur, Fatekharda, Basu, Palkhed, Amjhera and Dabhoi. His associate Malhar Rao was a goat-herd and had at first served in the Raja's contingent under Bande.[3] His daring and courage brought him to the notice of the Peshwa who persuaded him to take service with him. He knew the Satpura region like the palm of his hand and had fought with conspicuous bravery in the battle of Amjhera.[4] With these experienced soldiers Bangash was to contend now.

Bangash received his new appointment on 19th Sept. 1730. He marched towards Malwa at the head of 8200 horse and 2500

1. S. P. D. XXX, pp. 300.
2. Idem, pp. 304-6.
3. S. P. D. XXX, p. 233 and XVII, 1.
4. S. P. D. XIII, 33.

foot.[5] Liberal promises of aid in men and money were made by the Delhi Court, but none, it would be seen subsequently, were kept. Halting for days in his march for reinforcements from Delhi to join him, he at last reached Ujjain on 18th January 1731 too late to prevent the Marathas under Holkar from entering the province. Holkar even attempted to surprise the Governor's camp at Sarangpur while he was yet on his march, but the attempt did not succeed.[6]

The presence of Holkar near the capital obliged the Governor to take the field at once. He personally moved towards Dhar and sent his son Ahmed Khan with another force towards Sarangpur. Holkar fell back in the direction of Dhar, was engaged by Bangash's troops and was forced to evacuate his outposts at Dhar, Dipalpur, and Mandleshwar.[7]

Bangash's apparent success was due to the absence of the major part of the Maratha force in Gujarat. The rivalry between the Peshwa and the Senapati had flared up into an open rupture and both sides were preparing for the coming struggle. The Senapati had succeeded in winning over the disgruntled Pawar to his side and was negotiating with the Nizam for an alliance. The Senapati's hostile preparations obliged the Peshwa to recall his best troops from beyond the Narmada which contributed materially to the success obtained by Bangash over Holkar.

The Subahdar about this time made a wrong move which roused suspicions about his motives and lost him the favour of the imperial court and ultimately brought about his downfall. The Emperor though outwardly reconciled to Nizam-ul-mulk, distrusted his submission and looked on him as a rebel to be crushed at the proper time. He could not forget his defiance of imperial authority in Gujarat and Malwa after his withdrawal to the Deccan. The Governor of Malwa was expected to watch the movements of this rebel, and deal with him effectively should he find an opportunity to do so. Even the

5. Irvine, II, p. 249. 6. *Ibid*, p. 250.
7. J. A. S. B. 1878, p. 310.

troops of Bangash believed that they would some time cross swords with the army of the Deccan Subahdar. But when contrary to expectations, Bangash met the Nizam on the Narmada at the Akbarpur Ferry* on 17th March 1731, the party opposed to him at the court immediately used it against him to insinuate to the Emperor that the Pathan chief had entered into the schemes of the Nizam to dethrone him. Though no immediate action was taken by the emperor it antagonised him against the Pathan and made him unresponsive towards the latter's difficulties.

The meeting between the two Viceroys was an astute move on the part of the Nizam directed against his inveterate enemy the Peshwa. Bangash while yet at Sadhaura in Dec. 1730 on his way to Ujjain had received letters from the Nizam inviting him to meet him on the Narmada.[8] His recent experience in Bundelkhand had shown Bangash that the Peshwa was not a despicable foe and that he would have a hard time fighting him in Malwa single-handed. He therefore gave a willing ear to the overtures of the Nizam for joint operations against the Marathas. The Senapati was up in arms against the Peshwa and the Nizam felt that if he and Bangash would support the former, the Peshwa's power would be crippled if not completely destroyed. The two therefore met on 17th March and remained in conference for twelve days. Before their plans could be perfected the Peshwa had struck a decisive blow at his opponent and dispersed his troops. The scheme of the two chiefs fell to pieces, and each had to hurry back to his province to save it from the ravages of the Maratha horse.

Malhar Rao Holkar was at this time operating near Mandsor, while another Maratha chief (Antu?) was ravaging the country near Kayeth. Unrest made its appearance among the troops of the Governor, and the Raja of Kotah and other chiefs whom Bangash had asked to co-operate with him against the

* About 35 miles south of Indore and 40 miles S. E. of Dhar.

8. S. P. D. X, 70 and XVII, 8; Irvine II. p. 251; the correct date of S. P. D. XVII. 8 is Recd. 7 Nov. 1730.

Marathas, refused to move. From Mandsor Holkar marched on to Sarangpur in June 1731, engaged the Governor's troops but was forced to retire. Muhammad Khan went to Sironj and remained encamped there throughout the monsoon. He had begun to feel the pressure of the Marathas.[9]

After the monsoon the Marathas returned to Malwa in increasing numbers. Holkar was reported to be in the vicinity of Sironj at the head of 50,000 men. Sindhia, Pawar and others were following him. Bangash wrote to Delhi for help, but no aid came from that quarter.[10] He wrote to Shahu Raja, but was referred to the Peshwa.[11] The Nizam having come to an understanding with the Peshwa showed no anxiety to relieve the distress of his former ally. Bangash's little provincial force of 10,000 was unable to cope with the numerous Maratha hordes. The local Zamindars and chiefs found it convenient to make peace with the intruders rather than co-operate with the Governor in repelling their attacks. Bangash realised the helplessness of his situation and sought an understanding with the Maratha chiefs by granting them chauth for the year.[12] At the same time he informed the Court that without substantial reinforcements he could no longer hold back the Marathas. His appeals were replied with an order informing of his removal and the appointment of Sawaj Jai Singh as his successor (Sept. 28, 1732). Thus ended rather ingloriously the two years' Governorship of Muhammad Khan Bangash.[13]

So far had the Marathas entrenched themselves in their new conquests by now that the Peshwa thought it safe to divide Malwa among his chief captains. This was effected in July 1732 when Sindhia Holkar and the Pawars were assigned definite shares in the revenue of the province.

---

9. J. A. S. B. 1878, pp. 316-7.
10. J. A. S. B. 1878, pp. 321-2.
11. Idem. 12. *Ibid*, pp. 322-23.
13. There are few Marathi papers referring to Holkar's activities for 1731-32. Our main source is therefore J. A. S. B. 1878, part IV.

Sawai Jai Singh was appointed Viceroy for the third time to allow him to pursue the policy of appeasement which he had initiated in his previous term of office. The appointment of this powerful Rajput prince, the friend of the Amir-ul-Umara, signalised that 'the Mughal Court had at last awakened to the gravity of the menace'.

After the fall of Giridhar Bahadur, the Peshwa lay quiescent for some time. In 1730 February, Pawagarh, the south-western entrance into Malwa was wrested from Kanthaji Bande,[14] in 1731 April the Senapati's opposition was shattered at Dabhai. One more attempt of the Nizam to ruin his rival was defeated and the former very wisely entered into a secret pact with the Peshwa not to molest his southern territory while he pursued his ambitious policy to the North, carried his arms into Malwa and pushed his conquests over the Emperor's remaining dominions."[15] Thus having established himself over his domestic rivals and overawed the Nizam, the Peshwa was free to direct his full energies to the project so dear to his heart.

His first care was to consolidate his hold over his Bundelkhand Jagirs. They had been bestowed on him by the grateful Chhatrasal who died on 14th Dec. 1731. To effect a partition of the Jagir and to collect tribute from the Bundela Chiefs of Orcha, Datia, Narwar and Bhadawar the Peshwa despatched his brother in Bundelkhand in the cold weather of 1732. Chimaji left the Deccan in Oct. 1732, came up in Bundelkhand and appointed Govind Ballal Kher to carry out the details of the negotiations. By tact and suave temperament the partition was effected without the smallest hitch. The Peshwa obtained a Jagir valued at one lakh from Jagat Raj and another of a quarter and a lakh with the fort of Rajgarh from Hirdesa. It was

14. S. P. D. XXX, p. 297.

15. Elphinstone, p. 687. This compact was concluded in Aug. 1731 and ratified in 1732 Dec. when the Peshwa and the Nizam met at Rohe Rameshwar ; vide Raj III, No. 97 and S. P. D. XXX, No. 90, 91.

also stipulated that Bundelas would join the Peshwa's standard and give him aid when he would invade foreign territory or march on Delhi. Hirdesa with his eye on Orcha dreamt of extending his territory in that direction and promised to share that state with the Peshwa.[16]

The Rajas of Bundelkhand appealed to the Mughal Court for help against Maratha aggression. But before the Vazir had moved from Delhi,[17] and marched in the direction of the Marathas, the latter had retired after collecting dues. The Raja of Orcha and Rao Ramchandra pressed the Vazir to lead his army against the sons of Chhatrasal who, they represented, were in alliance with the Marathas and had given them a foothold in the province, and must be crushed. The Vazir advanced to the boundary of the territory of Raja Jagat Raj where he learnt of the formidable rebellion of Bhagwant Singh of Adaru in Ghazipur and the death of his brother-in-law Jan Nisar Khan, in a recent attack. Incensed the Vazir marched on Ghazipur and invested the place. Bhagwant Singh fled to the mountains. The Bundela Chieftains and Muhammad Khan Bangash once more urged the Vazir not to abandon the operations against the allies of the Marathas. The ease-loving Vazir however had begun to feel the severities of the campaign. His agents were sent to Hirdesa and Jagat Raj returned with evasive replies from the two Chiefs. The prospect of a monsoon campaign in the hilly Bundela country did not appeal to Qamr-ud-din Khan. He retired with his army, reaching Delhi on 28th July.[18]

While Chimaji's force was operating in Bundelkhand, another body under the joint command of Ranoji Sindhia and Malharji Holkar invaded Malwa. Commencing its march in December 1732, it arrived on the Narmada by way of Kansul. Here it divided, one force under Anand Rao Pawar taking the

16. S. P. D. XIV, 7-9, Br. Ch. 44. Also Prof. Potdar's paper.
17. The Vazir left Delhi on 21 Shawal, [27 March 1733], Irvine, II, p. 277.
18. S. P. D. XIV, 9.

direct road to Malwa, while Sindhia and Holkar struck a north west route, entered Gujarat, captured Champaner and plundered Umreth.[19] From here they secured an easy passage into Malwa to divert Sawai Jai Singh who was reported to be going against Chimaji Appa. The Maratha Commanders secured information that Jai Singh was encamped near Mandsor. Leaving behind their heavy baggage they pressed towards his camp and surrounded it. Jai Singh now persuaded Udaji and Krishnaji Pawar who were hovering about with their contingents, to join him. They could however bring little relief to Sawai Jai Singh and left him on the representations of Sindhia and Holkar. Jai Singh offered to pay the Marathas six lakhs of rupees in addition to the collections from 28 paraganas already made by them. The Maratha demand rose higher, and Sawaiji, being informed that the Emperor had moved out of the capital and was coming to his aid, decided to attack the Marathas. The rear of Jai Singh's army was engaged and plundered by Holkar who lost in the engagement only two hundred horses. Holkar retired to a distance of sixteen coss, but again returned to the attack. Jai Singh at last found it prudent to come to terms with the Maratha Chiefs, Sindhia and Holkar accepting the terms already proposed by Jai Singh and hostilities ceased for the season.[20]

Soon after this Sawai Jai Singh retired to his country of Amber and gave himself up to pleasure. " Aware of the downfall of the Empire he saw it was in vain to attempt to check Maratha invasion or to prevent the partition of the Empire."[21]

When the next campaigning season (1733 Oct.—1734 May) opened the Peshwa was sitting before Janjira vainly attempting to reduce the island castle. His Lieutenants however were not taking any chances. Sindhia, Holkar and Pilaji Jadhav were

19. S. P. D. XIV, 1 ; the correct date of the paper is 21 Feb. 1733.

20. S. P. D. XIV, 1, 2 and XV, 6 ; the correct date of XIV, 2 is 5th March 1733 and of XV, 6, March 7th 1733.

21. Tod II, p. 1212.

once more active in Malwa and Bundelkhand and keeping the enemy on the run. Sindhia and Holkar crossed the Narmada, reduced Barwah and proceeded to Malwa. There was a brush between Holkar and Yar Muhammad Rohilla of Bhopal in which many lives were lost. The Marathas then proceeded to settle the affair of Bundi where they had been invited by the deposed Budh Singh. This prince had incurred the enmity of the Amber Chief, Jai Singh, and had been obliged to flee his kingdom. His state was then reduced by the troops of Jai Singh, who seated on the vacant throne his nominee Dalel Singh. It was against this usurper that Budh Singh sought Maratha aid through Pratap Singh Hada. On April 22nd, 1734, the Marathas attacked the fort of Bundi and carried it after a severe fight. The Rani of Budh Singh out of gratitude for the aid given by her husband tied a *rakhi* thread round Holkar's wrist thus acknowledging him as her brother. The Marathas received 6 lakhs in money for their assistance.[22]

Pilaji Jadhav who had proceeded north-ward through Nemar went to Datia and Orcha. Laying these states under contribution he moved on to Gwalior, found the country desolate, proceeded to Bhadawar, received over 3 lakhs from that Chief and fell back on Narwar and leaving Chanderi to his left he returned to the Deccan about the end of April.[23]

Reports of the destructive activities of the Marathas were reaching the Delhi Court, but no one there was interested in resisting their advance. The Emperor, when questions of the state arose, went out on hunting parties or spent his time in visiting the gardens. The Vazir likewise went to his country house and the business of the State remained at a stand still. The Subahdar of Malwa, Sawai Jai Singh sat calmly at home

22. S. P. D. XIV, 11, 18 and XV, I. Marathi papers are silent about the Bundi affair. Sir Jadunath Sarkar in his Fall of the Mughal Empire, I, pp. 249-52 bases it on Vamsha Bhaskar. The correct date of XV, 1, is 2 May 1734 ; of XIV, 11 is 28 Dec. 1733.

23. S. P. D. XIV, 10, 13, 18; the correct date of XIV, 13 is 9 April 1734.

doing nothing, though he possessed an army of 30,000 horsemen and a large number of matchlockmen. The large sums he received from the Royal Treasury to defend the province he shared with the Marathas.[24]

Orders had been issued to the Mir Bakhshi, Khan-i-Dauran, to proceed against the Marathas as early as June 1733. But it was not before February 1734 that he was able to find out some one who would undertake the task for him. He persuaded his brother Muzaffar Khan, the Governor of Ajmere, to lead the expedition. When the Khan was at last ready to march out, the Marathas were reported to be retiring. Muzaffar Khan followed them as far as Sironj, where they surrounded his camp and by continuous skirmishing straitened his resources. The Khan contented himself with preserving the safety of his person and when after the Marathas had left he returned to the capital in June, all congratulated him on his able conduct of the war.[25]

Immediately after the rains of 1734, the Marathas renewed their activities. Pilaji Jadhav arrived in Bundelkhand with the Peshwa's son Balaji, and Vyankat Rao Ghorpade. He forded the Narmada at Ketughan on 28th December 1734 ; On 15th January 1735 he reached Amola in Orcha territory.[26] On his arrival in Bundelkhand he was joined by a son of Chhatrasal.[27] Sindhia and Holkar at the same time marched into Malwa.

" The Marathas had (thus during the last ten years) continued to extend their ravages and incursions to which they had been encouraged by receiving contributions in order to purchase their forbearance, wherever they appeared. When they saw no measures were taken to oppose their movements they recommenced operations in the next year. At length they assumed absolute dominion of those districts which formerly only paid tribute. By these encroachments, the frontier of the

24. Irvine II, pp. 278-79.
25. Siyar-ul-Mutakherin, pp. 243-44.
26. S. P. D. XXX. pp. 312-318.
27. S. P. D. XIV, 23.

Empire retrograded while they advanced. By the supineness and shameful neglect of the Emperor, they now occupied the territories as far as Gwalior and approached to the vicinity of Akbarabad.[28]

Two mighty armies therefore took the field and moved out to meet the invaders. The one under Vazir Qamr-ud-din Khan left the capital on 10th November and three months later came up with the Marathas near Narwar. As he commanded a well equipped force of 25,000 the Vazir was naturally anxious to engage the Marathas at close quarters.[29] Pilaji Jadhav on the other hand avoiding a general action fought two or three light engagements. Immobilising the Vazir's force by his rapid movements he put his artillery out of action and caused scarcity in his camp. With great difficulty the Vazir pressed on till he reached the Udit Singh tank near Orcha ; then on 14th February though it was the Id day (1 Shawal) the Mughal Army commenced its retreat in utmost silence to escape the Marathas. But intelligence of the enemy's movements was carried to the Maratha camp. Immediately surrounding the Mughal force, Maratha matchlockmen delivered the attack. The Vazir no longer able to continue the march took refuge in Orcha.[30] Leaving him in Orcha, Jadhav crossed the Betwa and turned towards Gwalior and the Jat country for raising collections. At Gwalior he surprised Sayyid Najm-ud-din, Ali Khan, Faujdar of Gwalior but released him with a Ziafat.[31] After the Marathas had moved out to the Jat country the Vazir left the position taken by him and advanced from Orcha to intercept Pilaji. The latter however was able safely to fall back on Sivpuri, Kularas, seizing a number of horses and camels from the enemy. The Vazir had failed miserably either to engage the Marathas or drive them out.[32]

28. Siyar p. 242. (Panini Office ed.) 29. S. P. D. XIV, 22.
30. Mss. Papers ref. Sardesai's Riyasat, Madhya Vibhag, I, pp. 353-4.
31. S. P. D. XXX, p. 318. 32. S. P. D. XIV, 22, 23.

Finding further resistance useless, the Vazir expressed his willingness to effect a compromise by paying a sum of five lakhs. But this offer was not acceptable to the Maratha Chief. Pilaji moved about for some time ; then on 4 Zilkad leaving Malwa, he re-entered Bundelkhand, picked up his baggage and retired to the Deccan by way of Chanda, Deogarh. On 5th June 1735 he reached Poona. Owing to the presence of the Vazir's forces in Bundelkhand the collection of dues fell off considerably* [33]

While Jadhav engaged the Vazir near Orch, his colleagues Sindhia and Holkar scored a brilliant success over the imperialists in the western theatre. Against them had advanced Khan-i-Dauran, Samsam-ud-daulah, Mir Bakhshi, the Emperor's favourite Chief. Commanding the best Mughal troops, and carrying choice artillery, Khan-i-Dauran left the capital in November, 1734,[34] was joined on the march by Sawai Jai Singh, Abhay Singh of Marwar, Durjan Sal of Kotah, till his army swelled to near two lakhs.[35] Resolved to sweep the Marathas out of Malwa the confederates entered the province by the Mukundra pass and reached Rampura in early February. Here their further advance was challenged by Sindhia and Holkar. Effecting their favourite encircling movement they stopped provisions reaching the huge conclave. Then abandoning the blockade they passed the rear of the Mughal army, crossed the Mukundra pass and by way of Bundi entered the territory of Sawai Jai Singh, denuded of its troops.[36] On Feb. 28th Sambhar was plundered yielding a rich harvest. The Governor

* *Note* : Persian chronicles wrongly place these activities in the year 1736. In that year Pilaji Jadhav was ill and did not proceed northward.

33. S. P. D. XIV, 21, 22, 23, 28 ; Two letters in Joshi Collection quoted at length in Sardesai's Madhya Vibhag, I, pp. 353-354 ; also Itihas Samgraha Aitihasik Charitren, letter of P. Jadhav at p. 68. The correct date of that letter is Feb. 1735.

34. Siyar p. 244.

35. S. P. D. XIV, 23 ; Itihas Samgraha, Ait. Charitren, letter at p. 68, gives the figures as 50,000 which is more correct.

36. S. P. D. XIV, 21, 23.

Fakhruddin Husen was stripped of everything he possessed in spite of the presents sent by him to the Maratha Chiefs. The Qazi of the place killed his women in the Hindu style and fought till he was struck down.[37] The news of the Marathas raiding their province caused consternation among Khan-i-Dauran's Rajput allies. They were now anxious to save their defenceless homes. The army therefore retraced its steps, moving towards Jaipur to seek the enemy. While Khan-i-Dauran was yet at Kotah, a meeting with the Maratha Chiefs was arranged by the mediation of Sawai Jai Singh on 24th March 1735.[38] Khan-i-Dauran agreed to pay 22 lacs of rupees to the Marathas as Chauth for Malwa and went back to Delhi which he reached at the end of April.[39] Holkar and Ramchandra Malhar went to Kalabag from Bundi while Ranoji Sindhia moved as far as Sironj, Rajgarh and Patan.[40] They returned to the Deccan in July. They had defeated the Mir Bakhshi of the Empire and in recognition of their services the Peshwa went forward to meet them at a distance of two miles from his capital.[41]

CHAPTER X

ATTEMPTS AT CONCILIATION.

Bajirao visits Jai Singh.

The policy of appeasement had been tried with disastrous results. Fresh concessions instead of satisfying the Marathas had called forth fresh aggressions. They had overrun Malwa and advanced upto Gwalior. The Emperor began to express dissatisfaction with the way in which affairs were going. It was openly discussed at the Court why Sawai Jai Singh who

37. Siyar-ul-Mutakherin, p. 244.

38. S. P. D. XIV, 24,26, 27, 57 ; XXII, 284 ; Rustam Ali, pp. 50-51.

39. Sarkar, Fall, I, p. 255.

40. S. P. D. XIV, 29.

41. S. P. D. XXII, 293.

had encouraged these aggressions should not be removed forthwith from the Subahdari of Malwa and Agra. The Turani party went further in their distrust; they charged Sawai Jai Singh with an understanding with his co-religionists and disloyalty towards the Imperial throne. Khan-i-Dauran, Sawai Jai Singh's friend and patron, pleaded the inability of the Imperial forces to contend with the Maratha hordes. He spoke of his conciliatory policy as having won over the Peshwa to the Imperial cause. For had he not, added he, sent his mother north on the pretext of a pilgrimage? The Peshwa would soon follow her with his family, come to Delhi, pay homage to the Emperor and prove the most loyal and the most active servant of the Crown. The Emperor, he further added, must congratulate him (Khan Dauran) and his friend Jai Singh on their sagacity in having secured such a powerful chief as the Peshwa as an ally and a servant for the grant of territories which were held by rebels and thieves (and which were therefore not yielding any revenues to the Imperial Government). Sadat Khan who so loudly advocated the policy of resistance and demanded to be placed in charge of Malwa and Agra, was a rogue and a cheat. His friendship with the Nizam he may use to place another prince on the throne. While the progress of the Maratha arms dismayed the monarch, the advocacy of his favourite minister and the logic of his argument seemed equally convincing and he wavered between the courses of action to be pursued.[1]

The discussions in the Imperial Court had their repercussions in the Courts of the Rajput Rajahs and were watched with interest by the agents of the Peshwa. The Peshwa's mother had gone north on a pilgrimage this year (1735).[2] And as she progressed towards Benares by way of Udepur and Jaipur, the occasion of her visit was used by these Chiefs to communicate their secret views to the Peshwa.[3] Jai Singh after

1. S. P. D. XIV, 39, 47.
2. She left Poona in Feb. 1735, vide S. P. D. IX, 11.
3. S. P. D. XIV, 39, 47 and XXX, 128, 131, 134.

a feeble attempt to check the Marathas in 1733 had left Malwa to their mercy. His attempt in August 1734 to organize a league of the Rajput princes for common defence had failed.[4] He hoped fondly he could retain the provinces and along with them his importance in the imperial council by banking on his friendship with the Marathas. He conveyed to the Peshwa's Vakil, that he ever guarded the prestige and importance of his Master (the Peshwa) because he distrusted the Turk (i.e. the Mughal Emperor). If the latter had triumphed over the Deccani forces he would have shown him scant regard. If the Peshwa would now extend him his support, he would yet retain the provinces ; otherwise they would be placed under the command of a hostile chief and the Peshwa would lose all the advantages he had obtained so far from their being in the hands of a friend. Let him with Sindhia, Holkar and Jadhav come north at the head of a large force ; he would give him twenty lakhs of rupees in cash (as Chauth for Malwa) and also pay his troops. They would then confer together and through the mediation of Khan-i-Dauran secure the Peshwa's demands and arrange a visit to the Emperor. If the demands were not accepted the Peshwa was at liberty to break off negotiations and pursue other measures.[5]

These proposals were followed by the ominous news of the Emperor having effected a reconciliation between the Vazir and Abhay Singh of Marwar and of his having appointed the former to the charge of Agra, Malwa and Gujarat. If Jai Singh joined the Vazir, with his troops, his territory was not to be molested ; otherwise no regard was to be shown to him.[6] The Padishah was greatly dissatisfied with Jai Singh's management of affairs and wanted to place them in abler hands. Saadat Khan suggested a simultaneous campaign against the Bundelas by reinstating Bangash in the Subahdari of Allahabad, and appointing himself to Patna. It was common talk that two armies would march southwards against the Marathas ;

4. Tod I, pp. 430-31.
5. S. P. D. XIV, 47.
6. S. P. D. XIV, 39.

the one led by Jai Singh and Khan-i-Dauran by way of Jai Nagar and the other by way of Gwalior under the command of Vazir Qamruddin Khan, Saadat Khan and Abhay Singh.[7]

The Peshwa felt he could no longer remain away from the scene; his presence at the head of a large army was necessary to defeat the machinations of the Turani party and wring more concessions by appearing to support the Hindustani leaders.

Tents were sent in advance on the auspicious day of 3rd October 1735 and the Peshwa commenced his march on the 8th.[8] Sindhia and Holkar, who had the management of operations in Malwa for the previous four years and had thus gained considerable experience in that region, accompanied him with several other captains of note—chief among them being Tukoji and Anand Rao Pawar, and Kanthaji Kadam Bande. On account of Pilaji's illness, the command of the Bundelkhand force devolved on his son Satwaji Jadhav, with whom was associated Baji Bhivrao.[9] The two forces commenced their march simultaneously, separating as they approached the Narmada.

The news of the Peshwa marching in person into Hindustan created a stir in the Courts of foreign rulers. For three years Imperial troops had struggled vainly against Maratha generals. Now the Master himself, the dreaded Peshwa, was going north and momentous changes were expected to follow in the wake of the invasion. The Nizam, ever watchful of his neighbour's movements, began mobilising his army; the Emperor called to his side Saadat Khan who had vaunted of his valour and of his readiness to check the advance of the Southerners.[10]

---

7. *Idem.*

8. S. P. D. XXII, pp. 168-69.

9. Persian authorities speak of Pilaji's Bundelkhand operations for the year 1735-36. The incidents they describe all relate to the previous year. See P. Jadhav's itinerary in S. P. D. XXX, pp. 313-8. In 1736 Jadhav was ill and later commanded forces in Konkan. He did not visit Hindustan that year. See S. P. D. XXII, 306-9: (pp. 168-70).

10. S. P. D. XIV, 40-42.

The Peshwa marked the commencement of his operations by a diplomatic offensive. He opened the campaign with proposals to the Hindu rulers of Rajputana to rally under his banner.[11] He was going north relying on the assurances of Sawai Jai Singh that his appearance beyond the Narmada at the head of a respectable force would dishearten the opposition of the Turani party and would persuade the Emperor to make far reaching concessions. The Chauth his armies were already collecting from Malwa and Bundelkhand, with the consent, open or secret, of the Subahdar. For this position he would obtain legal sanction and would also demand the transfer of the province to himself as Viceroy. But instead of formulating his demands in advance he decided to present them after his meeting and discussion with Sawai Jai Singh.

The Peshwa left the Deccan in October 1735.[12] By the end of November he had forded the Tapti at Nandurbar.[13] In December the hill fort of Kukshi was assaulted. Lunawara and Dungarpur were laid under contribution. On January 1736 the Peshwa was reported to have arrived in Banswara on the border of Mewar.[14] For the year last his agents had plied the Rana with their counsel that it would be to the utmost advantage for the safety of the Rana's state to make over the pargana of Banera to their Chief. The Rana was obdurate and procrastinated with the Maratha agents.[15] The Peshwa was now to try the effects of a personal persuasion. Sending away his hordes towards Shahpura, he arrived at Udepur in the first week of February, with a picked force of 8000[16] and was received with great ceremony by Baba Takht Singh, a Mewar Noble of the first rank and lodged in the Champa Bag grounds. On the next day after his arrival a Darbar was held in his

11. S. P. D. XXIX, 39 and Mss paper.
12. S. P. D. XXII, p. 168.
13. S. P. D. XIV, 42.
14. S. P. D. XIV, 50, 51.
15. S. P. D. XXX, 128, 131, 134, 143, etc.
16. S. P. D. XXX, 160.

honour where the Rana in person welcomed his noble guest. Gracefully waiving the honour of sharing the exalted seat with the Rana, the Peshwa sat just below near him and after formal preliminaries, opened negotiations for the cession of Banera district. The Rana promised him a tribute of one lakh and a half of rupees, but turned down the proposal of parting with his territory.[17]

While yet at Udepur, the Peshwa began receiving envoys from the various potentates. Ayamal, the Diwan of Jai Singh, arrived with rich presents of cash, jewellery, horses and an elephant, and on behalf of his master invited him to visit Jainagar.[18] On 4th February the Peshwa saw the famous Jalmandir at Udepur and left the Mewar capital on the 8th.[19] Mahadeo Bhat Hingne had been already despatched to the Peshwa carrying with him the terms Sawaiji would propose to the Emperor for acceptance. They consisted of a cash subsidy of twenty lakhs of rupees, a Jagir of forty lakhs in Malwa and a tankah on the territory of Dost Muhammad Rohilla.[20] The Peshwa's progress towards Jaipur was a triumphant march. The Imperial Government was anxious to come to terms with him,[21] while the Hindu Chiefs and Hindu populace looked on him as a deliverer for whom they were long waiting. On the 3rd March the Peshwa arrived at Bhamola near Jai Nagar.[22] On the 4th March the two leaders met with great éclat and conferred together on the policy to be pursued.[23] On 8th March arrived Yadgar Khan and another envoy to discuss and, if possible settle the demands of the Peshwa. Before start-

17. Tod I, p. 440, Fall of the Mughal Empire I, pp. 260-262 and Gauri Shankar Ojha in his History of the Rajputs.

18. S. P. D. XIV, 50-51.

19. S. P. D. XXX, p. 321.

20. S. P. D. XIV, 50.

21. Idem.

22. The place of meeting is given in Vamsha Bhaskar as *Bhambholao*, 30 miles due east of Ajmer and 19 m. S.-E. of Kishangarh.

23. S. P. D. XXX, p. 322. The entries in the Peshwa Rozkird, expenditure side, leave no doubt about the date of the meeting. The cover page giving the place of the Peshwa's camp is unfortunately lost.

ing the negotiations the Peshwa took care to receive 20 lakhs as the chauth of the province.[24]

While terms for a peaceful settlement were being discussed by the Peshwa, his armies were not keeping idle in the field. The force under Satwoji Jadhav and Baji Bhivrao had, as previously related, separated from the main army in November and struck a north easterly route.[25] It arrived in Bundelkhand in January 1736, Datia and Orcha paid tribute, as also the Zamindars of Suklora, Gujrola, Pachor, Uchat and Bhadawar. Hirdesa and Jagat raj, the sons of Chhatrasal, even agreed to join the Peshwa with their respective quotas should the latter arrive in Bundelkhand.[26] By February Baji Bhivrao reported to the Peshwa "There is no place in Bundelkhand (all having submitted and paid chauth) to which I can now advance. I cannot stay here and subsist my troops much longer. I wait for orders where I should proceed next.[27]

It was suggested to Baji Bhivrao by Hirdesa and Jagat Raj, his Bundela allies that he should cross the Jumna at Kalpi, and lay waste the Subah of Allahabad. But the Jumna was not as yet fordable and could not be crossed without boats.[28] The Peshwa was negotiating a peaceful settlement with the Imperial Government and disapproved the proposal of attacking its territory.[29] Baji Bhivrao therefore moved into Jadhav Hati in the direction of Gwalior. The Delhi Government apprehending that the Marathas would break in the direction of Agra, despatched Muhammad Khan Bangash to guard the fords of the Chambal near Dholpur. He arrived at Dholpur about 14th January, crossed the river and entrenching himself in a ravine, waited for the Marathas to attack him. Baji Bhivrao advanc-

24. Rustam Ali, p. 52.
25. S. P. D. XXX, 140-1, 172.
26. S. P. D. XIV, 52-56 and XV, 4, 8-16, 87-90, explain the activities of Baji Bhivrao for the year 1736. Some of these papers, esp. 8-16 have been wrongly placed by the editor in the year 1737.
27. S. P. D. XIV, 52. 28. S. P. D. XV, 16, 89.
29. S. P. D. XIV, 56.

ed to Nurabad, but observing that Bangash was not coming out in the open, assaulted Bagtini the stronghold of the Sikarbars. Bangash in the meanwhile moved to another difficult position between the Kuwari and the Chambal and refused to budge. He sent a Vakil to the Maratha Chiefs to seek terms.[30] As the Peshwa was himself negotiating a settlement with the Imperialists he recalled the Bundelkhand force and Baji Bhivrao joined the Peshwa near Ujjain about the beginning of May.[31]

A part of the Peshwa's force under Sindhia, Holkar, Bande and Anand Rao Pawar had been ordered to lay waste the territory of Abhay Singh of Marwar.[32] This prince was opposing Maratha ambitions and had connected himself with the Turani party,[33] which was bitterly hostile to Maratha demands. Abhay Singh was to be taught what a dangerous game he was playing in allying himself with the Turani party. From Dongarpur, Sindhia and Holkar advanced to Shahapur and from Shahapura entered the Marwar country. For two months the army lived on that territory. On 1st April Merta was assaulted and paid a fine. After Merta, Nagore, Ajmere were visited and laid under contribution. About the end of April the force rejoined the Peshwa.[34]

The Peshwa in the meanwhile had presented his demands to the Imperial Government. Through his envoy, Dhondo Mahadeo he asked for (i) a hereditary estate under the Crown, (ii) grants of mansabs and Jagirs for himself and his chiefs, (iii) cessation of hostilities against his army, (iv) the office of Sardeshpande of the Deccan, and (v) an indemnity to meet the war expenses. He also asked to be received by the Emperor in Court. Items nos. (i) and (v) were granted and promises of granting (ii), (iii) and (iv) were held out.[35] Another yad

30. S. P. D. XIII, 48 ; XIV, 55, 56.
31. S. P. D. III, 201.
32. S. P. D. XIII, 49 ; the correct date of receipt of the paper is 7 May 1736.
33. S. P. D. XIV, 39.
34. S. P. D. XIII, 49, XIV, 14 and Tarikh-i-Hind, P. 52.
35. S. P. D. XV, p. 92.

was presented by which the Peshwa asked for the Subahdari of Malwa and for thirteen lakhs of rupees to meet his expenses.[36] Both the items were granted. A further list called for Chimaji Appa, the Peshwa's brother, being presented with two lakhs of rupees in cash as he was a loyal and zealous servant of the Imperial Throne. This was granted.[37] The Peshwa then requested to be given the right to levy tribute from the Chiefs and Zamindars of Malwa.[38] On the top of this came further staggering demands :—

(i) The Subah of Malwa, inclusive of the states, to be granted in Jagir to the Peshwa and he to be appointed Governor of the Province.

(ii) Yar Muhammad Rohilla and Ijjat Khan to be ejected from Malwa and their territory to be made over to the Peshwa.

(iii) The forts of Mandu, Dhar and Raisin to be ceded. The territory upto the Chambal to be granted to the Peshwa in Jagir. He promised to continue those Chiefs in their estate who would pay him Nazzar.

The Peshwa to be given an assignment of 50 lakhs of rupees on the revenues of Bengal.

Allahabad, Benares, Gaya, and Mathura (all places of worship of the Hindus) to be ceded to the Peshwa

The Sardeshpandeship of the Deccan to be conferred on the Peshwa.

A Jagir of fifty lakhs in the Deccan to be granted to the Peshwa : The Shahzada to be appointed to administer the province ; a share to be given to the Peshwa in the revenues of the Deccan which may be collected with his aid. The cession of Shivner and Tanjore.[39]

36. S. P. D. XV, p. 93.
37. *Idem*.
38. *Ibid*, p. 94. These were Orcha, Datia, Narwar, Chanderi, Seondha, Sipri, Bhadawar, Kotah, Bundi, Rampura and Amjhera.
39. S. P. D. XV, pp. 95-6.

Starting with a request for the grant of the chauth of Malwa and some cash to cover his expenses, the Peshwa went on increasing his demands till at last he asked for virtual control over Malwa, Bundelkhand, Bengal and the Deccan. This almost took away the breath of the Mughal Court. Compromise is possible only when the two parties can agree to a minimum of concessions. The Imperial Government decided to fight rather than make an ignominious surrender. As long as the Peshwa remained in Malwa with his troops it procrastinated merely to gain time.

CHAPTER XI

THE PESHWA'S DASH ON THE IMPERIAL CAPITAL.

The Peshwa for a time remained in Malwa guiding peace proposals. At the end of May he left for the Deccan and reached Poona on 24th June.[1] His generals Sindhia, Holkar and Pawar continued in Malwa to complete the negotiations and conclude the final agreement. On 25th June Ranoji Sindhia in a strongly worded despatch to the Maratha ambassador at Delhi, asked him to obtain from the Court the long promised farman of the Viceroyalty and the chauth of Malwa and cash to meet the expenses of his force.[2] The farman was at last issued on 29th Sept. 1736 bestowing on the Peshwa a Jagir, a Mansab, the mahals of his watan as well as a dress of honour, a Jegha and a Sarpech.[3] All that Jai Singh could persuade the Emperor to grant to the Peshwa was the deputy Governorship of the province, which fell far short of the latter's demands, and the renewal of hostilities was inevitable.

1. S. P. D. XXII, 333.
2. Rajwade, VI, 95-97 ; these three papers should be placed in 1736.
3. S. P. D. XV, p. 86 ; XIV, 62 refers to the farman. It should be dated 23 Jamadi-ul-Akhir ; the date of the issue of the farman is 29 Sept. 1736 and not 8 Sept. as given by the editor.

Calling to his standard a vast force of fifty thousand horse, the Peshwa commenced his march on 12th Nov. 1736.[4] By rapid marches he arrived in Malwa and effected a junction at Bhilsa with the troops which had been quartered in the province for the monsoon.[5] Except for the strongholds of the Rohilla Chiefs, the province had for all practical purposes become a Maratha principality. This island of opposition to Maratha influence could no longer be suffered to remain. The Peshwa therefore directed his arms against the refractory Yar Muhammad Rohilla, invested him in Bhopal and forced him to pay a contribution of five lakhs of rupees (December 1736).[6] Bhilsa was next attacked and carried after a week's fighting (13th Jan. 1737).[7] The province of Malwa thus completely subdued could no longer be used to support the huge hordes the Peshwa was leading. He therefore struck off north east, overawed the Bundela feudatories of Orcha, Datia, Narwar[8] and at the end of February 1737 arrived near Bhadawar. The Raja of Bhadawar commanded a well equipped army, in addition to 50 war elephants. Having received assurances of being supported with all his resources by Saadat Khan of Oudh, he refused to pay the annual tribute and prepared for fight. He was however betrayed by his brother who went over to the Marathas and revealed them the secret of the Raja's defences. On his advice the Peshwa divided his army ; while one part delivered a frontal attack on the Raja's force, the other detachment made a detour and entered the city of Ater from the rear. Unable to defend his capital any longer the Raja sought safety in the fortress. There he was closely invested and was so much harassed

4. S. P. D. XXII, 339, 341 ; according to Br. Ch. Appendix 46, his plan was either to march on Delhi or descend into the Doab.

5. S. P. D. XV, 5, XXX, 192 ; The junction was effected on 5th Jan. 1737. Bhopal was reduced prior to this.

6. S. P. D. X, 27 ; the date of the paper is (recd.) 19 January 1737.

7. S. P. D. XV, 5.

8. Itihas Samgraha, Aitihasik Charitren, p. 69.

that he at last made his submission (18th Feb.) and agreed to pay twenty lakhs in tribute and ten elephants.[9]

The Peshwa's arrival on the northern borders of Bundelkhand, hardly 70 miles distant from Agra, constituted a menace of the first magnitude to the Empire which had to be warded off. Large armies were equipped and put in the field under the command of the Vazir and the Mir Bakhshi. Imperial farmans were sent out calling other Mughal Chiefs and Rajput princes to rush to the defence of the capital with their quotas. Jai Singh in response started from his capital with a force fifteen thousand strong and a park of artillery. Abhay Singh of Marwar followed with his contingents of Marwaris.[10] Saadat Khan of Oudh was moving swiftly and was reported to be approaching Agra.

The Peshwa had undertaken the expedition with the express object of overawing his opponents into granting his demands by a demonstration of armed might and instead he found the Mughal armies converging on Agra and effectively barring his path northward in the direction of the Capital. It therefore became absolutely necessary to break up this concentration of enemy forces. To create a diversion and prevent junction of the enemy at Agra he despatched a strong detachment of ten thousand troops under the command of some of his ablest chiefs Malhar Rao Holkar, Satwaji Jadhav, Baji Bhivrao and Ruprai Adaru in the Doab to lay waste the territory of Saadat Khan. Holkar's troops crossed into Doab and marched on swiftly in a northerly direction leaving behind a trail of fire and destruction.[11]

Itimadpur and Firozabad in the Doab opposite to Agra were laid under the sword and the Marathas reached Jalesar when they were sighted by the advance column of Saadat Khan's army. Marching day and night from Itawa Saadat Khan had arrived near where the Marathas were plundering.

9. S. P. D. XV, 18, 47 ; Peshwa Rozkird and Rustam Ali, p. 53.

10. S. P. D. XV, 18.

11. S. P. D. XV 47.

His vanguard of 12 thousand commanded by his nephew Mansur Ali Khan marched slightly ahead of the main army and contacted enemy troops.

Thinking they were encountering the entire army of Sadat Khan, the Marathas attempted their favourite encircling movement. Mansur Ali retired to the main army fighting, and the Marathas who followed him, found themselves opposed to a force six times their number. Nothing but a swift retreat could save the Maratha detachment from utter destruction. Swerving round they made for the Jumna, with the Khan's army in close pursuit. In the confusion of the retreat the force lost its direction, missed the ford by which it had entered the Doab and had to sacrifice its baggage to the enemy. A number of casualties were also suffered. Holkar had evidently been surprised, little imagining that he would be overtaken by the Khan's army. His flight at the last moment alone enabled him to bring his force back and join the Peshwa at Kotila near Gwalior. This happened on 12th March 1737.[12]

Saadat Khan followed the flying troops of Holkar and crossed the river by means of a bridge of boats near Agra and awaited the arrival of the armies of the Vazir and the Mir Bakhshi to start operations against the Peshwa.[13] The Peshwa was foiled in one more attempt to dissolve the concentration of enemy forces and had to think of other plans. Retiring to a little distance from Agra he sent away his baggage and camp followers, under heavy escort of his Bundela allies, Jagat Raj and Hirdesa, and Baji Bhivrao. The temporary withdrawal of the Peshwa's troops created an impression that demoralised by the recent setback, the Marathas could no longer face the imperialists and were making for the south.[14]

The Vazir and the Mir Bakhshi were marching towards Agra with numerous forces to join Saadat Khan. It was neces-

12. S. P. D. XV, 17, 22, 27-8, 47, XXX, 198, 365-6 and Rustam Ali, pp. 53-54.

13. S. P. D. XV, 17, 27 ; Rustam Ali, p. 54.

14. Letter of Pilaji Jadhav in Itihas Samgraha, Ait. Ch. p. 69 ; S. P. D. XV, 24, 34, 38.

sary to destroy the Khan's force before this could happen, but the khan having taken up a strong position near Agra the light Maratha horse that made up the Peshwa's army, was unable to deal the smashing blow that would shatter the Khan's force ; neither could it manoeuvre rapidly in its present grounds near the rivers Chambal and Kuwari where the terrain was full of ravines and was unsuitable for rapid movements of cavalry. The Peshwa therefore decided to shift his ground and move out into the open.[15]

Saadat Khan had communicated his recent success over the Peshwa's detachment in glowing terms. He claimed to have destroyed two thousands Marathas, to have captured several leaders of note and to have sent two thousand more to a watery grave ; he boasted of soon driving away the Marathas beyond the Chambal. The Peshwa was determined to let the Emperor know how empty was the claim made by the Khan and how little trust could be placed in his words. Either the Khan's force must be wiped out or the Peshwa should show himself at the capital and put it to the sword. As the Khan was not coming out, the Peshwa chose the latter alternative.[16]

The march on the capital in the face of two armies moving towards Agra was not only a daring but a most hazardous enterprise. Its success, no doubt would force the hands of the feeble monarch, but the difficulties it presented looked almost insurmountable. Another man in the Peshwa's place would have flinched before them and beaten a hasty retreat, thus imperilling the position Maratha arms had won in the north. A serious blow and a setback to the nascent Maratha power would have resulted from withdrawing from the contest at this critical hour. The spell of Maratha invincibility would be gone. Knowing that the morale of the fighting force decides the issue of a battle much more than superiority of numbers or of equipment, the Peshwa determined to take the risk. Sending away his heavy baggage and other impediments to Bundelkhand

15. Peshwa's own account in the letter in Br. Ch. App. 27.
16. Idem.

he made a dash on the capital, so swiftly and secretly, that none of the Mughal Commanders were aware of his whereabouts till he was actually in the vicinity of the Capital. Avoiding the direct Delhi-Agra highway, the Peshwa followed an unfrequented route through the hilly country of the Jats and Mewatis and appeared before the Capital on 29th March, 1737.

In vivid language the Peshwa reported the event to his brother : "I was resolved to let the Emperor know the truth, to prove that I was still in Hindustan and to show him the Marathas at the gates of the Capital. We marched through the country of the Jats leaving the direct route. Khan Dauran and Bangash reached Agra and met Saadat Khan who had already arrived there with his army. My Vakil Dhondo Pant was with Khan Dauran. Saadat Khan sent him a message that Bajirao's army had been dispersed ; that he had fled beyond the Chambal, and it was no longer necessary to honour his envoy : he should be dismissed forthwith. Dhondo Pant was therefore sent away and arrived in my camp. We pressed on avoiding contact with the Vazir's army that passed near us. On 7 Zilhej (29th March, Tuesday) leaving the Barapula and the Kalika temple to our right, we arrived near the capital. I now changed my plan of sacking the capital. I knew that the Emperor and Khan Dauran were inclined to grant my demands, but that the Mughal faction was opposed to this conciliatory policy. I did not want to drive our friends to an extremity by committing sacrilege on the capital. I therefore sent letters assuring the Emperor. Our people seized some elephants coming out of the city and plundered at the temple of Bhawani where there was a fair. As I apprehended mischief to the city from the contiguity of our troops, I moved on to the jhil tank." [17]

Panic and consternation spread over the Mughal capital. Since the Marathas had arrived near the city it was concluded that the two armies sent against them had been overwhelmed and nothing was left to the Emperor, but to sue for peace on

17. Br. Ch. No. 27, (App.).

the Peshwa's terms or retire beyond the Jumna. To guard against surprise however, on the advice of the Mir Atish, Saduddin Khan, defensive works were put up and guns placed at intervals from the city to the enemy's encampment at the Jhil tank and the force on garrisoning duty at the capital was sent to hold up the enemy. Many of the younger nobles and courtiers who had never seen war before, but nevertheless boasted of their courage, made up this force. When the Peshwa was changing his grounds the next day (Wednesday) some of these chiefs thought that the Marathas afraid to attack, were falling back. Mir Hasan Khan Koka, Roz Afzunkhan, Amir Singh, Raja Shivsingh and Muzaffar Khan at the head of eight thousand troops advanced beyond the protection of their artillery and tried to engage the Maratha vanguard. Jadhav lured them on and sent back notice that the enemy was coming on. Bajirao at once perceived the advantage he had obtained and directed his veterans Malhar Rao Holkar, Ranoji Sindhia, Tukoji, Jiwaji and Yashwant Rao Pawars, Manaji Paygude, Govind Hari to support Jadhav. The Maratha horse advanced for battle, enveloped the Mughal column and routed it. Raja Shiv Singh and a number of Darbari nobles were slain. Mir Hasan Khan was wounded, 250 to 300 of the Emperor's bodyguard fell. 400 men were wounded. Roz Afzunkhan, Amir Khan, Muzaffar Khan and other Khans fled into the city. 2000 horses were captured, 5 or 6 thousand fled; Indraji Kadam, an officer of Ranoji Sindhia, had two of his fingers shot off. Very few men were lost on the Maratha side.[18]

The Peshwa had attained his object. His sudden appearance at the capital proved how very hollow were Sadat Khan's claims of his sweeping victory over the Marathas and of his being able to drive them beyond Narmada ; it demonstrated to the Emperor the futility of the policy of opposition advocated by the Turani leaders. The fair capital of the Mughals, the

18. Br. Ch. No. 27 ; S. P. D. XV, 37, 47 ; Irvine's account is slightly different in details. I base this on the Peshwa's letter printed in Br. Ch. and Jadhav's letter in Ait. Ch. pp. 69-71.

ancient city of Delhi, now awaited to be sacked and despoiled of its splendour and wealth by its new conqueror. But the Peshwa was not a barbarian cast in the mould of an Atilla or a Chengiz Khan. He had made a dash on the capital not to lay it under sword and fire, but to enforce on the Mughal Government the policy of concessions advocated by Jai Singh and Khan Dauran and favoured by the Emperor personally. The Peshwa rightly imagined that his mere appearance at the gates of the capital would force the hands of the Emperor. On 31st March he disappeared as suddenly as he had appeared two days earlier.

There was another strong reason for his sudden departure. Vazir Qamr-ud-din Khan who was moving towards Agra, learnt of the Peshwa's march on the capital while yet at Kaman Pahari[19] and immediately ordered a march back. On Wednesday (30th March) at noon the Peshwa was informed of the approach of the Vazir's army and decided to retire at once. In the evening after the Marathas had marched a distance of 10 miles they sighted near Badshahpur the Vazir's army. After a long and tiring march following a heavy engagement, the Peshwa was in no mood to attack the Vazir. Neither could the Vazir array his forces for battle, as his artillery and a part of his men were yet on the road. There was a brush between the two forces in the failing light of the day ; one elephant and a few horses were seized by the Marathas and then they moved another eight miles before encamping for the night.[20]

The leaders of the Mughal armies near Agra were utterly confounded by the course of events and found themselves in a quandary. Saadat Khan had arrived at that place on the 16th March and was joined by Khan Dauran on 23rd. While they were yet congratulating themselves and celebrating the recent success over the Marathas, news was brought to them of the march of the Peshwa on the capital and his arrival near Delhi. The Khans at once broke up their camp and hastened towards

19. About 65 miles from Delhi.
20. Br. Ch. App. 27 ; Jadhav's letter in Ait. Ch.

the imperial city. They came up with the Vazir on Thursday, 31st March ; but by that time the Peshwa was reported to have reached Rewari.[21]

Thus ended in smoke the proud boasts and wild schemes of the Mughal chiefs to chastise the Peshwa. While the Emperor yet wavered between a policy of appeasement as opposed to that of resistance and asked his chiefs to hold their hands, Saadat Khan had attacked a Maratha detachment and dispersed it. Magnifying this minor gain into a big victory, he spoke of beginning a campaign to sweep away the invaders beyond the Chambal. The Emperor was taken in by his vaunting claims and bestowed on him high honours and a *dress* for ridding him of a nightmare. He received a rude awakening when within a fortnight the Peshwa in person, of whose discomfiture the Khan had boasted, appeared before the capital. The Emperor felt nothing but disgust and contempt for this braggart and refused to grant him an interview or appoint him to the Subahdari of Malwa and Gujarat.[22] Saadat Khan left for his province of Oudh which the Marathas once more threatened to lay waste.[23] Bangash was ordered to hold on at Agra, while Abhay Singh went back to Marwar. Summer having now advanced the Vazir and the Mir Bakhshi retired to their mansions in the capital.[24]

Sawai Jai Singh all this while remained an idle spectator of events. The forces he commanded could have enabled him to cut off the retreat of the Peshwa's army through his territory by way of Rewari, Kotputli, Manoharpur and Lalsot, had he had the will to do so. The Marathas were lightly armed, the terrible privations they had suffered during the last fifteen days had rendered them unfit for facing the respectable force of Jai Singh. The Rajput was operating in his homeland and had the resources of his state at his service. The Marathas on the

21. Idem, also Rustam Ali, pp. 54-55.
22. S. P. D. XV, 29 ; Rustam Ali, p. 55.
23. S. P. D. XV, 23 ; 30-32.
24. S. P. D. XV, 29, 30.

other hand were in alien country cut off from even their base of operations and could have offered little resistance to the serried phalanx of the Kachwa cavalry. But Jai Singh's sympathies lay with the Marathas which made him look on quiescently while the empire's provinces were one by one overrun and despoiled by them. The revenues of Malwa he was sharing with the Marathas since 1732 : Last year he had advised the Emperor to appoint the Peshwa to the Deputy Governorship and thus abandon the province to him. While imperial forces were frantically running about to save the capital, this Rajput Chief, one of its leading nobles, was conferring with the Peshwa's Vakil and thanking his master profusely for looking on him as his brother and not molesting his territory.[25] From Rajputana the Peshwa entered Bundelkhand to pick up his baggage.[26]

The Mughals had made a supreme effort to bring the Marathas to book. They had put in the field four fine armies amounting to over a hundred thousand men equipped with ample funds and military stores. In the absence of capable generals to lead them these splendid armies had merely tired themselves out with marching and counter-marching without coming to close grips with the enemy. By his clever strategy the Peshwa had outmanoeuvred his opponents and completely immobilised them. The Turani party which opposed Maratha ambitions was discredited in the councils of the Empire where the influence of the Hindustani leader, Khan-i-Dauran, the friend of Jai Singh, the advocate of the peace policy, once more became supreme.[27]

25. S. P. D. XV, 23.

26. S. P. D. XV, 38 ; The Peshwa was at Somavali on 29 Jilhej and at Sironj in May ; S. P. D. XV, 38, 42.

27. S. P. D. XV, 30.

CHAPTER XII

THE BATTLE OF BHOPAL

(1737-1738)

Having established in the Imperial Government influence favourable to Maratha demands the Peshwa looked forward for an early cession of Malwa and compliance with his other claims. But a new combination of forces thwarted the immediate realization of his ambitious schemes and challenged his supremacy in the imperial councils. This was an alliance of the Viceroy of the Deccan with the Imperial Government.

Nizam-ul-mulk, the Viceroy of the Deccan was a servant of the Crown and professed himself to be so. Having realised that the empire was disintegrating he had retired to the Deccan in 1724 and assumed independence in everything but name. His professions of submission had never deceived the Delhi Court, which looked on him as a rebel and only awaited a favourable opportunity to crush him and recover the vast dominions of the six provinces of the Deccan. Its Malwa Governors had secrét instructions to bring this rebel to book whenever an opportunity should present itself.[1] The Nizam was not unaware of the veiled hostility of the Crown towards him and kept himself well-informed of happenings at the Court. But he had realized with the Marathas the want of energy of the Mughal Government in which he found his best defence. Another factor which kept his superior fully engaged and worked in his favour, was the expansionist policy of the Peshwa in pursuance of which the latter had crossed the Narmada and was overrunning imperial territory.

The Nizam however knew the direction from which another and a greater danger threatened him. There was no love lost between him and his Maratha neighbours. Their aggressive policy marked them out as the common enemy of the Empire, as well as of its Deccan Viceroy. Their claims of Chauth

1. S. P. D. XIII, 10 and Ahwal-i-Khwaqin, as quoted by Irvine, II.

and Sardeshmukhi introduced a baneful principle in his Government of the Deccan, made a mockery of its sovereignty, and reduced him, (the Nizam) to the position of a tributary of the Maratha state. As the Marathas insisted on collecting their dues by means of their own officers, an authority superior to and undermining his own was established in the Government which made the existence of his state precarious and his subordination most galling to him. To oppose the claims of the Marathas and break up the chains that bound him became therefore the watchword of his policy. Direct opposition against the superior military strength of the Marathas being out of question, the Nizam encouraged one rival claimant against another for the Satara Gadi, fomented discord among rival groups at the Court and actively supported the Peshwa's enemies in an effort to secure his release from the tribute.

His first attempt to assume complete direction of his affairs was defeated at Palkhed in February 1728. His second attempt to embroil the Peshwa in his domestic feuds was likewise foiled when the Peshwa forestalled him and overpowered Dabhade in the battle of Dabhai in 1731 April. To save his uncertain existence the Nizam at once sought an understanding with the Peshwa, and a secret compact was concluded by which "it was settled that Asaf Jah should support the Government of Baji Rao, while the other carried his arms in Malwa, 'and pushed his conquests over the Emperor's remaining dominions.' The Nizam's object was to turn the Peshwa's energies and resources in directions other than his own ; nor is it unlikely that he expected the latter to expend his strength and suffer a set back in his policy of northward expansion, Events however belied the Nizam's expectations. The weakness of the empire revealed itself more and more glaringly as the Mughal-Maratha struggle developed and Mughal arms suffered reverses after reverses. Instead of being checked and driven back, the Peshwa reached the very gates of the capital and threatened to subvert the Empire itself.

With an envious eye the Nizam looked on the progress

of Maratha arms beyond the Narmada. Their successes against Bangash, Jai Singh, Khan Dauran, Vazir Qamruddin Khan increased his anxiety. In the summer of 1735 while the Vazir was struggling against Pilaji Jadhav near Narwar, the Nizam attempted to reinforce the former with a detachment of five thousand horse and went to the length of asking Pilaji Jadhav to retire.[2] The Peshwa's march to the north (1736 Feb.), his meeting with Sawai Jai Singh and the subsequent negotiations were watched by the Nizam with the gravest concern and discussed at his court day and night.[3] He was always apprehensive that the Mughal diplomats would turn against him his own device of involving the Marathas in hostilities with them. His apprehensions proved true to a letter. In the demands made by the Peshwa on the Imperial Government one was for conceding him a new right over the Subah of the Deccan—the right of Sardeshpande—and another for appointing the Subahdar of the province with his consent. The claim of Sardeshpandeship was promised by the Imperial Government as thereby it expected the Marathas to distract the Nizam.[4]

But the 1736 negotiations proved abortive. In the next campaigning season the Peshwa invaded the north with a formidable army and reducing Bhopal, Bhilsa, Chanderi and Ater, made a dash on the capital. It was suicidal for the Nizam to look on events placidly while the bulwarks that held back the Marathas were being demolished one by one. He decided to make common cause with the Imperial Government to save it and save himself thereby.[5]

While the Nizam lay encamped at Burhanpur reports reached him on 31st March (1737) of disaster having overtaken the Maratha detachment that had crossed into the 'Doab'.[6]

2. B. I. S. M. Quarterly, XII, 4.
3. S. P. D. X, 93, & XIV, 43.
4. S. P. D. XV, p. 92 says the right of Sardeshpande was promised on condition of payment of Nazar. P. 96 says it was not granted.
5. S. P. D. X, 27.
6. S. P. D. XV, 17, 22.

This was heartening news. The Nizam made up his mind that the time to strike had arrived. On 8th April he sent back his heavy artillery and moved to Hindia ford.[7] To protect his dominions from the inroads of the Marathas in his absence Abdul Rahim Khan and Anarul Khan were posted in Khandesh with a force of five thousand. His son Nasir Jang held Aurangabad with another force of ten thousand. Chandrasen Jadhav kept vigil over Bijapur and Bir Pathri, while Shujaat Khan was directed to watch the activities of Raghuji Bhonsle.[8] To dispel suspicions of his movements the Nizam conveyed to Raja Shahu and the Peshwa assurances of his friendly sentiments towards them. His earnest desire to pay homage in person to his liege-lord and wash away the infamy of being looked on as a rebel was, he gave out, the sole cause of his making the journey to the feet of the Emperor.[9] But his professions deceived nobody. The Peshwa's reporters had uttered warnings about the Nizam's unfriendly attitude several times before.[10] The Peshwa was once more cautioned against the danger. Deoji Somwanshi wrote to Chimaji Appa to put the Peshwa on guard against the Nizam's friendly declarations. He told him that the Nawab's fear of being ousted from the Subahdari of the Deccan had urged him to undertake this journey, that he had been advising the Imperial Court not to surrender to the Marathas and had offered to make the Empire's cause his own.[11] The attitude of the Imperial Government stiffened since getting these assurances from the Nizam. It invited the Nizam to the Court for discussing plans of common defence and broke off negotiations with the Peshwa.[12]

On the 19th April the Nizam reached Bhamgarh.[13] His march to the north at this crisis was meant to revive the flagging spirit of resistance among the Mughal Court and therefore

7. *Ibid.* 25.
8. S. P. D. XV, 26,
9. S. P. D. X, 34, XV, 26.
10. S. P. D. X, 27, 91, 94, XIV, 43.
11. S. P. D. XV, 26.
12. S. P. D. XV, 33.
13. S. P. D. XV, 27.

menaced the Peshwa's position. To defeat this move the Peshwa called on his brother to attack the Nawab's territory and keep him engaged in the south.[14] But Chimaji being then in close grips with the Portuguese over Bassein was unable to move out to hinder the Nawab's march.[15] Awaji Kawde's small detachment in Khandesh was defeated by Jamaluddin[16] and the Nawab moved on freely into Malwa.

The Peshwa who had returned to Bhadawar after the dash on the capital was awaiting peace proposals from the Mughal Court. He was informed that the Court refused to discuss matters relating to Maratha claims till the arrival of the Nizam.[17] The Peshwa knowing full well that a coalition between the Imperial Government and the Nizam would threaten his new conquest and which must therefore be prevented at any cost, marched in the direction of the latter and came up with him near Sironj in the middle of May.[18] He was wise enough to know what reliance to place in the Nizam's declarations of friendly sentiments. To reach Delhi without loss of time the Nawab had rid himself of his heavy baggage and was marching with light troops amounting to not more than twenty thousand.[19] The news of the Peshwa's appearance at Delhi and of the dissolution of the several armies sent against him reached him while he was yet at Sironj.[20] The Nawab had expected to attack the Marathas in the rear while the Imperial forces faced them in front, now found his position untenable. He had been caught up by the Peshwa at a point* where he could expect no immediate reinforcements either from his son or from Delhi. Nothing but a miracle, it seemed, could save him and his force from total annihilation and a miracle did happen. To Jadhav who was deputed to the Nawab to comprehend the secret object of his visit to the Emperor, the

14. Br. Ch. Appendix No. 27.
15. S. P. D. XV, 27, 39; XIV, 45.
16. S. P. D. XIV, 45, XV, 25.
17. S. P. D. XV, 33, 21.
18. S. P. D. XV, 42.
19. Idem.
20. Idem.

*Sironj is 225 miles from Agra and 215 from Burhanpur.

Nizam repeated his friendly declarations and showed him so much regard as to dupe him completely.[21] He was allowed to move on unmolested and was escorted part of the way by the Peshwa's troops. Moving by way of Kalapani, Shahdora, and Budha Dongar the Nizam reached Delhi by the end of June.[22] To remove the least suspicions about his dark intentions he went to the length of dismissing the Maratha cavalry that had accompanied him so far from the south.[23]

Bajirao's conduct in giving the Nizam a free passage remains inexplicable. The Nawab was not an unknown factor or an utter stranger to the Peshwa. He knew him as a crafty, cunning and intriguing diplomat, ever ready to avail himself of domestic feuds among the Marathas and whose policy had been one of consistent opposition to their ambitions. The Nizam's declarations of his repentance for his past misconduct towards the Crown and his anxiety to make atonements for it at this particular moment were such as could carry conviction to none, much less to the Peshwa. But in spite of this the Peshwa chose to believe in the professions of his adversary and as a result had to prepare for another trial of arms.

It may be argued that since 1732 the Nizam had agreed to give the Peshwa a free hand in his northern conquests and had kept quiet while the Peshwa's armies were operating in distant lands and that he even sent away a part of his troops to the Deccan so as to make his move appear innocent. But that was not of material importance. The Imperial Government lacked not men and resources but capable leadership. This the Nizam amply supplied and buoyed it up for fresh resistance.

On his arrival at Delhi the Nizam was received by the

21. S. P. D. XV, 48, 44, 45, 49 ; XIV, 59, 60. The last two papers should be dated 30 May, 2 June 1737. No. 48 XV should be dated 28 May 1737.

22. S. P. D. XV, 45, 49 & Rustam Ali, p. 56 : on 3rd July he had his first audience of the emperor.

23. S. P. D. XV, 44, 49 ; also XIV, 59. No. 44 XV, should be dated 29 May 1737.

Vazir in person. The best residence was placed at his disposal. The Emperor lavished on him all kinds of favours appointing him Wakil-i-Mutlaq. The Mughal Court looked on the Nizam as a saviour who was to rescue the Empire from the wild barbarians of the South. Whatever he asked for or suggested was granted. During the last fifteen years the Maratha power had expanded enormously engulfing Gujarat, Malwa and Bundelkhand and now their northern boundaries impinged on the province of Agra so near the capital itself. Jai Singh's policy of appeasement had proved a failure and was discredited. On (17 Rabi-ul-akhir) 3rd August he was deprived of his charge and the Nizam's eldest son Firuj-jang was appointed Governor of Agra and Malwa. A sum of sixty lacks of rupees was paid to him to equip his army which the chief nobles of the Court and Rajput princes were asked to join.[24] The Nizam abandoned the defensive strategy followed by his predecessors. He would carry the war south and would not wait for the Marathas to cross the Narmada after the close of the rains and start their career of devastation.[25] With an army of thirty thousand and a fine park of artillery the Nizam left the capital to seek and if possible, destroy the enemy. He marched through Bundelkhand where he was joined by Saadat Khan's troops under his nephew Mansur Ali Khan, the Rajas of Orcha, Datia, Sabhasing Bundela and several other chieftains, till his force swelled to seventy thousand in addition to hundred and twenty cannon drawn by elephants and 3,000 camels carrying rockets and swivels.[26] On 12th November the army reached Dhamoni.[27] About the middle of December it arrived near Bhopal by the route of Sironj.[28] The Maratha outposts were to be seized,

24. S. P. D. XV, 53.

25. Br. Ch. Appendix, 134.

26. S. P. D. XV, 56, 58, XXX, 207 ; also Br. Ch. app. 134, but the Peshwa in his letters places it at 35,000 which would appear to be more correct from the defensive tactics of its commander, at Bhopal. The rest were perhaps the Bungahs.

27. This is a surmise from No. 56 of XV.

28. Br. Ch. Appendix No. 33 and S. P. D. XV, 56-59.

their garrisons to be thrown back and then the Maratha force which would dare advance against the Imperial army was to be crushed between the force striking from Hyderabad and the one the Nizam was leading personally. But the Peshwa refused to act according to the dispositions of the Nizam. To the mighty preparations of the Imperial Govt. to wrest from him his new conquests he was determined to give an effective reply. He called up his detachments from the south, from before Bassein and at the head of 80,000 troops invaded Malwa crossing the Narmada near Punasha in the last week of November.[29] Another strong force of ten thousand under Chimaji Appa took up a position on the Tapti to prevent succour going to the Nawab from the Deccan.[30]

While the Nizam yet awaited reinforcements from the south to join him, the Peshwa came up with him near Bhopal on 15th December. The Nawab instead of going straight for his enemy awaited the Marathas to attack him, taking up a position near the town with the lake at his rear and a nullah protecting his front. This encouraged the Peshwa to take up the offensive. His troops advanced and delivered the attack against the centre of the enemy held by the Rajputs despite the heavy fire of their guns. Ranoji Sindhia, Pilaji Jadhav, Sayaji Gujar and other Siladars engaged the enemy at close quarters taking a heavy toll of killed and wounded. The Nizam without risking further, sought shelter behind the walls of Bhopal. His artillery and the defile of the nullah prevented the Peshwa from pressing the attack home. He retired to a distance and invested the Nizam in the fort.[31]

The City of Bhopal had now to provide for the immense mass of humanity making up the Mughal army, as well as their camp followers. The place was completely blockaded and no grain or grass could pass in from outside. Soon the small supply in the town was exhausted ; for a day the horses and

29. Br. Ch. Appendix No. 134.
30. S. P. D. XXX, 207.
31. Br. Ch. Appendix 33, and Rajwade VI, 117.

camels subsisted on the bark of trees and water reeds. Even this could no longer be obtained. The Rajput and Bundela troops now repented of the folly of having joined the Nizam. Their baggage being held up in the town they could not effect their escape from the fort, nor could they leave their entrenched position to engage the enemy for fear that they may not be supported by the Nizam's Mughal troops. The Nizam on his part suspected the loyalty of the Rajputs and was not prepared to risk the rest of his army. Men and animals famished for want of food and to their great annoyance the Marathas day and night threw in rockets in the huddled mass of the Mughal soldiery and caused great confusion in their camp.[32]

The Nizam called help from the Emperor at Delhi and his son as well. The Foujdar of Shahjahanapur Mir Mani Khan who tried to succour the Mughal army, was cut up on the way with 1,500 men.[33] The Emperor had not yet forgotten the fright given him by the Peshwa last year by his sudden appearance. He had sent with the Nizam his best troops, his best guns and an ample supply of money. If that was not going to save him, there was no use denuding the capital of the remaining troops. "When the request of the Nizam for reinforcements was presented to the Shah he told his ministers he would not give them leave to depart but that they should accompany him when he would move out in person."[34]

The Nizam's hope of succour now centred on reinforcements from Aurangabad. Courier after courier raced to Aurangabad from the Nawab calling for aid. The Peshwa likewise wrote to his brother to hang on the southern army and not let it cross the Narmada. As large issues depended on the decision of the battle he suggested Chimaji should call to his side the contingents of Dabhade, Gaikawad and Bande. The Maharaja was appealed to persuade Fatesingh Bhonsle, Sarlashkar

32. Br. Ch. Appendix 33.

33. This happened previous to the Nizam's investment in Bhopal. See 58 XV, No. 207 XXX.

34. Br. Ch. Appendix 33.

Raghuji Bhonsle and a host of other Maratha Chiefs to march into Khandesh.[35]

A fresh army consisting of some of the best Maratha cavalry in the Nizam's service was preparing to leave for Bhopal when disaster overtook the Nizam's Berar force. Raghuji Bhonsle who was moving into Khandesh at the Peshwa's behest found his path blocked by Shujaat Khan, attacked his force and destroyed it completely.[36] This reverse sealed the doom of the army besieged in Bhopal. Nasir Jang could ill spare forces for relieving his father when his own position in the south[37] was not safe.

The condition of the beleaguered force was fast deteriorating all this while. The coarsest food became a rarity, while fodder for the animals could nowhere be obtained. The Nizam's attempt to extricate his army by a clever ruse was foiled by the Peshwa's watchfulness.[38] As the last means of rescue the Nizam abandoning his equipment in Bhopal and Islamnagar, began retreating under cover of a powerful artillery and number of swivel guns. The Peshwa did not relax the blockade. Surrounding the moving columns he marched with them harassing and galling them with matchlock fire and showers of rockets. No relief could be obtained on the way. The Nizam unable to hold out any longer begged for terms through Ayamal, the Dewan of Jai Singh. On 26 Ramjan (7th January, 1738) at Duraha Sarai he signed the convention promising to grant to the Peshwa :

(*i*) The whole of Malwa,

(*ii*) The complete sovereignty of the territory between the Narmada and the Chambal ; and

35. Br. Ch. Appendix 33.

36. S. P. D. XV, 82 and XXX, 207. The correct date of XV, 82 is Dec. 1737.

37. S. P. D. XXX, 207.

38. Br. Ch. App. 34 ; Kavyetihas Samgraha Patren, No. 27, which refers to this incident is dated Paush Badya Chaturdashi which is a misreading for Chaturthi.

(*iii*) To obtain a confirmation of it from the Emperor,

(*iv*) And to use every endeavour to procure the payment of 50 lacs of rupees for war expenses.

Immediately the convention was signed, the blockade was raised and food was sent in to feed the starving troops. The Rajas in Malwa and Bundelkhand waited on the Peshwa in ceremony and the Nizam returned to Delhi.[39]

The victory of Bhopal marks the zenith of the Peshwa's triumphant career. He accomplished the conquest of Malwa which he had set before himself since he came to the Peshwaship. Creating powerful armies out of divergent elements of Maratha Siledars, Bajirao invaded the north, brought to grief one imperial army after another sent against him, acquired immense territory till the Maratha outposts reached the Jumna and the Chambal. The early incursions of the Maratha horse assumed under him serious proportions. The disaster of Amjhera first opened the eyes of the Imperial Government to this menace from the south. But the measures it adopted to fight it were feeble, half-hearted and lacking in consistency. The friendship of Jaisingh enabled the Marathas to plant their power firmly in Malwa. The later attempts of the Mughal Government to oust the Marathas failed on account of the pusillanimity of its leaders and want of energy in its administration. By defeating the confederate armies at Bhopal the Peshwa established the supremacy of Maratha arms in India and announced the birth of a new Imperial Power.

After the Nizam's departure, the Peshwa set about chastising the Rajas who had helped the Mughal cause. Ranoji Sindhia and Holkar were sent against Kotah to which the Peshwa advanced about 6th February, laid waste the district and besieged the town. The Rao fled to Gagron and made peace by promising to pay a tribute of ten lakhs.[40] From Kotah the Peshwa moved into the country of the Ahirs. The Ahirs'

39. S. P. D. XV, 66 ; Br. Ch. Appendix No. 35, 116.

40. S. P. D. XV, 68 and Br. Ch. App. 136.

country was overrun and Kurwai was invested.[41] Reducing Kurwai he went towards Datia and Orcha and then retired to the Deccan, reaching Poona on 15th July.[42] This was his last and most important expedition.

CHAPTER XIII

NADIR SHAH'S INVASION.

Its effect on Maratha Expansion.

The convention signed by the Nizam by which the province of Malwa was surrendered to the Peshwa was yet to receive the formal sanction of the Emperor. Though the Empire held its frontier provinces loosely, its heart was sound. Such immense resources in men and money the Empire commanded that an able leader should not have found it difficult to hold back the Marathas. Bajirao had succeeded in wresting a province or two from the Empire, but had done no vital damage to the main structure. The total overthrow of the Mughal power was yet far off and would have demanded from the Marathas greater sacrifices than they had made so far. But a terrible calamity overtook the Empire and dealt it a fell blow from which it could never recover. Nadir Shah swooped down upon India and with one stroke destroyed the edifice of centuries. The Empire of the Chagtais was showing signs of decay, but none expected it to meet the ignominious end it met at the hands of the Persian adventurer.

Nadir, a soldier of fortune, raised himself to the highest position in Iran (1736) by sheer daring and generalship. While reducing south Afghanistan he found many rebels escaping towards Kabul which was then a Mughal province. His protests to the Governor or to the Court at Delhi went unheed-

41. S. P. D. XV, 69.
42. S. P. D. XXII, 380.

ed : his messengers were cut down on the road. This was sufficient reason for Nadir to invade India.[1]

Whatever the immediate cause for his march the real cause was, as Anand Ram Mukhlis remarks, the utter weakness of the Mughal power.[2] The Monarch was sunk in pleasure and knew nothing of the important trust he was called upon to administer ; the men gathered round him—his councillors—were sycophants and flatterers ; the defences of the empire were in neglect ; the army was ill-paid and ill-disciplined. No wonder foreign potentates cast covetous eyes on Hindusthan.

Nadir Shah reduced Kabul in June 1738 and then with a formidable army of 55000 Kazalbash troops commenced his march on Delhi. On 14th November he surprised the Pathan defenders of the Khyber pass and secured the north west gate-way of India.[3] Within four days he reached Peshawar ; there informing himself of the fords of the several rivers his army was to cross, he resumed his march, arrived before Lahore on the 10th January. The Governor of Lahore after a feeble attempt to oppose the Persian, surrendered (12th January) and saved the city from destruction by paying a fine of twenty lakhs of rupees.[4]

The news of the fall of Kabul and Nadir's preparations to invade India were received at the Court with the utmost unconcern. While the Turani and Hindusthani factions were yet immersed in their petty squabbles further intelligence arrived of the Persian having forced the Khybar pass and reached Peshawar. The menace could no longer be neglected. Farmans were issued to all Chiefs, Subahdars, Rajput princes, and the Peshwa to come to the aid of the Empire.[5] The Peshwa's army

1. J. Fraser, Hanway and Malcolm are the standard histories describing events in Persia. The three chapters on Nadir Shah in "Later Mughals" come from the able pen of Sir Jadunath Sarkar.
2. Anand Ram, p. 77, (in Elliot & Dowson, Vol. VIII.).
3. Anand Ram, p. 78.
4. Anand Ram, p. 80.
5. Rajwade VI, 130.

being concentrated at Bassein for the final assault, he was in no position to respond to the farman immediately.

The imperial army mustered about one lakh and marched out of the capital on 10th January. The Emperor joined it on the 27th near Panipat. As Lahore had been occupied by the enemy it was deemed inadvisable to proceed further than Karnal. Here the Mughal army encamped and waited to be joined by Saadat Khan. Nadir Shah's spies had informed him of the enemy movements. He attempted to intercept the Khan's march; though the main army escaped, Nadir secured the Khan's baggage. Enraged at this Saadat Khan attacked the Persian troops. What began as a partial action (13 Feb.) soon developed into a general engagement in which the Indian army was routed. Khan-i-Dauran was killed; Saadat Khan was made a captive. He lived for a month more only to betray his master and bring on on the innocent population of Delhi untold miseries. It was through Saadat Khan's treachery that Nadir Shah increased his demand of indemnity from fifty lakhs to twenty crores, made Muhammad Shah and his ministers prisoners, arrived at the capital and laid the city under sword.[6]

The appearance of a rival in a field which he considered as his own and his meteoric progress took the Peshwa by surprise. His reaction to this sudden upheaval was one of bewildered amazement. This revolution threatened to destroy the hegemony acquired by Maratha arms in the imperial councils. If Nadir Shah was to stay in India and found a new dynasty subverting the Mughal line—and reports spoke of the Persian adventurer having declared himself Emperor of India

6. Anand Ram, Pp. 81-90 and the two Nawabs of Oudh by Dr. Ashirbadi Lal Shriwastava. The details of the fighting and the subsequent massacre are omitted as being unnecessary for the purpose of this chapter which aims at giving the reactions the event produced on the Peshwa's policies. Graphic details of the massacre in the capital and Nadir's rule may be obtained from S. P. D. XV, 71-76; 80; XXX, 225-6, 229, Rajwade VI, 131, 133-4; 137, Itihas Samgraha, Aitihasik Tipanen, II, 6, Br. Ch. App. 41, 42 and two letters cited in the book at pp. 117 and 119.

and of his intention of marching south—Maratha supremacy would be gone and their new conquests beyond the Narmada would be imperilled. The Peshwa recognised the seriousness of the menace and asked his brother to conclude the war with the Portuguese and set free the forces locked up in Konkan.[7] Projects of a coalition of the forces of the Rajput princes with those of the Peshwa began to be discussed.[8] All hopes, all eyes were turned to the Peshwa who spoke confidently of making a stand against the tornado that was sweeping over the land and saw in the upheaval the opportunity for realizing his ambitious policy of totally destroying Muhammedan power in the south and acquiring preponderating influence in the Imperial Councils at Delhi.[9] But the projects did not materialise. It was useless moving against Nadir without adequate troops. The Peshwa refused to move unless joined by his troops then engaged before Bassein.[10] The citadel of the Portuguese fell on the 12th May, but by that time Nadir had turned his back on India[11] and was returning to his country. The Peshwa broke up his camp at Burhanpur and returned to Poona on 27th July.

Nadir inflicted such a blow to the Mughal authority that it could no longer make any serious opposition to Maratha ambitions. Within twenty years the Marathas overran the provinces of the empire one by one and were masters practically of the whole of India.

7. S. P. D. XV, 75 and 72.
8. *Idem* and Itihas Samgraha, Ait. Tipane, II, 6.
9. Br. Ch. letters on pp. 117-20.
10. S. P. D. XV, 72.
11. Nadir Shah left Delhi on 7 Safar, 5 May, 1739, vide S. P. D. XV, 80, and Irvine II, p. 375.

CHAPTER XIV

THE SALSETTE CAMPAIGN.

(1737-1739)

We now enter on another glorious chapter of Maratha expansion—the conquest of Salsette and Bassein from the Portuguese. The wresting of the mighty Bassein fortress and the destruction of the Portuguese power in Salsette peninsula were indeed remarkable exploits for the Marathas. What has added particular interest to the campaign is, that in the struggle for Bassein the Marathas were matched against a western people who regarded themselves in every respect superior to and invincible by orientals ; the interest is heightened when we bear in mind that the Marathas attacked a foe who was posted safe behind natural defences strengthened by human ingenuity ; it is further enhanced when we find that the besiegers attacked with swords and matchlocks while the besieged resisted with the best artillery of Europe. The campaign of Bassein is a shining example of Maratha heroism, of human courage triumphing over seemingly overwhelming odds. The struggle was fought grimly on both sides, the Portuguese gallantly resisting till further opposition was hopeless.

Rise of the Portuguese Power in India.

The establishment of the Portuguese power in Salsette dates as far back as 1534. Within thirty years of the rounding of the Cape of Good Hope by Vasco Da Gama, Portuguese fleets had visited almost all western coast of India and had ruined the trade of their rivals, the Moors, and had dotted the western coast with their factories. In 1531 a great Portuguese fleet collected by Nuno da Cunha for the capture of Diu failed to make any impression on its fortifications and returned to Goa, leaving Antonio de Saldanha with sixty sails to plunder the Cambay ports ; on his way south Antonio destroyed Balsar, Tarapur, Kelwe-Mahim and Agashi. In 1532 Nuno collected another fleet and advanced against Bassein then garrisoned by 12,000 men of the Sultan of Cambay. The Portuguese dashed

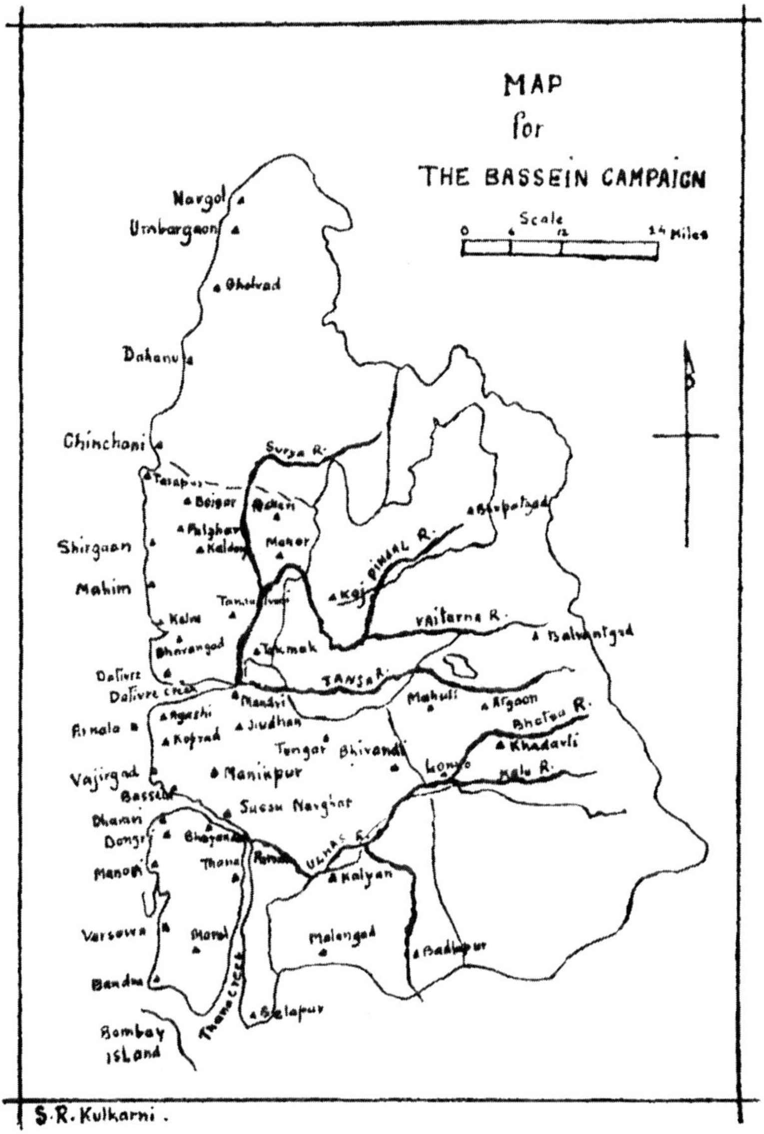
MAP
for
THE BASSEIN CAMPAIGN
Scale
0 6 12 24 Miles
Nargol
Umbargaon
Dahanu
Chinchani
Surya R.
Boisar
Palghar
Shirgaon
Manor
Mahim
Kelwa
Vaitarna R.
Bhavangad
Balvantgad
Tansa R.
Mandvi
Mahuli
Argaon
Bhatsa R.
Agashi
Arnala
Kopra
Jivdhan
Khadavli
Tungar
Bhiwandi
Vajirgad
Manikpur
Kalu R.
Bassein
Dongri
Bhayandar
Sussu Narghar
Ulhas R.
Kalyan
Thana
Manori
Versowa
Marol
Malangad
Badlapur
Bandra
Belapur
Thana Creek
Bombay Island

S. R. Kulkarni.

against the port, took it by assault and razed the walls. Thana and Bandra were forced to pay tribute. The coastal towns between Bassein and Tarapur were burnt and an attempt was made to take Daman. Bahadur Shah of Gujarat who then held sway over this territory, found it convenient to come to terms with the Portuguese and ceded them Bassein and its dependencies and agreed that Gujarat ships bound from Cambay for the Red Sea should touch at Bassein, carry Portuguese passes and should not act in concert with the Turks. In return the Portuguese were to aid Bahadur Shah against Humayun in regaining his kingdom.

The relations between the Portuguese and the Kings of Gujarat underwent many vicissitudes, but the Portuguese successfully warded off the Muslim attacks against Bassein in 1540, against Diu in 1538-1546. In 1556 the hill fort of Asheri and the important station of Manori on the Waitarana river were occupied by them. In 1560 they secured the belt of the coast from the Waitarana to Daman from one of the Gajarat Nobles. Daman was strongly garrisoned and in the same year the Portuguese beat off an attack of the Mughals. In 1570 the Portuguese withstood the combined hostility of the Kings of Bijapur and Ahmednagar. In 1583 Akbar attempted to capture Bassein and Daman, but meeting with stiff resistance he retired.

Its fortunes decline in the 17th century.

From the beginning of the seventeenth century, however, the days of Portuguese greatness were past. About 1580 having fallen under Spanish domination the Portuguese had to join hands with Spain in its luckless war with Holland. As Holland was the bitter enemy of Spain, it began attacking Portuguese ships in all parts of the world and in 1599 Dutch fleets appeared in Indian waters. In 1609 the Portuguese became involved in war with the native powers ; the Subhadar of Chaul declared war against the Portuguese and harassed their shipping. Two years later Malik Ambar the Nizam Shahi Minister sent an army against Bassein and Thana. In 1612 Portuguese prestige received a serious blow when four English ships defeated their fleet off the mouth of the Tapti near Surat. In 1640 Portugal made itself independent of Spain and began to evince fresh interest in its eastern possessions. But it had now lost its supremacy as a sea power.[1]

The succeeding fifty years formed a peaceful interlude to the Portuguese possessions in Salsette. A canker however had set in in their body politic and the long respite availed them little. In their contact with the natives their character deteriorated and their religious zeal and proselytising activities made them unpopular with their Hindu subjects. As Sir Jadunath Sarkar puts it, "The smallness of the population of Portugal for maintaining a colonial empire, the suppression of the national energy during the sixty years of Spanish domination, and the ruinous war with Holland and the rapid moral decline of their settlers in Asia—all made the Portuguese in India a decadent power, anxious only to hold their own and timidly averting an armed encounter with every other state by employing friendly appeal, patient endurance and diplomatic evasion."[2]

In 1660 there appeared on the horizon a small cloud no bigger than a man's hand that was in the course of the next century to burst with a thunderclap. This was the rise of the Maratha power. A new factor was introduced in Konkan politics by the advent of Shivaji. He captured Kalyan from the Sultan of Bijapur in 1657, and thus established himself as a neighbour to the Portuguese.

Portuguese contact with the Marathas.

On 16th August 1659 Fransisco de Melo a Castro and Antonia de Souza Coutinho, captains of Salsette and Bassein respective-

1. Bombay Gazetteer, Vol. XIII, part II, pages 451-54 ; Cambridge History, Vol. V, pp. 1-27, Sir Denison Ross's chapter on the Portuguese in India ; Danvers, the Portuguese in India ; Prof. Commissariat in his history of Gujarat devotes about six chapters to the struggle between the Muhammedan rulers and the Portuguese on the west coast.

2. Sir Jadunath Sarkar, "Shivaji" (3rd edition, p. 362.)

ly, wrote to their king that "Shivaji, son of Shahaji, a Bijapur Nobleman, had reduced the country round Chaul and Bassein and that he was fitting out a fleet at Kalyan and Bhiwandi. They had therefore instructed their Captains to challenge Shivaji's ships at sea."[3]

Shivaji soon lost Kalyan to the Mughals who tried to come to terms with the Portuguese and secure their aid against Shivaji. The Portuguese were not anxious to connect themselves with the Mughals and the negotiations broke off. In 1667 there was war between Shivaji and the Portuguese which went on intermittently till 1670 when by the treaty the Portuguese agreed not to molest his vessels at sea, while Shivaji on his part consented to allow Portuguese ships to shelter in his ports.[4]

In 1670 Shivaji once more occupied the province of Kalyan and reduced the hill forts of Karnala and Mahuli, dominating the province.[5] In spite of the treaty signed in December of the same year, a Portuguese fleet attacked Shivaji's ships near Daman and captured twelve which they carried to Bassein.[6] In 1672 Moropant Pingle led an army to the hilly part of the Thana district and reduced the Koli states. He attacked Ghor Bandar and demanded from the Portuguese for the first time the Chauth which they used to pay these Koli rulers.[7]

In 1674 Shivaji himself appeared at Kalyan and threatened Bassein.[8] In 1677 he threatened to lay waste Daman if the Chauth formerly paid to the Koli Rajas was not forthcoming.[9]

For the next two years the Portuguese stood in dread of an invasion from the Marathas for their refusal to give passage to a Maratha fleet sailing to Bombay to attack the Sidi's fleet nestling in Bombay harbour.

3. Pissurlencar in Shiva Charitra Pradeep, p. 178.

4. Patra Sar Samgraha, 1175, 1184, 1212, 1233, 1246 ; [Treaties of 1667 and 1670 are given in their English translation in Shiva Charitra Pradeep by Sir Jadunath Sarkar, pp. 2-5.]

5. *Ibid*, 1294-5.

6. *Ibid*, 1369.

7. *Ibid*, 1473-78, 1480.

8. *Ibid*, 1658, 1671, 1686-7.

9. *Ibid*, 1908, 2002-3.

Shivaji died in 1680. He avoided war on his three frontiers and was conciliatory towards the Portuguese. Hostilities against the Portuguese were however declared by his son Sambhaji.

In 1683 the Portuguese unwisely entered into an alliance with the Mughals which proved disastrous to their cause. As soon as Sambhaji heard of the alliance he descended into Konkan and laid siege to Chaul, which the Portuguese compelled him to raise. The Viceroy in person led another force against Maratha territory in the south, ravaged it and advanced against the fort of Ponda. Sambhaji with lightning speed appeared near Ponda, cut off the Portuguese communications with Goa and forced the Viceroy to retreat. At every step the Portuguese force was harassed by charges of horse while Maratha sharpshooters fired continuously from the hills at the retiring enemy. In his retreat the Viceroy had to abandon his baggage and siege train and before he reached Cumbarim island the Marathas had taken a heavy toll of his force. They followed the retiring enemy, overran Bardes and Salsette and on the 25th November 1683 took the Island of Santo Estavaso. The forts of Rachol, Tivim, and Chapora fell into Sambhaji's hands and the town of Margao surrendered. At last it appeared that the Marathas would force a passage into the island of Goa, the last retreat of the Portuguese, and drive them into the sea. In despair the Viceroy called for divine mediation placing in the hands of the corpse of St. Xavier the staff of his office. The prayers of the Viceroy were as it were heard ; a Mughal force that was advancing against the Marathas made a timely appearance and forced Sambhaji to abandon operations.[10]

For the next twenty-five years the Portuguese suffered little molestation from the Marathas. The latter power was engaged in a life and death struggle with the Mughals and had enough trouble at home to worry themselves about their navy

10. Orme. Hist. Fragments, pp. 156-160 ; History of Aurangzeb by Sir Jadunath Sarkar, Vol. IV, pp. 269-71, Danvers II, 367-80.

or their maritime possessions. The rise of Angria made little difference ; though Kanhoji often molested Portuguese shipping at sea, he was not powerful enough to attack their territory. In the long drawn struggle with the Mughals the Marathas emerged victorious over their rivals establishing their rule to the foot of the western ghauts. By the treaty of 1718 concluded by the Deccan Subahdar Husain Ali and later confirmed by the Emperor, the latter acknowledged his defeat and made to the Marathas a formal surrender of their territory. In 1719 Kalyan and Bhiwandi were evacuated by the Mughal garrison and occupied by Ramchandra Mahadeo on behalf of the Peshwa, who now became the next door neighbour to the Portuguese.[11]

Revival of Maratha Power in Konkan.

The revival of Maratha power was watched with anxiety by the Portuguese. Shahu while pursuing the fugitive queen Tarabai had sent an embassy to the Portuguese Viceroy from Bhudhar Garh. The Viceroy while making professions of friendship to both parties refused to compromise himself with either.[12] The same attitude of neutrality was maintained by the Portuguese in 1719 when the Marathas came down to take possession of Kalyan and Bhiwandi. The Governor Gonsalves afraid that any aid given to the Mughal Subahdar of Kalyan would involve him in war with the Marathas and invite their hordes to his fertile districts, not only refused him direct assistance but also prevented the Sidi from carrying succour to the Mughals by way of Bassein creek.[13] Immediately on the establishment of their power at Kalyan the Marathas opened their demands of Sardeshmukhi (or 1|10th of the revenue) against the Portuguese. The Governor declined this demand pointing out that his country was not subordinate to the Mughal, and his grant therefore could have no effect for the

11. S. P. D. XXX, 308, 339 ; Peshwa Rozkird Mss, Rajwade, II, p. 38.

12. Pissurlencar, p. 1.

13. *Ibid*, p. 4.

Portuguese territory.[14] This happened in 1719 and though there was lull for some time, the trouble which was to end in a big conflagration may be said to have begun from this time.

Bassein and Thana were greatly valued by the Portuguese. The territory of Goa was much smaller then and besides the island of Goa included only Bardes and Salsette, while their Konkan possessions or the Province of the North stretched along the coast from Cheul in the south to Daman. The districts were fertile, rich in forest, thickly populated and brought a fair return to the treasury and their wealth was the source of the prosperity of many a Portuguese family in Goa. They were surrounded by rivers navigable several miles into the interior. The conquerors had bestowed great care on the defences of the territory. "They had built places of special strength at Bassein, Asheri, Tarapur, Mahim, Daman, Cheul ; had raised royal fortifications at the headquarter of each subdivision ; guarded the entrances to their territories with forts and stockades ; they armed several of their colleges and monasteries and in each village the proprietor built a watch-tower or a moated grange. The hill of Asheri which wanted little help from art, was strongly guarded from the time of its capture in 1556 ; the mighty fortifications of Bassein belong to about the close of the 16th century. Thana fort was begun in 1734 and almost brought to finish in 1737. Of creek bank defences the most notable were four wooden stockades at Sopara ; of fortified custom houses the chief at Manor, and fortified religious houses are mentioned at Yerangal near Versowa and at Bandra in Salsette."

The system of Portuguese defences.

"In the north-east of Asheri and Manor, a line of forts along the east or left bank of the Waitarna guarded Kelwa-Mahim from the raids of the Koli chiefs of Jawhar.

"South of the Tansa river the fort of Mandvi (about 15 miles north-east of Bassein) and the stockaded post at the

14. Pissurlencar in Como se Perdeu Bacaim.

subdivisional town of Saivan (five miles east of Mandvi), guarded the rich lands of Sopara and Bassein from attacks along the left or south bank of the Tansa valley. The Tungar and Kamandurg range, running south from Mandvi, protected the eastern frontier as far as the valley of the Kamwadi or Bhiwandi river and the Bassein creek. The entrance to Bassein along the right or north bank of this creek was blocked by a line of forts, Kambe about two miles west of Bhiwandi, then Ju-Nandikna, Gava, Phiringpada, Paigaon, Sassu Navghar and the striking fortified hillock near the sub-divisional town of Kaman. Further south there was a fortlet named Santa Cruz on the river bank opposite Kalyan and on the main-land across from Thana were watch-towers or granges. Another row of watch-towers guarded the coast from Shirgoan fifty miles south to Dantivra at the mouth of the Waitarana."[15]

Degeneracy of Portuguese Character in the 18th Century.

The military defences of the Portuguese thus looked almost perfect, but were miserably lacking in soldiers who could hold them manfully. Decadence had set in, and in the 18th century Portuguese "Society was rotten to the core. The morals of the community were extremely lax. Profligacy had become the predominant and fashionable vice, and men gave themselves up to sensual pleasures peculiar to oriental life. The public administration was equally tainted. Justice was bought and sold ; public offices were put up to sale ; and the martial spirit of the natives degenerated into effeminacy, sloth and indolence."[16]

Abbe Raynal's testimony is very decided. He regarded the Portuguese as a decaying race. " The religious zeal which once inspired them with energy and generous courage, was afterwards manifested only in ferocity and served to stifle all scruples about pillaging, cheating and enslaving idolaters. As

15. Bombay Gazetteer, Vol. XIII, Part II, pp. 456-7.

16. Fonseca, Sketch of the City of Goa, p. 168 ; Da Cunha, Antiquities of Chaul and Bassein, p. 144.

they pretended to be endowed with authority over the kingdom of Asia by a decree of the Pope, they chose to suppose that a power to seize the property of individuals was also conferred upon them. Demanding tribute from the ships of every country, ravaging the coasts and insulting native chiefs they became the scourge and terror of all natives, bordering upon the ocean. Nor was their treatment of one another better than of foreigners. They were divided into factions and amongst all avarice, debauchery and cruelty prevailed. Many of them had seven or eight concubines whom they employed as menial servants. Effeminacy pervaded their armies and they lost the courage for which they had once been celebrated. No Portuguese pursued any other object than the advancement of his own interest, there was no zeal, no union for the common good".[17]

Mismanaged state of affairs: defence neglected.

This degeneracy of character was reflected in the mismanaged state of their public finances and the neglect of defence works. A large part of the revenue was appropriated by churches and religious orders leaving hardly sufficient to carry on the government efficiently.[18] The report made by the officer (1727) sent to examine the defences revealed how loose and corrupt was the entire management. It made several useful suggestions about putting the defences in order and raising the discipline of the soldiers. It also recommended that friendly relations should be established with the Marathas by giving them yearly presents.[19]

Improvements on these lines were commenced by the Portuguese at several places. But they forgot the main suggestion about maintaining amicable relations with the Marathas. By their harsh treatment of their Hindu subjects and impolitic handling of their foreign policy the Portuguese

17. Abbe Raynal as cited by Anderson, in *The English on the West Coast,* p. 16.
18. P. S. 1609 and Cambridge History, V, p. 18.
19. Thana Gazetteer, II, pp. 490-1.

found themselves embroiled in a war with their powerful neighbours.

The way the Portuguese had administered the province had not conduced to its prosperity and contentment.[20] A mere handful of Europeans they dreamed of turning their conquests into Christian lands; in their religious zeal they overshot the mark. The Salsette Chronicle says " The Portuguese rulers entertained evil disposition. They confiscated the watans of the land-holders, forced whole villages to embrace Christianity at the point of the sword. On the death of the head of the family the minor children were taken possession of by the priests and forced to kiss the Cross. Many fled to the south. Hindus were forbidden to practise their religious rites and social ceremonies. Temples were destroyed and on their ruins were raised churches. Brahmin priests were driven out of the land. The entire village was punished should it be found ever so guilty of publicly worshipping according to its religion. Men of position and high standing were falsely accused to the priests and whether guilty or innocent, forcibly converted."[21]

Religious Persecution.

Maratha plans for invading Salsette date as far back as 1720. As soon as the Peshwa's rule was established in Kalyan the silent discontent of the populace became vocal. The mal-

The intrigues of the Hindu population.

20. S. P. D. XXXIV, pp. 92, 202.

21. Salsette Chronicle, pp. 2-4; Grose, 'A Voyage to the Indies', p. 69; English Factories in India, Vol. XI, p. 144, Ovington, pp. 206-7: Sir Denison Ross's authority is important on this point. In his chapter on the Portuguese in India in Cambridge history, Vol. V, this learned author ascribes the ruin of that power to its mistaken religious policy towards its native subjects. In the preamble to the grant issued by the Peshwa to the Anjurkars in 1741 is recounted the horrid tale of Portuguese persecution of their Hindu subjects. This should silence the contention of Modern Catholic writers that this phase of Portuguese activities was a thing of the past. Salsette chronicle, Grose are all contemporary authorities. The references to the Portuguese in the Factory Records do not speak of them in complimentary terms.

contents took heart and in the name of religion invited the Peshwa to invade their land and free them from the alien yoke. The ringleaders of the movement were the Naiks of Anjur. Formerly natives of Bandra the coming in of the Inquisition in Salsette in 1580 forced the Naik family to leave their homeland and fly to Anjur. Two generations of the family resided in the village in want and poverty cherishing one dream—the dream of establishing once more their religion in the land of their birth. They appealed to Sambhaji for deliverance; they repeated their application to Kanhoji Angria and Dabhade. Their chance came when the Peshwa's power was established in the village in want and poverty cherishing one dream the Peshwa's Subahdar Ramchandra Mahadeo, unfolded to him the miserable plight of the Hindus in Salsette and won him over to his cause and through him exacted from the Peshwa a promise of undertaking the conquest of the Portuguese Province of the North.[22]

Proselytising zeal and the consequent persecution of their Hindu subjects were not a new phase of the Portuguese rule; what was new was the rise of a powerful Hindu state on their borders and almost encircling their Konkan settlements; in 1719 the Marathas occupied the Kalyan province and began extending their conquests in the direction of Jahwar and Ramnagar. But the Peshwa did not feel himself sufficiently strong to attack the Portuguese immediately. Maratha forces however began penetrating Portuguese possessions. In November 1723 a small force under Pilaji Jadhav invaded the southern part of Surat; on its way back it raided Portuguese territory and attacked Saibana and Gokhirve. A treaty was concluded on 10th January 1724, by which both parties agreed not to molest each other.[23] Expeditions into Karnatak and Malwa and the war with the Nizam and Sambhaji of Kolhapur engaged the

Slow penetration by the Peshwa.

22. Salsette Chronicle, pp. 5-19.
23. Pissurlencar in Como se perdeu Bacaim, p. 6, footnote.

attention of the Peshwa, and the invasion of Salsette had to be put off from time to time.[24]

Ramchandra Mahadeo died in the early months of 1728 and was succeeded by his brother Krishna Rao Mahadeo. A man of querulous temperament his regime of three years was a failure. He led an expedition against Ramnagar and on his way back burnt Nargol and other villages belonging to the Portuguese. The Portuguese retaliated by attacking Kalyan which was saved by the bravery and heroism of Shankaraji Phadke, Gangaji Naik Anjurkar and others.[25] Kalyan was once more threatened by the Portuguese in 1730 when the Peshwa recognising the incapacity of Krishnarao Mahadeo sent Pilaji Jadhav at the head of a small force. Jadhav carried war in the enemy's country. Kambe, a Portuguese outpost near Bhiwandi, was attacked in June 1730; two country vessels that sailed up the creek with reinforcements were captured by the Marathas and the guns found in them were used to batter down the walls. The whole garrison fell into the hands of Marathas and was sent to Kalyan. The attempt of the Commandant of Bassein to dislodge them was foiled.[26]

After Kambe had been reduced the Marathas planned to surprise Salsette. But before the expedition could start the Portuguese Governor took prompt measures to fortify the fords leading to the island, prepared his small force for receiving the enemy and at the same time appealed to the English at Bombay to aid him in the defence of the place. The preparations of the Governor and the reinforcements arriving from Bombay obliged the Marathas to withdraw from their project.[27]

24. This affair was under discussion in 1726 and in 1729, 30, 32, 34; see Rajwade VI, 26 and the correspondence between the Peshwa and Kawle in the App. of Madhyandin Shukla Yajurveda Brahmananchi Mahitee; also S. P. D. XVI, 5.

25. Salsette Chronicle, p. 26.

26. Danvers, Vol. II, p. 296, Pissurlencar, p. 7.

27. Forrest, Home series, p. 48 and Pissurlencar, p. 8.

In February of the next year the Marathas appeared before Manora. "On 1st March they gained possession of the neighbouring country and cut off the water supply of the fort. In spite of the heavy fire kept up from the town the Marathas succeeded in constructing entrenchments within pistol-shot, but reinforcements arriving from Bassein on 5th March obliged them to abandon the siege and retire to the hills. Here they were attacked by the Portuguese and suffered several casualties." [28]

The Peshwa being at this time threatened by a coalition of the Nizam, the Bangash and the Dabhade, had to call up his armies dispersed in several places. For a time Kalyan became denuded of troops and the pressure on the Portuguese was relaxed; they now made several raids into Maratha territory. "On 2nd October 1731 a force of 208 Portuguese and 562 sepoys arrived at Trumba and attacked the village of Panwell belonging to the Marathas, drove them out and set the place on fire." On 17th January 1732 representatives of the Portuguese and Marathas arrived at Bombay for the purpose of negotiating terms of peace and a treaty was concluded restoring *status quo ante bellum.*[29]

Peace had been made by the Peshwa under the pressure of circumstances. It could not be expected he would abide by it for long. In India at this time arrived Conde de Sandomil with strong ideas against Asiatics. A vigorous man he immediately set about organising the administration, speeding up the defences and making his country once more formidable and respected by the native powers. To the island of Salsette he appointed as General of the North Dom Louis Botelho, a gentleman high in his confidence as well as in that of the home authorities. He was to carry out vigorously the Viceroy's new policy and push on the work of the defences for the planning of which

Policy of vigorous offensive of Conde de Sandomil: Thana fortifications commenced.

28. Danvers, Vol. II, pp. 397-8.
29. Danvers, Vol. II, pp. 398-400.

was sent a skilful and experienced Engineer Andre Reberro Coutinho. Embarking at the end of April 1734 they arrived at Bassein on 8th May and set on the scheme of the fortifications. The Engineer surveyed the situation, carefully prepared his plans and work was started immediately.[30] A general tax was levied on the populace for meeting the heavy expenditure of the defences. They were also ordered to furnish labour and ships for the works. The heavy taxation and the demand for labour created discontent among the populace and so harassed them that, in the words of Danvers, "in desperation they invited the Marathas to take possession of the island".[31]

The Portuguese involved in the family dispute of the Angrias.

The Portuguese in the meanwhile by their impolitic handling of the Angrian situation found themselves involved in a bitter family dispute and ranged against the powerful Peshwa. With a view to strengthen their position, in 1735 they first supported Manaji Angria in his revolt against his brother Sambhaji; when he refused to cede them territory promised for their aid, they sided with the latter in an attempt to dislodge the former from Kolaba. Manaji this time invited the Peshwa to his assistance and succeeded in beating back Sambhaji and his new ally, the Portuguese. The Peshwa had cultivated great dislike for Sambhaji and hated him; when the Portuguese, his erstwhile enemies, appeared in support of his cause, they became the particular object of his hatred. The possession of Rajkot at Chaul was hotly contested by both sides, and the Peshwa to relieve the pressure at Chaul meditated a surprise attack on Salsette. He was however advised that the invasion would excite against him the jealousy of the English and the Sidi and would involve him in heavy expenditure. Being just then destitute of means for undertaking a big venture the plan was held in abeyance.[32]

30. Pissurlencar, p. 13.
31. Danvers, II, p. 402 and Pissurlencar; S. P. D. XVI, 11.
32. S. P. D. XVI, 6, 13, 14, 17, 25 and XXXIV, 1, 2, Brah-

Coutinho went back to Goa by the end of 1734 and his plan of the defences was modified so as to expedite the work. By April 1737, excepting the watch-towers, looking over the river side, the main fortifications were nearing completion.[33]

The Marathas invade Salsette.

On their side the Marathas watched the progress of the works with an uneasy mind. They realised that once these defences were ready their passage into Salsette would be barred and they therefore determined to strike.[34] In February 1737, the Peshwa's brother Chimaji Appa was appointed to command the expedition and sent in advance Shankaraji Pant Phadke, Ramchandra Hari, Chimnaji Bapuji, the Anjurkar Naiks and others, to proceed with their preparations and make dispositions with the utmost secrecy. By March 1737 a large force collected in the neighbourhood of Kalyan and hung on ominously. As soon as arrangements were perfected Appa left Poona on Thursday night on the fourth day of Chaitra (24th March) and arriving at Badlapur Saturday evening (26th March) heard two distant salvos of guns. These had been fired by way of signal by the advanced Maratha parties who acting on the secret advice of their informant, had crossed the ford at low tide at Kalwe, attacked the St. Jeronimo tower, put the small garrison to sword and secured the passage into the island of Salsette. Soon the entire advance force had crossed over to the island, while the main army under Appa followed them with baggage on the next day.[35]

The Portuguese garrison surprised, retires to Karanja.

The firing of the cannon was also heard in the town of Thana. The Governor sent a small party of soldiers to enquire into the cause of the firing and report to him. Little did they know what fate awaited them. They all fell into the

mendra Swamichen Charitra, P. 69 : all these papers must be placed in 1735.

33. Pissurlencar, p. 14. 34. S. P. D. XVI, 8, 13.

35. S. P. D. XXII, 348-50, Salsette Chronicle, p. 37 ; Pub. Dept. Diary, Vol. X, pp. 71-3.

enemy's hands and not one of them returned to tell what was happening at the waterfront. Soon the Convent of St. Augustine was ablaze and there was commotion in the native town. The Governor realized too late that the enemy had forced the passage and were coming up. Frightened out of his wits he called together a council of his officials and asked their advice. A general retreat was decided upon, and on the 27th the Governor and the officers and their families with six companies of soldiers sailed away to Karanja leaving a detachment to hold the fort de Reys. These handful men were so overcome with fright that on the next day they abandoned the fort not caring to destroy either the artillery or even to take away their colours.[36]

On the 27th and 28th the entire Maratha force had crossed over into Salsette, and took possession of the fort and the town. Detachments were immediately sent out to reduce the remaining fortified places within the island and to dislodge the enemy from the ports of Bandra and Versowa.[37]

While one army under the main command was operating against Salsette and had forced its way into the island, another (2200 strong) moved against Bassein and hoped to gain admittance inside the walls by the same stratagem. But the plan miscarried; the Portuguese Commander of Bassein had been warned of enemy movements and had in consequence posted strong patrols at all fords and outposts and had taken every precaution against surprise. When therefore the second force under Shankaraji Phadke moving secretly by night from Mahuli arrived on Saturday evening (March 26th) at the Rajawal ford which it expected to cross without any difficulty, it found its way blocked by a party of Portuguese guards. Nothing daunted the Maratha Commander swiftly moved a party about 150 strong below the Rajawal

A second force moves against Bassein, but fails to surprise the place.

36. Pissurlencar pp. 18-9 and Pub. Dept. Diary, X, pp. 71-73, Salsette Chronicle, p. 39. S. P. D. XVI, 41.
37. S. P. D. XXXIV, 23, 24.

point and asked it to attack the outpost from the rear. The attack succeeded and the entire Portuguese guard was cut down. But the interval that had elapsed between the arrival of the force and the commotion at the ford was sufficient to warn the garrison of what was happening and they doubled their vigilance. The element of surprise was gone. The second force had succeeded merely in entering the district or island of Bassein, but had failed to secure entrance inside the walls.[38] The two forces acting simultaneously had succeeded in their objectives in varying degrees. The main army under Chimaji Appa to round off its conquest had only to reduce Bandra and Versowa, while that under Shankaraji Phadke found itself stopped outside the formidable walls of the Bassein fortress. Ways had to be devised for achieving these different objectives.

Mopping up operations at Salsette, but Bandra and Versowa hold out.

Appa's work appeared easy of accomplishment. The main force of the enemy had evacuated the island and only a few parties held on at detached outposts. If they could be dislodged from them not only would the entire island of Salsette be cleared of the enemy, but Bassein itself would be threatened from the south. To this the Maratha Commander now bent his energies. His first care was to secure Thana harbour and the creek leading into it from Karanja. A strong detachment under Narayan Joshi marched against Parsik three miles east of Thana, on the mainland and occupied it on the 3rd of April. The same detachment then moved further south and attacked Belapur or Sabajo as the Portuguese called it. Belapur resisted for some time, but surrendered on 28th April. Santa Cruz near Kalyan, as also Marol in the island of Salsette, were given up by the defenders at the first summons.[39]

38. S. P. D. XVI, 42 and XXXIV, 20, 21. No. 25 discusses plans after the failure of the attempt to surprise Bassein.

39. S. P. D. XVI, 46, 47, 56-59; S. P. D. XXII, 119; and Public Department Diary No. 10, pp. 110-1.

It was equally necessary to occupy the two island ports of Bandra and Versowa to prevent the enemy from landing a force and delivering a surprise attack. Versowa was defended by a fortalice and had a good harbour. A party of 500 horse under Honaji Balkawade was despatched against it on 27th March. Ill-equipped for siege operations Balkawde vainly tried to carry the place by escalade but was driven back with heavy loss. The port remained open to the enemy and was strengthened by reinforcements carried in by D'Souza Pereira.[40]

Bandra presented similar difficulties to the invaders. The party that advanced against the place found itself facing fire from three quarters. The Jesuits of the mission had called in to their aid the English of Bombay. They in self-defence supplied to the Jesuit fathers arms, ammunition and a company of 50 soldiers and these combined with their armed galivats posted in the Mahim creek, in keeping a steady fire and arresting the progress of the Maratha horse. The Portuguese were further reinforced by succour brought them by Joao de Souza Ferras, Captain of Salsette, and Bandra beat back attack after attack of the Marathas. The batteries prepared by the Maratha Captain Khanduji Mankar were silenced by the superior fire of the enemy. Attempts at escalade proved costly and unavailing and with the breaking in of the monsoon Mankar was forced to abandon siege operations and retire into cantonment.[41]

Gains in the Bassein Sector.

The results in the Bassein sector were almost similar. Maratha horse being held up before Bassein, overran the open country and one after another detached outposts were either abandoned by their commandants or capitulated after a little resistance. Jivdhan surrendered on the 1st of April, to Barwaji

40. S. P. D. XVI, 50, XXXIV, 24 ; also Pissurlencar p. 20, and Danvers II, p. 403.

41. S. P. D. XVI, 143, 50, 52, 64, 65, XXXIV, 35, 37, 39 ; Pub. Dept. Diary, Vol. X, pp. 71-73 ; also Pissurlencar.

Takpir.[42] Takmak and Kamandurg followed suit,[43] Tandulwadi was occupied on 2nd May.[44] Mandvi stood a siege of about ten days,[45] as also Manori,[46] both passing into Maratha possession on 16th and 20th May respectively.

Another valuable Maratha gain in this quarter was the island of Arnala (or Ilhas da Vaccas as the Portuguese called it). The Maratha Commander Shankaraji Pant in his despatch dated 13 April reported the capture of this island at the mouth of the Waitarana. The place had been neglected by the Portuguese; Shankaraji Pant winning over the local Kolis sailed into the harbour, landed parties and took possession of the island. Realising its excellent strategic situation he immediately started defensive works and garrisoned the place with a strong party.[47]

These gains important in themselves were inconsiderable and of little value so long as the fortress of Bassein remained in Portuguese hands. The cidadel was as it were the symbol of Portuguese rule in Konkan and was then regarded as one of the strongest places in India. A mile and a half in circumference and dacagonal in shape, its walls rise from thirty to forty-five feet from the ground. They are built of black stone and about five feet thick deriving their chief strength from the situation among swamps. At each corner of the dacagon there are four sided bastions which were all mounted with artillery in those times. To the south of the fort flew the Bassein creek or river; the west was washed by the Arabian sea; on the eastern side was a belt of marshy land overflown by tidal waters. The only side from which the fortress could be approached by

Siege of Bassein, its difficulties.

42. S. P. D. XVI, 44, 118; The correct date of the letter No. 118 is 1 April, 1737 and of 143 is 29 March, 1737.
43. Raj. II. p. 76.
44. S. P. D. XVI, 61.
45. S. P. D. XXXIV, 164, 168, 171, 175 and XVI, 62-3.
46. S. P. D. XXXIV, 59, 189.
47. S. P. D. XVI, 37, 40, XXXIV, 40; Salsette Chronicle, p. 42.

an enemy was the north. Here the ground was loose sand and without vegetation or shelter of any kind to the enemy outside. The formidable walls of Bassein laughed at the efforts of the Maratha commander to reduce the place without the means of battering down the defences. Shankaraji Phadke pitched his camp in advance of the native town and watched for the enemy to come out.[48]

The Commandant of Bassein Pedro Guedes de Megalhaes lay secure within the walls. So long as his sea communications remained open and he could draw provisions, arms and ammunitions from Goa and outside he felt sure of holding out indefinitely. On the sea the Peshwa could claim not one single ship. His protégé and ally Manaji Angria possessed a fleet of country crafts quite inferior to the Portuguese navy and hardly able to challenge it at sea. Without the support of a navy the Maratha Commander was helpless against Portuguese vessels moving in and out of Bassein and bringing relief to the beleaguered place. The Portuguese however shared the like disadvantage. Cooped up in the walls of their forts they were unable to prevent the enemy calling in reinforcements. The struggle thus developed into a contest of exhaustion, the question resolved itself as to who could hold longer and wear out the other and would be decided only by the superiority of one of them in resources, men and money and in generalship. The Portuguese power was internally weak and decaying and when the Marathas pressed the attack with unusual vigour and tenacity, it was sapped to its foundation ; it crumbled and fell never to rise again.

Let us however resume the thread of the narrative and describe the Portuguese attempts to defend their position. On the first approach of the Marathas, the Commandant came out to meet the invaders with a company of Grenadiers and four

The Garrison of Bassein reinforced by the arrival of the Governor.

48. For the description of Bassein fort see Thana Gazetteer, Vol. XIV, pp. 28-34, Da Cunha's Bassein, pp. 207-8, and S. P. D. XXXIV, 25, XVI, 42, 44-5.

of Native Infantry. When, however, he saw the Maratha horse rushing like a tidal wave to meet his small force, he discreetly retired to the shelter of the walls. The arrival of Dom Louis Botelho from Karanja eight days later heartened the defenders. They were further cheered by the news of large reinforcements having been shipped them from Goa.[49]

When the news of the disaster of Salsette reached Goa, the Viceroy realised the magnitude of the danger and with the greatest promptitude fitted an expedition of 300 soldiers and a large store of money under the command of Pedro de Mello, an able and experienced officer. De Mello was instructed to open negotiations with the English and Sambhaji Angria to secure them as allies for repelling the invaders.[50] Arriving with his troops at Bassein on 17th April De Mello strengthened the defences and invited the English of Bombay to make a common cause with him. He advised them that it was in their interest to declare war on the Marathas and cooperate with him. The English were doubtful of the Portuguese being able to fight the war to a successful conclusion and politely declined the offer, agreeing however to supply the Portuguese with arms, ammunition and such other warlike stores and withhold the same from the Marathas.[51]

In the meanwhile a hue and cry was raised against the luckless General, Dom Louis Botelho to whom was ascribed the loss of Salsette. He was removed from his post, to which was appointed another experienced General, Antonio Cardim Froes. Cardim took his passage in an English ship and arrived at Bassein on 12th May, 1737.[52]

The General's first care was to keep his communications

49. Salsette Chronicle, p. 41, Pissurlencar ; p. 21, Danvers II, p. 403.

50. Public Dept. Diary X, p. 113 ; The Diary places the number at 300 ; Pissurlencar, p. 23.

51. Public Department Diary, X, pp. 114-16, 124-25.

52. Public Dept. Diary No. 10, p. 116 ; S. P. D. XXXIV, 116, 175, XVI, 55 ; Pissurlencar, P. 24.

with Goa and Bombay open, and then reinforce such places as were still resisting the enemy. His line of communication to the south was lately being harassed by a Maratha battery at Dharavi, just south of Bassein. Within eight days of his arrival Cardim had landed a strong party of 300 men, led them to the Maratha positions and delivered a surprise blow. Unable to stand the enemy's fire the Marathas broke and fled and the battery was destroyed.[53]

Portuguese attack on Dharavi: the Maratha battery destroyed.

Another column under Brito de Silva marched to the relief of Manori then reported to be invested by Awji Kawade and Barwaji Takpir. Just when he had arrived in sight of the place, Brito had the misfortune to learn that the place had surrendered that very day. Nothing remained for Brito but to fight his way back. His small force was surrounded and attacked by Maratha horse, but the brave soldier with consummate skill and a well-directed fire held them back in check and reached Bassein in safety on 21st May.[54]

The Indian monsoon now set in in all its fury entirely cutting off the Portuguese northern possessions from their base at Goa. With rivers inundated and roads knee deep in mud all military operations had to be suspended and a general inactivity was enforced. But the belligerents knew no rest. The Marathas were anxious to force the issue and bring hostilities to a conclusion before the end of the monsoon would enable the beleaguered garrison to receive reinforcements. They now attempted to take the place by escalade. The first attempt was made on 30th May, but was beaten back. Another made on 28th June and on a bigger scale, met with a similar fate, the Marathas losing over two hundred in dead and wounded. Night and day vigil was kept by the Portuguese on the ramparts—especially the north side where the Marathas had pitched their

Attempts of the Marathas to take Bassein by escalade.

53. S. P. D. XXX, p. 346; Danvers, II, 404; Pissurlencar, pp. 29-30.

54. S. P. D. XXXIV, 59, XVI, 67 and Pissurlencar, pp. 30-31.

camp—and their smallest movements could not escape observation of the inmates.[55]

The Marathas in the meanwhile gained a small advantage at Murdhah. A Portuguese force under Carvalho was lured beyond the protection of its guns in pursuit of a party of Maratha horse and completely destroyed.[56] Heartened by this success and weary of the long waiting enforced by the weather, yet another assault was attempted on 4th September this time led by Baji Bhivrao, a trusted Captain of the Peshwa. Three thousand men equipped with ladders moved under cover of night and rushed to the walls. The Portuguese had received intelligence of the coming attack and as soon as the Marathas were within cannon range, an inferno of fire opened on them. In spite of shells bursting round, the Marathas manfully struggled near the wall for over an hour, but could not secure a foothold. Their ladders were hurled down and their ranks were thinned by a withering fire. Utterly discomfited they retired leaving the ground strewn with their dead.[57]

The Bassein garrison receives further reinforcements.

With the break of the monsoon military stores, men and money began to pour into Bassein. Two ships carrying reinforcements from Portugal arrived in Goa on the 4th and 20th September respectively. Ambitious projects for the defence of Bassein and wresting of Salsette from the Marathas were debated in the Court at Goa.[58] The Peshwa was in the midst of a big offensive against the Nizam heading the Mughal Court and had collected a formidable army to crush his opponents. To guard his rear he had posted his brother Chimaji on the Tapti with another army which had necessitated withdrawing part of the force operating in North Konkan.[59] This naturally put the

55. Pissurlencar and Salsette Chronicle, p. 43.
56. Pissurlencar p. 34.
57. S. P. D. XXII, No. 359 and XXX, p. 349; Rajwade VI. 114-5; Salsette Chronicle p. 43; Pissurlencar p. 35; Danvers II, p. 406.
58. Pissurlencar, pp. 38-39.
59. These activities are detailed in the chapter, Battle of Bhopal.

Portuguese in high spirits and gave them hopes of recovering their lost domains.

The first convoy consisting of a large quantity of rice, gunpowder and a hundred thousand Xeraphins arrived at Bassein in October. In the next month 1500 soldiers—500 Portuguese and 1000 native sepoys—arrived with another large supply of money and reinforced the garrison. Local militia was also raised in the Daman district and plans for an attack on Thana began to be examined and the English once more invited to co-operate.[60]

Maratha attempt to reduce Mahim ends in disaster.

The Marathas in the field however were not idle. Taught by the terrible losses inflicted on them in frontal assaults on the walls of Bassein, they determined to resort to blockade and starve out the garrison. Success in this new strategy depended on their being able to sever the enemy's line of communication with Goa as well as to reduce the Daman district to prevent it from supplying the needs of the besieged. A strong detachment under the command of Mahadaji Phadke, brother of Shankaraji Phadke was despatched towards this quarter. Crossing the Dantiwara creek in the beginning of November Mahadajee appeared before Mahim and summoned the garrison. Another force under Malhar Hari attacked the minor post of Shirgaon two miles north of Mahim, but failing to take it, commenced siege operations. The Mahim garrison also held out; Mahadaji Phadke reinforced by another detachment sent by the Peshwa under Ramchandra Hari, felt himself strong enough to carry the fort by mining and assault. The place was surrounded and batteries began to be feverishly put up for pounding the walls. The Portuguese General learning of the threat to Mahim, held over his project against Thana and moved succour

60. Pissurlencar and Public Department Diary, X, p. 304; Plans for an attempt to regain the fort of Thana were being considered since July. Cardim had sent an envoy to the English at Bombay with definite proposals. The proposals were not accepted. Pub. Dept. Diary X, pp. 179-83; Salsette Chronicle, pp. 44-45.

to the beleaguered place. The first relief party landed on 7th December, gained admittance without fighting. Repeated sallies were now made by the inmates against advance posts of the investing force, but proved unavailing. They were unable to shake off the Marathas and the ring began to close tightly round Mahim. Fresh reinforcements were despatched. Their landing on 20th December was contested without success. The third relief party and the largest, consisting of over 800 sepoys was brought by Pedro de Mello, Mestro de Campo, in person and fought its way to the fort. On 23rd December about noon the entire Portuguese garrison sallied forth and attacked the Maratha lines. Mahadaji Pant through overweening confidence had advanced his batteries dangerously near the walls without sufficient cover. A barrage of fire from the fort artillery drove back the supporting troops, while the Portuguese infantry attacked the isolated batteries and demolished them. The advanced positions were stormed all along the line and wiped out. Mahadaji Phadke was trapped in one of the advance posts and fell with a number of his lieutenants. Unable to withstand the enemy's pressure the Marathas abandoned the siege and retired to Shirgaon. Here they were followed by De Mello on the next day, attacked and dispersed. The victorious captain then headed a strong column for the relief of Asheri hard pressed by the enemy. Marching through tortuous stony paths and warding off the blows of the enemy De Mello appeared near Asheri on the 16th of January (1738). So much had the Maratha force been shattered and so completely demoralised that the news of the march of the Portuguese was sufficient to induce the Maratha Commandants, Pantaji Moreshwar and Hari Sadashiv, to raise the siege, dismantle the nearby post of Manori and seek safety in a junction with the force that had retired from Mahim. De Mello then marched back to Bassein and was received with public honours by the Governor and a mass was read to commemorate the occasion.[61]

61. S. P. D. XVI, 73, 74, 76-81, 96, 98-103, 105-6, XXXIV, 8,

After this the Portuguese once more turned their attention to Dharavi (or Dongrim of the Portuguese records). The place occupied an excellent strategic position which the Marathas had been quick to perceive and had used it against the enemy last summer. A battery they had mounted in that place did very good execution harassing enemy shipping in the harbour and was demolished by the Portuguese after heavy fighting. The interval of the monsoon had been utilised by the Marathas to fortify the point and erect guns which began annoying Portuguese vessels once more. The garrison depended for its food supplies on Bombay, Cheul, and Daman and could not allow the enemy threaten its life-line. Cardim realised his mistake in not keeping a garrison in that place and now directed another attack against it. Under the ruse of attacking Thana he sailed up the creek and then turning back on 17th February early morning delivered the blow. While the main force of 1500 was contesting the landing with the Marathas, another detachment under the General sailed round, disembarked in the rear and charged Maratha positions. Yet another division held back the horse from Thana that had rushed to the relief of the out-post. In the fighting that ensued the Maratha garrison after suffering terrible losses broke under pressure of the enemy's fire. Leaving three battalions to hold the place under an experienced officer, Cardim retired to Bassein.[62]

Maratha garrison at Dharavi annihilated.

The debacle of Mahim and the reverse at Dharavi stemmed the tide of Maratha advance and damped their efforts. One large force of 4,000* had been routed and dispersed and

Maratha forces demoralised. Appa's arrival.

49, 81, 150-35 and Br. Ch. letter on pp. 76-79. This long letter gives all the graphic details of the Portuguese attack on Maratha lines; also S. P. D. XXII, 367 and Salsette Chronicle pp. 45-46.

62. Salsette Chronicle, p. 46. Pissurlencar amplifies this from Portuguese papers, pp. 49-50; S. P. D. XXXIV, 111 and Peshwa Rozkird.

* According to the Peshwa's despatch of 9 Nov. 1737 (Br. Ch.

another destroyed. The remaining forces operating before Bassein and defending Salsette became demoralised and desertions on large scale began to be reported from everywhere. The men developed a veritable terror of the Portuguese fire and decamped at the least rumour of enemy movements.[63] The moment seemed ripe for the Portuguese to strike their final blow. But the blow never came. Portuguese reinforcements received from Goa had been dissipated in fierce onslaughts on enemy positions at Mahim and Dharavi and strengthening the forts that yet remained in hand.[64] The English on whom the Portuguese relied for expelling the Marathas from Salsette, thought it " imprudent to risk in an attempt that did not promise of success." In their opinion " the force the General commanded was not even capable of maintaining the field against the Marathas, not to speak of an attempt on Thana."[65]

The Peshwa's signal victory over the Nizam at Bhopal on 7th January 1738 released large forces locked in that struggle. Chimaji Appa at the head of 12000[66] horse and foot hastened to the Konkan theatre of war and arrived at Kohaj on 10th February [67] once more to direct the campaign in person. The new militia consisting of Arabs and Kanarese footmen had proved worthless and were discharged their places being taken by old Maratha veterans.[68] The inspiring presence of the Commander gave a fillip to the drooping spirits of the Maratha armies ; [69] their camps began to hum with bustle and activity. The old costly strategy of frontal attacks on fortified positions without support of heavy artillery was abandoned.

pp. 76-77) the strength of the force besieging Mahim was 3200. It was reinforced later.

63. S. P. D. XXXIV, 111.

64. Salsette Chronicle, p. 46.

65. Public Dept. Diary, XI, p. 59 consultation dated 1st March 1738. The Marathas had kept themselves informed of the proposed attack on Salsette. See S. P. D. XXXIV, 130-31, Rajwade, VI, 118.

66. Public Dept. Diary, XI, p. 59.

67. S. P. D. XVI, 75.

68. S. P. D. XXXIV, 52. XVI, 124.

69. S. P. D. XVI, 108.

Continuous harassment, it was realised, would ultimately sap the enemy's limited strength;[70] parties of Maratha horse under Honaji Balkawade and Dhondopant raided the Daman district and laid it waste.[71] Defensive works and stockades confronting Portuguese castles were commenced almost on the entire front.[72]

The Portuguese now began to show signs of exhaustion. The activities in the Maratha camp had a depressing effect on them. The enemy was overrunning the entire northern province; the revenues were at a stand still, the militia raised for the war swallowed up the treasure received from Goa. To maintain it at that strength[73] required more supplies which Goa could no longer spare. With the enemy surging round him like sea, the Portuguese General felt himself in the midst of a whirlpool and in utter despair threw up his command and retired to Goa on 11th April. To that onerous post now succeeded Pedro De Mello, Mestro de Campo, who had distinguished himself in the recent fighting.[74] The Viceroy appealed to the English to mediate in the dispute, but so long as the Portuguese were unwilling to relinquish their claims to the island of Salsette, accommodation was not possible.[75]

Portuguese defences exhausted. Cardim retires.

An empty treasure forced the new General to demobilize the large force raised by his predecessor, keeping only 500 natives in addition to the Portuguese complement and to seek safety behind the defences of the walls. The circumstances dictated that he should pursue tactics by which the Marathas would again be tempted to repeat the costly attacks of the

70. Rajwade VI, 118.

71. S. P. D. XXXIV, 120.

72. S. P. D. XVI, 43, 113, 119, XXXIV, 26, 105, 161-2. The last two letters should be dated 20 March, 1738.

73. According to S. P. D. XXXIV, 111, the strength of the Portuguese force was 4000.

74. S. P. D. XXXIV, 99, 120, XVI, 122, 125, Danvers, II, p. 407.

75. Pub. Dept. Diary XI, p. 125.

last year. On 2nd July a column of Portuguese soldiers sallied forth and pretended to engage the Maratha lines; when the Marathas advanced for battle it retired; the fort artillery then roared forth spreading destruction among their ranks. The attack cost the Marathas over two hundred in casualties, 84 being counted as dead. When this was repeated a number of times the Marathas refused to be taken in, and waited for the return of the fair season to begin the grand assault.[76]

Portuguese desperate attempt to take Thana.

Yet another supreme effort was made by the Portuguese to retrieve their fortunes. The news of the disaster had reached the mother country in March 1738. A force of 1000 picked soldiers with ample war material was immediately shipped to India. This arrived at Goa in October and was ordered to proceed at once to the theatre of war. De Mello reinforced with fresh troops from Europe struck on the bold plan of attacking the fort of Thana.[77] On 24th November the Portuguese force sailed out of Bassein harbour and rounding the Bombay island, moved up the Thana creek. The shallow waters round Thana allowed only small gallivats to approach the walls and in consequence the Portuguese General was unable to bring his heavy artillery into action. Two days heavy cannonading from a distance having proved ineffective De Mello with a few officers, approached the walls for observing the enemy's defences, when a stray shell from a Maratha gun burst near him and killed him on the spot. The death of their General had a depressing effect on the expedition; the fleet returned to Bassein in a mood of despondency.[78]

The plan of the attack examined.

The failure of the attack on Thana marked definitely the turn in the tide of the Portuguese fortunes. They had staked their all on the

76. Danvers II, 407; Pissurlencar p. 53, amplifies the account of Danvers.

77. Danvers II, p. 407; also De Mello's letter to the Bombay Council, dated Oct. 28th, 1738, Pub. Dept. Diary XI, 263-65.

78. Pissurlencar p. 58 and Danvers II, pp. 407-8; Also Salsette Chronicle p. 47; Peshwa Chronology.

expedition. The English and the Sidi looked on the struggle anxiously and in dread of Maratha hostility, pretended neutrality while they helped the Portuguese as much as their means would permit. The success at Thana was to be the signal for these neutrals to declare their common interest with their neighbour and throw in their lot with him, and make a joint war on the Marathas on an extended front. The English had been watching the progress of the war from its commencement and knew of the immense superiority of the Marathas in men and resources. The attack on Thana appeared to them as vainglorious and they had advised the Portuguese Commander that "their force was inadequate to attempt any decisive action or to carry on a violent war and had given it as their reason for not hazarding a rash and abrupt declaration of hostilities against the Marathas."[79] They had from the beginning discouraged the idea of attacking Thana. The Maratha hold round Bassein however was tightening and the Portuguese General anxious to engage the English in the struggle and thus retrieve his desperate situation, conceived the wild project of this assault. The project had been mooted as far back as 1737 November, but was abandoned when reinforcements of the year were dispersed in the attacks on Mahim, Asheri, Dharavi and rehabilitating other Portuguese posts. By itself the plan was a sound one; the fort watching over the river side occupied a key position; its possession would open the gates of the island to the Portuguese force, and would isolate the Maratha garrison. Knowing its importance the Marathas had bestowed great care on its fortifications. They had hastily reconstructed the watch towers and made the place almost impregnable.[80] The buildings round the castle had been razed, and the ground made clear of obstacles which would offer shelter to an investing force. Batteries had been mounted in position and the place garrisoned by a picked Maratha force under the command of Khanduji Mankar. If the plan had any chance of

79. Pub. Dept. Diary, XI, pp. 263-65; also pp. 59-60.
80. S. P. D. XXXIV, 78, XVI, 43, etc.

success in 1737, it had none now. But a drowning man clutches at a straw and De Mello heedless of the warning of his friends and subordinates, appeared before Thana. Before the grand assault could develop the General himself was killed and the grandiose scheme ended in smoke.[81]

The Marathas plan a new strategy.

The initiative now passed to the Marathas and it is necessary to narrate their activities since the summer of 1738. On account of his failing health Appa went back to Poona on 29th May.[82] The Maratha Generalissimo in his three months' campaign had stopped the rot, checked the Portuguese advance and prepared defensive works everywhere for enabling his forces to keep the field during the monsoon.[83] He realised however that the army surrounding Bassein though large enough to hold the open country, was inadequate and ill-equipped for reducing the fortress, (which was) the nerve centre of the enemy's activities and the symbol of his rule in North Konkan ; that Bassein would hold out so long as it continued to be provisioned and reinforced from Daman and Goa. With the advice of his brother, Bajirao Peshwa, Appa planned a new strategy for smashing the enemy after the rains. The entire forces at the command of the Peshwa were to be hurled against the Portuguese ; all the resources were to be employed for destroying their authority in Konkan.[84] A pincer like movement was to begin at the southern and northern extremities of the enemy's territories which was to converge on Bassein. Pre-

81. Duff refutes the charge made by the Portuguese that the cannon which killed their commander was pointed by an English gunner. Bombay letter to the Court of Directors dated 3rd Jan. 1739 is clear on this point. " What he mentions of the gunners going from this island to and attributing the loss of the late General to their expertness is an absolute falsity ; there were two soldiers and a seaman deserted from this island to Thana *the day after the Portuguese made the attack on Fort Dos Reys,* who were returned by Condajee Mankar.

82. Raj. VI, 120.

83. S. P. D. XVI, 119-20, 152 ; XXXIV, 136, 150-1, 161, etc

84. Salsette Chronicle, p. 47.

parations on large scale were started and the Peshwa's foundries at Poona, Kalyan, Bhiwandi began to turn out munitions in huge quantities.[85]

The rains calling a temporary halt to major operations, the interval was utilised by the Marathas in putting their previously abandoned out-posts in a posture of defence. New points of vantage like Danda Khatal were fortified[86] and patrols of Maratha horse began to ravage the country round Mahim and Tarapur often crossing the Surya river into Daman district. On occasions there were clashes between them and parties of the enemy, in one of which Capt. Pereira lost his life, while on another Capt. Piemental was surrounded and destroyed with his men.[87]

Daman invaded.

The monsoon retreated in November when Ranoji Sindhia with a numerous horde entered the Daman district, overpowered the small garrisons of Nargol, Khatalwad, Umbergaon, Dahanu and laid the country under fire and sword.[88]

In the south the Goa province was invaded by Vyankatrao Ghorpade in cooperation with the Sundah Rajah and the Sawant of Wari. Entering by the Digi pass Ghorpade descended into Concolim province and reached Margaon without opposition. As Goa had been denuded of troops, the Portuguese could offer but feeble resistance. Margaon fell on 15th January (1739) and the whole of Salsette province with the exception of Rachol and Marmagoa passed into Maratha hands. The fort of Fonda was taken over from the Sundah Rajah on 19th February. On the 22nd the Sawant of Wari marched into Portu-

Invasion of Goa.

85. P. D. (Mss). S. P. D. XXII, 121 shows the number of guns brought into action by the Marathas against the fort of Bassein.

86. Danvers, II, p. 407.

87. S. P. D. XXXIV, 204; Pissurlencar, pp. 54-55.

88. Pissurlencar, p. 68. Danvers II, p. 408, Salsette Chronicle p. 48, S. P. D. XVI, 127.

guese country. Leading his troops against the fort of Tivim he took it by escalade and then attacked Coloale. From Coloale he marched upon Xapora and soon the entire Bardes district was overrun by his troops.[89]

In the North affairs were moving to a like crisis. Chimaji Appa with a formidable army composed of the flower of the Peshwa's troops marched into Konkan;[90] arriving at Saygaon on 23rd December he was joined by Shankaraji Phadke from Bassein with 2200 troops.[91] Mahim was invested on 30th December. Batteries were prepared and began pounding the defences. Mines were laid and carried to the foundations of the walls. On 9th January 1739 the Commandant begged for terms.[92] Kelwe and Shirgaon, two small forts in the vicinity were stormed the next day and the garrisons put to the sword.[93] The Marathas then marched on to Tarapur. Tarapur put a still more stiff resistance. But lack of man power made counter attacks expensive and counter attack is the only method by which defensive works can be maintained intact. Under cover of their artillery the Marathas carried mines to the walls which blew up on 24th January. Waves after waves of Maratha soldiers rushed towards the breaches only to be met with a withering fire. At last their enormous superiority in number began to tell. Completely exhausted the defenders laid down their arms. The Commandant Luis Veloz had fallen fighting, but many prominent officials and over 4000 soldiers were taken prisoners. On the Maratha side the casualties were equally heavy. Baji Bhivrao, the Peshwa's trusted captain and friend was killed

Appa arrives, Mahim, Shirgaon Tarapur, Asheri surrender, January, 1739.

89. S. P. D. XVI, 147, 150, 160 and Pissurlencar, pp. 70-80.
90. According to Pissurlencar, p. 62 the total strength of the force besieging Mahim was computed at 60,000.
91. S. P. D. XXXIV, 141.
92. P. D. (Mss) and Forrest, Maratha Series, p. 27; Pissurlencar, pp. 62-64.
93. *Ibid.*

by a shot while leading an attack. The place commanded the communications with the hill fort of Asheri to which a column proceeded under Haripant and occupied the stronghold on 3rd February without firing a shot.[94]

Success in Salsette.

Minor successes were obtained in the island of Salsette opposite Bassein. Versowa which had continued to resist for the last two years was abandoned on 9th February.[95] Dharavi was pounded and battered into submission by Khanduji Mankar and surrendered on 7th March.[96] On the advice of the English the defences of Bandra were demolished on 25th March.[97]

Isolated plight of Bassein.

Bassein was now completely isolated and the Maratha forces began to converge upon the place. The siege of that fortress had continued without interruption since April 1737, but had produced little effect so far as the garrison had been able to draw freely supplies from outside. But the two years fighting had completely dried up the Portuguese resources. The entire province of the North had passed into Maratha hands. Supplies from Goa were no longer available as Goa was hard put defending itself against the enemy who had made his appearance at the gates and was pressing the attack home.[98] The Portuguese had not a single ally or friend to whom they could turn for assistance. Their relations with the English were never very amicable and the latter were deterred from em-

94. Br. Ch. App. 49, S. P. D. XVI, 130, 136, S. P. D. XXII, 389; Forrest, Maratha Series, p. 27 and Pissurlencar, pp. 64-65.

95. Forrest, Maratha Series, p. 28; According to S. P. D. XXXIV, 150-1 it was invested by Khanduji Mankar since January 1739.

96. Operations against Dharavi commenced on 13th Feb. 39 (S. P. D. XVI, 138-9), and were finished on 7th March (S. P. D. XVI, 141); also 131-5, 140, 142. The correct date of 132 is 3 March, of 133, 1st March, 1739.

97. Forrest, p. 34.

98. Forrest, Maratha Series, p. 29.

broiling themselves in the struggle through fear of the Marathas. The Sidi had been humbled and shorn of his territories. The situation appeared desperate, but the Portuguese garrison refused to haul down their flag preferring death to an ignominious end.

Final assault on Bassein.

*Chimaji Appa at the head of his numerous force arrived before Bassein on 7th February and immediately began preparations for storming the place.[99] A passage had to be forced by partially or wholly demolishing the walls, and this was possible on the northern side owing to the peculiar situation in which the fortress stood. Within fifteen days of Appa's arrival his forces "had carried their approaches by sap and mine to the foundation of the wall which it was their intention to blow."[100] It was the opinion of expert Portuguese and English Engineers that "the ground being loose sand near the sea side where the water did not permit mine of any depth, no mine could be carried deep enough in the ground to injure or endanger the walls, and as the works of the Marathas would be superficial, the best way to annoy them was by sally or raining shells plentifully on them"[101] and to this the Portuguese now resorted. Bombs were thrown and combustible matter was poured on the approaching mines. The fort artillery roared day and night and destroyed the Maratha works.[102] With a grim determination the Marathas fought the enemy back. They replied to the Portuguese with their weapons. One-hundred and thirty four cannon and sixty mortars poured their fire upon the town and the fortifications and silenced the enemy's guns.[103] It was estimated that during the three

* For the account of the final assault, see S. P. D. 162, XVI, Brahmendra Swamiche Charitra, Appendix No. 52, and one excellent Marathi letter published in Pissurlencar's book. Also Forrest, Maratha series, pp. 36-40.

99. Br. Ch. App. No. 52.

100. Forrest, p. 30. 101. *Ibid*, p. 31.

102. Sylveira's letter quoted by Forrest, p. 30.

103. S. P. D. XXII. 121.

months 45,000 shells were thrown inside the fort.[104] Breast-works were put up and under their cover the Maratha mines approached the walls.[105]

Again and again the defenders implored the English for supplies of gun powder, shots of different sizes, money and provisions. The English complied on a cash and carry basis, sending 200 barrels of gun powder and 4,000 shots in February and some treasure in April.[106] This merely served to prolong the struggle, but the issue was no longer in doubt. John Xavier Pinto, the Captain of Bassein, was killed by a musquet ball, Martinho De Sylveira, the General and successor of Pedro De Mello, was hit by a bullet on 4th April while inspecting the defences.[107] The Marathas relentlessly pressed the siege and with the greatest tenacity succeeded at last in carrying "thirteen mines to the cortines and bastions."[108] On the fateful day of 2nd May, 1739 in the early hours of the morning the drums beat, the mines were ignited and a terrific explosion blew up the San Sabastian and the Remedios towers. The Marathas rushed to storm the breaches, but were thrown into confusion by the late detonation of some of the mines.[109] Unmindful of the rocks flying at them, they pressed on recklessly. The Portuguese hurried up to the breaches and defended themselves with muskets and hand grenades and repulsed attack after attack. On the next day another big mine was sprung, making a fresh breach. Wave after wave of the Marathas dashed against the breach and fought with the utmost resolution and tenacity. Though repulsed several times they returned to the attack and at length gained a lodgment in the bastions.[110]

104. Pis. Appendix.
105. Br. Ch. App. 52, S. P. D. XXXIV, 193.
106. Forrest, Maratha Series, pp. 31 and 36.
107. Pissurlencar.
108. Forrest, Maratha series p. 39, consultation dated 7th May, 1739.
109. Br. Ch. App. 52; S. P. D. XVI, 162.
110. *Idem*; Forrest, p. 40.

The action had now lasted for two days. 800 of the Portuguese officers and rank had been killed; their ammunition was nearly exhausted and the remnant of the garrison was completely tired out and harassed. The place being no longer tenable the white flag was hoisted on 4th May, and an officer was sent to Appa to treat of a surrender. On the 5th capitulations were signed allowing the garrison the space of a week to evacuate the town.[111]

Befitting a true soldier, Chimaji Appa granted the enemy most honourable terms. The Portuguese troops were allowed to march out of the town with full military honours, and a free passage was given to them as well as to Portuguese families along with their movables and effects. Vessels of war in the harbour were allowed to sail away with their artillery. Appa generously agreed to grant religious liberty to all those who chose to remain in the district. One article provided for the exchange of prisoners, while yet another agreed to maintain the privileges of three Churches in the Province.[112]

The campaign against the Portuguese which had lasted over two years, thus ended in a resounding success for the Marathas. It forms one of the most glorious pages of Maratha history. The strategy adopted on the occasion was a novel one, foreign to Maratha methods of warfare. This was perhaps the first major campaign in which giving up their traditional methods of fighting the Marathas invested the enemy in what was then regarded as an impregnable fortress and showed amazing courage, skill and perseverance in storming it. Their losses were heavy. Appa in a letter to the Maharaja himself admitted that his casualties of dead and wounded in the last fighting amounted to near five thousand[113] while the total losses in the two years' fighting reached the staggering figure of 22,000.[114] But the cost of an offensive is always

111. Br. Ch. App. 52; consultation dated 7th May, 1739 in Forrest, Maratha Series, pp. 40-41.

112. Terms of capitulation given by Forrest, at pp. 40-41.

113. Br. Ch. App. 52.

114. Forrest, Maratha Series, p. 78.

heavy and the aggressor must be prepared to pay it. The success or failure of a campaign is to be judged not by the number of persons killed or wounded, but by how far the objectives of the war have been realised, how far the destruction of the enemy forces has been achieved. Looked at from this point the campaign must be pronounced a complete success. A smashing blow was given to the enemy; the Portuguese power which had thriven in Salsette for two hundred years was destroyed root and branch. With one voice the nation acclaimed Appa as its national hero, the Saviour of their Faith.

The gains to the Marathas may be summarised in the words of Danvers: "They acquired the entire northern province, twenty-two leagues in length, viz. from Varsowa to Daman, with their four chief ports, three hundred forty villages, and a revenue of 2,50,000 rupees. They gained besides Bassein eight cities, twenty fortresses, two fortified hills, the famous island of Salsette with the city of the same name and the island of Arnala. Daman escaped as also Chaul and Diu.

"The losses of the Portuguese at sea were equally heavy and of the greatest consequence to the state whose vessels had been always respected. The value of the implements of war, ammunition lost in the various fortresses, cities and ships exceeded 2,500,000 rupees exclusive of 593 pieces of artillery several being of bronze and of large calibre.[115]

On 12th May, 1739, the Marathas entered the fortress[116] and on the 23rd, at an auspicious moment, the ochre coloured Maratha flag was unfurled on the walls of Bassein[117] and proclaimed the incorporation of the mighty citadel and the province of Salsette in the Maratha Empire.[118]

---

115. Danvers, II, p. 411. 116. Br. Ch. App. 52.

117. S. P. D. XXII, p. 72.

118. The convention giving away Bassein and its dependencies is given by Pissurlencar, in two Marathi papers in the Appendix of his book. It was signed at Goa by the much harassed Viceroy before Bassein had actually capitulated. The final treaty was concluded late in 1740 after protracted negotiations through the mediation of the English: Vide Public Dept. Diary, Vol. XIII.

CHAPTER XV

THE PESHWA AT HIS RAJAH'S COURT.

In mediaeval polity, political power rested in the hands of the highest executive—the crowned prince or when he happened to be feeble and unfit to rule, it was gathered by his chief adviser or advisers. Shivaji directed all the activities of his State and ruled as well as reigned. Though he received advice from his ministers and accepted their suggestions, the responsibility for formulating the policy was his : the final authority rested solely in him, and his ministers were merely his secretaries—his servants who carried out his orders. His successors did not possess his tireless energy and came to rely more and more on their counsellors. Sambhaji resigned his authority to his minister Kalasha, while in Rajaram's time the exigency of the situation required that the Chhatrapati should give a free hand to his chiefs. In his absence in the Karnatak Ramchandra Pant Amatya directed Maratha activities on his own initiative, while even at Jinji Rajaram resigned himself to the advice of the able Pralhad Niraji.

In the interregnum from Sambhaji's capture in 1689 to the home coming of Shahu in May 1707 conditions in Maharashtra were abnormal and the machinery of administration as devised by Shivaji completely broke down. From the welter of the struggle with the Mughals emerged not a compact, homogeneous state, but a loosely knit organisation of powerful chiefs operating on their own behalf and owing but a nominal allegiance to the central authority. In the Satpura region (Berar, Khandesh and Baglan) Chiefs like Bandé, Dabhadé and Parsoji Bhonslé had dug their claws in and had established themselves by their own unaided prowess ; lower south, the Gangathari was the sphere of influence of the Sarlashkar and the Senapati ; the Mawal region was held by the Sachiv, while the maritime districts fell to Kanhoji Angria. Thorat, Chavan and Ghorpade carried on the struggle in the southern region now known as the Satara and Bijapur districts. These and a host of minor chiefs raised their own forces, fought the Mughals and made collection of revenue from which they reimbursed their expenses. Shahu who had returned home with a mere handful of body-guards, was called upon to establish his superior claims against the protege of Tarabai and set up his authority over these warlords. At first the patriotic tradition of his grand-father, and the bitter memory of the sufferings of his father, and the support of Zulfiqar Khan enabled him to hold his own against his rival. But these advantages by themselves would not have sufficed to make his position secure had he not been assisted by an exceptionally able minister, Balaji Vishwanath. Balaji's experience as revenue collector taught him where to find money and how to raise it: the smaller chiefs, the Khatavkars and Thorats, were put down one by one with a strong hand; the dominance of the Kolhapur party was undermined by creating dissensions within it; the more powerful warlords were persuaded to recognise the superior authority of Shahu by making their subordination least burdensome in consequence of conceding to them their conquests. The biggest triumph of Balaji Vishwanath's diplomacy was the treaty he concluded with Husen Ali legitimatising the conquests of the various warlords and securing wide sources of revenue for his Sovereign.

Having shared with the Raja the cares of the State and the changes of fortune, in his capacity of Peshwa, Balaji Vishwanath had thus come by the year 1720 to occupy a unique position; he was not merely the Raja's servant, he was his friend, guide and philosopher. The council of eight in which the Rajah's influence was supreme had disappeared with Shivaji, its place now being taken by a council in which the Peshwa enjoyed the highest status and the greatest confidence. Balaji Vishwanath exercised the king's authority over the chiefs in such an unpretentious and persuasive manner that it left no galling or rancorous memories. He himself was not a great military leader and though latterly he came to command considerable forces, his military authority was exercised only for restoring order and quelling disturbances in the territory directly under the king and in no way impinged on the spheres of other feudatories.

The character of Raja Shahu perpetuated the feudal tendencies of the time and helped the transfer of power into the hands of the ablest of his chiefs—the Peshwa. Shahu had the misfortune of having spent his formative years as a prisoner in the enemy's army. In the Mughal camp he was treated kindly and his physical needs were attended to, but in his captivity he could not receive that education which could have fitted him to be a ruler over a turbulent people. His long imprisonment in the Mughal seraglio enervated him and made him incapable of leading armies in fields, sharing their hardships and dangers, and exercising his authority in a way that his people would feel it. The sufferings he had undergone and the changes of fortune he had seen, left an indelible mark on his character. The sceptre and crown, the marks of regal authority, left him cold. He had developed a kindly and saintly disposition which preferred to leave the administration in the hands of his able Peshwa and contented itself with a kind of paternal influence over his activities. But he took a just pride in the achievements of his grandfather, gloried in the greatness of the heroic struggle waged by his people and foresaw the great future that awaited them. Himself incapacitated by circumstances from participating in the fulfilment of the great destiny of his people, he had the wisdom to lend his moral support and resign power into the hands of his able minister.[1]

In a confederacy the different units are independent in their spheres and only unite for the common interests. The Sovereign or the monarch represents the unifying principle, the principle that gives a common direction to the activities of the separate units. If this unifying authority is weakened, if this common bond is relaxed, the centrifugal tendencies

1. For Shahu's character and views please see Chitnis, pp. 25, 60-62 ; 81, 82, 85 ; Br. Ch. letter at p. 119, S. P. D. XXX, 222 ; III, 129 ; XVII, 12, etc.

raise their head, each separate chief seeks his own interest unmindful of the common purpose, and even harming the general interests, for his selfish end. The feudal state is therefore always in danger of losing its cohesion by the weakening of the monarchical bond.

Shahu neither by character nor by education, was fitted to exercise the authority so essential to hold together these loose elements, but he had the wisdom to allow himself be guided by an able minister. To this delicate position succeeded Bajirao when he was hardly twenty. The other chiefs who feared the Peshwa's preponderance in the council, advised the King that he would bring ruin on the state by resigning himself to an inexperienced youth. The grateful Rajah however set aside the objection and confirmed Bajirao in his father's office. The correspondence between the Rajah and his minister well brings out the relations existing between them. In the early days of Bajirao's premiership the tone of the Raja's letters is often critical and expressive of annoyance at the Peshwa's absences from Satara.[2] By defeating the Nizam, the leading Mughal Chief of the day, the Peshwa not only saved the state and upheld the authority of his Sovereign, but gained a place in the Rajah's confidence which nothing could shake.[3] His successes in Malwa and Bundelkhand by adding to his resources, strengthened his position at home and made him respected abroad. Deepsingh, the special envoy of the Jaipur Rajah, reported that he was "the only true leader of men among the Marathas. With the exception of Bajirao he could see no statesman true of his word, trusted by his Sovereign, beloved by his troops and capable of shouldering heavy responsibilities."[4] Even Anand Rao Sumant had unwillingly to speak of him as "the eye of his Sovereign, a faithful servant of the Crown."[5] When the dispute with the Senapati flared up, most of the chiefs, all the Marathas as the writer reports it—

2. S. P. D. XVII, 28, Shahu Rozkird 15, Rajwade VI, 16.
3. S. P. D., III, 123.
4. S. P. D. X, 66.
5. S. P. D. X, 59, 60.

Pawar, Bande, Gaikawad, Dabhade, the Pratinidhi — alienated from the Peshwa by his growing influence, wished secretly for the Peshwa's ruin, and negotiated with the Nizam,[6] but the Rajah never for a moment wavered in his support. On one occasion Umabai Dabhade was coming to Satara and there was a chance of her passing the spot where the Peshwa lay encamped. The Rajah fearing for the life of his minister, conveyed him a secret warning to avoid a brush up with the wrathful lady.[7] In the Janjira campaign when in Dec. 1735 the Sidi surprised Bankot and threatened to advance, the Raja called on the Peshwa to save the situation. He expressed his trust in Bajirao in memorable words. "We depend on you for everything. Who else would serve the state in the hour of peril?"[8] On another occasion he spoke of Bajirao as "the man with iron nerves."[9] Still on another occasion while expressing his utmost pleasure at the glorious successes obtained by the Peshwa, he warned him of tarnishing his fame by his rapacious practice of selling justice to the highest bidder.[10] The Rajah's heart beat with pride when he heard of the Peshwa's victories, but he often felt that the pace of the Peshwa's conquests was too fast and would land him in a dangerous corner.[11]

The methods of the Sovereign and the Minister were different, but their objective was the same. Shahu looked not to supplant the Mughal Emperor, he would rather be the Emperor's friend and mentor, would lend his sword arm to his support and thus acquire control over the imperial policy.[12] The reverence felt by him for the throne of the Chaghtais expressed not the servility of a subordinate to his Superior, but the sympathy which a man of culture—a noble soul—feels for an ancient relic, for a fallen cause. In the hands of Bajirao this attitude was rightly transformed into an attempt at poli-

6. *Ibid*, 70. 7. S. P. D. XII, 57.
8. S. P. D. III, 129. 9. *Ibid*, 135.
10. S. P. D. XVII, 52. 11. *Ibid*, 47.
12. S. P. D. XV, No. 72, XXX, 222; Satara Vol. 2, No. 268; the same letter printed in Br. Ch. at p. 119; Shahu Bakhar, p. 106.

tical hegemony in the north : the sword arm of the Maratha state was wielded so ably by his Peshwa as to fulfil the wildest dream of the monarch.

The Peshwa (and his agents) always remembered that his authority emanated from the Crown and had its roots in the confidence placed in him by the Sovereign.[13] He attended on the Raja on occasions, and when away on distant expeditions explained his motives and activities through his resident brother or his deputies, the Purandares. The Rajah's needs and comforts were promptly looked after.[14] But as the years rolled by and the Peshwa's resources increased with his conquests and his influence grew, the Rajah who chose the ease of his palace receded into the background. The Peshwa's visits to the court became rare and of shorter duration,[15] the affairs being managed by his deputies. Possessing a magnificient army with which he had dealt such crushing blows to his enemies and had acquired vast territories, the Peshwa came to be looked upon as the power behind the throne, and foreign potentates preferred to send their envoys and negotiate with him rather than with the figurehead at Satara. His dynamic personality so overshadowed that of the monarch that when Gordon visited the Satara Court in July, 1739, he reported, "Bajirao is so powerful that he makes small account of the Raja...as his power is uncontrolled by whomsoever, the Rajah is compelled to an exercise of an outward civility to him. The sentiments of most are that Bajirao has in view to throw off his allegiance to the Rajah." He therefore warned his masters that "although a civil correspondence with the Rajah may not be amiss, care must be taken that he is not solicited for what interferes with Bajirao whose authority at court is even such, that in the absence of the Raja, and contrary to the advice of the seven principal counsellors, he can enforce a complete obedience to his sole mandates."[16]

13. S. P. D. XVII, 98, XXX, 137, III, 128.
14. S. P. D. VIII, 15, 16, 18-29, 31, etc.
15. S. P. D. XVII, 28 and Br. Ch. No. 30 (App.).
16. Forrest, Maratha Series, pp. 78-80.

The adroit Inchbird who "by experience was well versed in nature, customes and manners of the Gentoo governments round Bombay" and who had been at this time deputed to Chimaji Appa "to treat of several matters and dependencies of great importance to the welfare of the island" reported to his superiors that "although they allow Your Honours' compliments to the Sou Rajah to be a piece of good policy, they greatly resent your not consulting them in it first: and although I have been at much pains to persuade them to the contrary, yet they still persist as they were our neighbours we ought first to have made our application to them."[17] Discussing the articles of the treaty he was negotiating with Chimaji and his council he adds, "in the eighth article they lord it over you and the Shahu Raja also and say that you shall not apply to him upon any account without their previous advice and consent."[18] As a result the council was convinced "that treating with the Shahu Raja directly as matters are circumstanced, would be to no purpose, as Bajirao's power is so firmly established that such a step would give him a jealousy that we were aiming at subverting his interests in these parts."[19]

This acquisition of the supreme power by the Peshwa was resented by the lesser chiefs, like the Pratinidhi, the Sumant, Angria, Dabhade, Pawar and others. Most of them ranged themselves against the Peshwa on one occasion or another, but were unable to wrest that power from him. The Pratinidhi consistently opposed the Peshwa's growing ambitions, but lacking his rival's military ability, his personal influence with the sovereign could avail him little. This man allowed himself to be duped by the Nizam and was prepared to commute the all-prevading claims of Chauth and Sardeshmukhi over the Deccan for a small territory. By secretly

17. Forrest, Maratha Series, p. 72.
18. Forrest, Maratha Series, p. 74.
19. Consultation of Nov. 1739, Vol. XII, pp. 481-82, Pub. Dept. Diary.

negotiating for the acquisition of the fortress of Raigarh he forestalled the Peshwa, roused his hatred and doomed the expedition to failure. In 1730 he was reported to be secrectly aiding the Dabhade party in their revolt against the Peshwa.[20] Feeling mortified at the Peshwa's resounding successes, the Pratinidhi rushed into fitting out expeditions in the Karnatak,[21] but nothing came of the projects as he possessed neither the skill of his rival nor was prepared to risk his money in raising adequate forces for the enterprise. He and his friends forgot that what gave the Peshwa his preponderance in the royal council was the military strength acquired by him by years of successful warfare. It was equally open to them to raise armies and lead them to foreign conquests, but like their master they loved the repose of the Court and in consequence slowly faded into insignificance.

But the Peshwa cannot altogether be absolved from the charge of using his opportunities for self-aggrandisement. Imperious by temperament and habit, he brooked no rival to his authority; those of the feudatories who refused to submit to his superior power were either destroyed or went over to the enemy and their energies were lost to the nation. The authority which his office gave him was used by him for enlarging his own resources and promoting his own interests. Not only were the northern conquests retained by him as his Jagirs, but so also were the territories acquired by him from the Sidi and the Portuguese. His dealings with Dabhade Senapati and Angria were to say the least, unfair and impolitic. Had he shown a little more regard for the rights of others and a little more disposition for conciliation, the dispute with the Senapati could have been settled amicably and hostilities avoided. By acquiring for himself the new conquests from the Sidi and the Portuguese he circumscribed Angria's influence and destroyed any possibility for the Angria expanding into a great

20. S. P. D. X, 65; and XII, 57, 74.
21. S. P. D. XXX, 171, XVII, 46.

maritime power.[22] While he could put in the field myriads of light horse for his northern conquests, he grudged to spare a respectable contingent for the war against Chavan that the Rajah was personally directing.[23] As the most trusted servant of the Crown his duty lay in harmonising the differences of the feudal chiefs by his selfless mediation. He cowed them by the force of his armed might, subordinating them to his authority. Even the Rajah on occasions felt the overgrown power of his minister and expressed his displeasure in sharp reprimands.[24] When he found the Peshwa's troops opposing his cousin in 1736 he remarked, "the Pant Pradhan is gone north without my orders; I get reports of his formulating mighty plans with the Emperor. Formerly he gave protection to the Sidi; fomented discord in the Angrian family and now he dare sent troops against my kith and kin." [25] On another occasion he expressed similar sentiments, saying "The Peshwa has done me real service only on one occasion—in repelling the Nizam. Otherwise his activities and conquests have been for self-aggrandisement." [26]

Thus by 1739 the Peshwa had reached the apogee of his power that led Gordon to think (wrongly) that he had in view the throwing off his allegiance to the Rajah. The control of Maratha policy had passed from the Sovereign to the Peshwa; the political revolution that became patent to all after the Rajah's death in 1749 was already an accomplished fact.

22. Forrest, Maratha Series, p. 79; S. P. D. XXXIII, 460 (p 384) contains Manaji Angria's complaints against the Peshwa. The correct year of the letter is 1734 and not 1738 as given by the editor.

23. S. P. D. XVII, 72.

24. S. P. D. XVII, 67-8.

25. S. P. D. XI, 23.

26. S. P. D. III, 123.

CHAPTER XVI

THE FINALE—ACHIEVEMENTS & CHARACTER.

During the last year and a half of his life the Peshwa appears to have lost the energy and buoyancy we meet in him from the beginning of his career. His activities become paralysed : his actions are halting. His fondness for his mistress Mastani brought on a crisis in his life which almost estranged him from his family. In Mastani's company he transgressed the rules of eating and drinking imposed on him by his caste and religion, which lapse raised a storm in his household and in the hide-bound Brahmin society of the day. The Rajah was appealed to to wean the Peshwa from his free habits : vows by the Ganges water were exchanged and as a last resort the woman was forcibly separated from her lord and kept under close surveillance.[1]

From this domestic discord the Peshwa sought escape in the field. In November 1739 he left Poona[2] and marched toward the Nizam's territory. Anxious to secure his routes into Hindustan which passed through the latter's country, he now demanded of the Nizam's local representative to grant him that part in Jagir. The demand was turned down and hostilities ensued. Nasir Jang was invested in Aurangabad, but fearing to be starved he moved out in the direction of Tisgaon and Kharadi followed closely by the Maratha horse. (7 Feb. 1740).[3] The two parties soon came to terms (27 Feb.) Nasir Jang bowing before the storm and granting to the Peshwa the district of Nemar demanded of him.[4] After fraternising the two armies separated, the Peshwa moving towards Burhanpur.*

---

1. S. P. D. IX, 30-34, 36 ; Raj. VI, pp. 30-31, Itihas Samgraha, Ait Tipanen II, 7. For a complete account of the Mastani affair vide the paper of Prof. Rao in the 1940 report of the Indian Hist. Records Commission.

2. Raj. VI, p. 28. 3. Purandare I, 138, 139.

4. S. P. D. XXII, 144, Br. Ch. App. 55 and Raj. II, p. 85.

*The account given by Persian authorities is different. I give here

He had received little news from Mastani and lingered here for some time. While encamped at Rawerkhedi on the

a detailed translation from Hadiqa-i-Alam and Sir Jadunath's comments on it. It would explain why I reject the Persian authorities.

HADIQA-I-ALAM, VOL. II.

(Written about 1802).

Literal translation from the Persian original, p. 187 :

When a fissure appeared in the empire of Hindustan in consequence of the coming of Nadir Shah, Baji Rao engaged in seizing the jagirs of the mansabdars of the Deccan which had been granted by the Emperor and by Asaf Jah, I. After the return of Nadir Shah from Hind to Persia, Nawab Nizām-ud-daulah Nāsir Jang, sending an envoy to Baji Rao, made overtures (or proposals) for an agreement. At that time Baji Rao withdrew his hand from the confiscation of the jagirs.

After two years, in 1152 A. H. Baji Rao, uplifting the standdard of hostility to Nizam-ud-daulah Nāsir Jang, began to attempt to wrest the kingdom of the Deccan from the hands of this Prince of Islam [who was then acting as deputy for his absent father] and having assembled a force, alighted in the southern side of Aurangabad. Nawab Nizamud-daulah, with the troops he had in the city marched out of Aurangabad with the object of carrying on a holy war and ravaging the infidels' seat Poona. After fighting, he became victorious, and beating the enemy, carried his victorious banners to the further [i.e., south] side of the river Gang [Godāvari], and from 17th January to the *Qurbāni Id* (Id of sacrifice which fell on 18th Feb. 1740), for one month and a few days there was the *qurbāni* (slaughter) of men and the flames of fighting and killing continued to blaze up. Although the enemy's force was 50,000 horsemen and the army of Islam did not amount to ten thousand, every day the holy warriors of Islam, displaying activity, pushed the infidels back; Baji Rao [P. 188] saw that he would gain nothing from fighting and inclined towards peace. He came and had the honour of interviewing Nāsir-ud-daulah. Nawab Nizam-ud-daulah, with a view to laying down the foundations of friendship, granted the districts (*Sarkār*) of Khargon and Hāndia as jagir to Baji Rao. After this peace had been concluded, Baji Rao in the manner of a defeated party (*maghlubāna*) turned towards Mālwā and reached the bank of the Narmada.

[COMMENTS : On the first occasion it was Nizam-ud-daulah himself who solicited Baji Rao to make peace. On the second oc-

Narmada he contracted a fever on 23rd April : after a short illness he passed away on Monday, the 28th April (Waishakh 13th day)[5] mourned by his family, by his King, and by his people. "He died as he had lived," says Sir Richard Temple, "in camp under canvas among his men and he is remembered to this day among Marathas as the fighting Peshwa or the incarnation of Hindu energy."[6]

The political career of this remarkable man has been fully studied and his influence on his country's destinies explained in the foregoing pages. His achievements may be summed up as "the establishment of supremacy in the Deccan and of political hegemony in the north." Prudence and self-defence dictated such a policy. Shivaji created an independent Maratha state by rallying round himself patriotic bands : the independent existence of this state was challenged by the Mughal Government, its territories overrun, armies dispersed and its ruler Sambhaji beheaded. The Maratha people recovered their independence after a most heroic struggle. But so long as a powerful neighbour could assail it, they could never rest in security. By defeating the Nizam the representative of the Mughal and the only other power that counted in the Deccan, Bajirao forced him to acknowledge that he could never hope to weaken the Maratha authority either by sowing dissensions or by a trial of arms so long as the Peshwa was at the helm

---

casion (1) plenty of Muslim soldiers on Nāsir Jang's side were slain, because an orthodox Shia writer like our author would not use the word *qurbāni* (sacrifice) for the slaughter of infidels. (2) No victorious party in its senses ever grants two rich districts to the vanquished party ; the reverse of it is the experience everywhere. Therefore, we must discount the fanatical boast of the Nizam's courtier-historian and conclude that Nāsir Jang was himself anxious to make peace and placate Baji Rao, so as to secure his powerful aid in the rebellion against his own father Asaf Jah I, which he was then planning ; the terms, all favourable to Baji Rao, were settled at their private interview. Asaf Jah I, himself had thanked Baji Rao for his aid in the battle of Sakarkheda.]

5. S. P. D. XXII, P. 89.
6. Sir Richard Temple, Oriental Experience, I, p. 390.

of affairs. The Nizam granted the Maratha claims of Chauth and Sardeshmukhi over his territory and accepted a subordinate position. The maritime districts of Maharashtra held by foreign powers were recovered from them : the Sidi was driven from the mainland and his power for mischief permanently crippled. The Portuguese authority in north Konkan was destroyed and their province came to form a division of the Maratha state. Dabhade and such other chiefs as tried to break away from the central authority by forming alliances with foreign rulers were taught a stern lesson. Thus by giving his people a dominant position in the Deccan, Bajirao secured their homeland from foreign aggression which position it continued to enjoy for more than half a century afterwards.

Such an achievement alone would have been most creditable and given the Peshwa a permanent place in the history of his country. His policy however extended beyond the security of his homeland. He aimed at establishing Maratha hegemony beyond the Narmada. Gifted with a majestic imagination, he realized as few of his contemporaries did, that the time had come to challenge the Mughal authority in the north. He perceived that the far-flung empire of the Mughal had lost its vitality and was tottering to its fall, and he hastened to grasp that power. For this purpose he cleverly utilised the mutual jealousies and hatreds prevailing among the court factions of Delhi. His successes over Giridhar Bahadur and Muhammad Khan Bangash established his hold over Malwa and Bundelkhand, while his victory over the Nizam at Bhopal defeated the final attempt of the Imperial Government to wrest his northern conquests from him. He had now secured bases from which to direct further expansion. Within twenty years of his death the Marathas were masters of the imperial capital and dictators of imperial policy.

What was the secret of the Peshwa's success? What enabled him to fill all these twenty years with resounding victories? The answer must be sought in his character and his able generalship. He had all the qualities that made him a tower of strength to his state—character, persistence and energy, high purpose, abounding faith and courage and an intimate knowledge of the political situation. His early training under his father, a masterful personality, inculcated in him habits of strenuous activity and patient perseverance, qualities so essential for ensuring success. In a sea of unrest he spent his childhood at Saswad, Poona, Satara, with the din of battle ringing in his ears. While barely ten years of age he began to accompany his father in his expeditions and acquainted himself first hand with the peculiar Maratha character and the problems confronting his nation. Thus when he succeeded to the Peshwaship he brought with him all this experience with the dashing energy of youth. Within ten years he had established his reputation at home and abroad. Deepsingh described him as "a man true of his words and trusted by his King."[7] Foreign potentates like Jai Singh, the Nizam, Saadat Khan[8] and Bangash vied with each other in seeking his friendship. Maratha Siledars confident in his leadership, flocked to his banner perferring to serve under him rather than under any other commander.

In the memory of his countrymen Bajirao remains a soldier first and last. He was never so long at home as in his camp. Throughout the twenty years of his Peshwaship he was ever on the move, marching and fighting, living on the simplest fare and sharing the hardships and toils of his men. His personal courage endeared him to his soldiers while his example inspired them. He walked fearlessly into the enemy's camp and sought to gain his point as much by personal meetings as by an appeal to arms. Liberal in rewarding merit, he was strict in exacting discipline and work. Cowardice and remissness were the two things he hated most in his men, and when he detected the least sign of them he came down upon the offender with a heavy hand.[9] Not only were great chiefs

7. S. P. D. X, 66.

8. S. P. D. XIV, 9 contains certain overtures to the Peshwa from Saadat Khan.

9. S. P. D. III, 112, XXXIII. 207. and Br. Ch. letter dated 9 Nov. 1737 at pp. 76-77.

rewarded for their gallant conduct in action, but even common soldiers were stimulated to exertions by promotions and inams. When Raja Shahu had occasion to express doubts about the efficiency of the Peshwa's infantry, he was immediately contradicted by Fatesingh (who was no admirer of the Peshwa) with the remark, "that the Peshwa was not neglecting his infantry, that he kept his entire army in good trim and ready for any emergency."[10]

He had an eye for recognising ability wherever it might happen to be; caste and class were no bar to promotion. Holkar and Sindhia who rose to the first rank under him had been just common soldiers under his father: Govind Ballal Kher was a personal attendant. When he had made his choice he placed entire confidence in his chiefs stimulating them to exertion by his example. Under him rose to fame Pilaji Jadhav, Sindhia, Holkar, the Pawars, the Retrekars, the Phadkes, Vinchurkar, Bundele and a host of minor chiefs.

If Bajirao was great as a soldier, he was greater still as a general. Sir Jadunath Sarkar calls him 'a heaven-born cavalry leader.' His skill lay in manoeuvering large bodies of cavalry with surprising speed. It was the Peshwa's celerity that brought the Nizam down to his knees in 1728 and forced him to sign the treaty of Mungi Shevgaon. His lightning speed enabled him to surprise Bangash at Jaitpur in 1729 and outwit the imperialist commanders before Agra in 1737. With speed he combined the element of surprise. Clever general that he was, he acquainted himself with the situation of his opponents and delivered his attack at a point where it was least expected. Bajirao kept his plans to himself, carefully obtained minute information of the enemy forces[11] and then moving by unfrequented paths, appeared before the enemy only to cause consternation. He thus kept the initiative of his campaigns to himself and left the enemy guessing. The

10. S. P. D. XXXIII, 254.

11. In his Rozkird there occur frequent entries showing sums expended in getting intelligence of the enemy.

Palkhed campaign, the Peshwa's offensive against Janjira, his dash on Delhi all bear out the above remark. At Palkhed after tiring out his enemy with marching and counter marching he came upon him in a difficult tract of country and cut off his water supply. In the 1737 campaign he retired to a little distance from Gohad and then making a long detour marched on Delhi. So secret were his movements that the defenders of the capital could not for some time believe that the Peshwa had succeeded in eluding their armies.

The light equipment of Bajirao's armies made their greater speed possible. Well knowing his own weakness in artillery, the Peshwa avoided closing with his adversary : he drew him out of his cover, surrounded him with his numerous hordes and cutting off his supplies brought him to his knees. This was how the Nizam was defeated at Palkhed and Bhopal.

Cool and unmoved by a situation of even the utmost danger, the man was full of resources and ready to meet any emergency. The strong detachment sent by him into the Doab in 1737 was routed and had returned in utmost confusion. Three large armies blocked his way towards Agra. Any other person in his position would have quailed and beaten retreat, imperilling his new conquests. Bajirao rose to the occasion and by his superior tactics and mobility baffled his enemies. Courteous in his manners he made war like a gentleman. Never in his correspondence does a vile phrase about his enemies escape him though his opponents (e.g., Asaf Jah) choose to call him "villain". He had the ancient capital of the Mughals at his mercy, but he preferred to retire rather than lay it under the sword. When the Nizam, hard pressed at Bhopal, opened negotiations and desired the Peshwa to withdraw to a little distance, the Peshwa agreed, out of deference for his opponent's age.[12]

But with all his achievements Bajirao cannot be hailed as a great constructive genius fit to rank with Shivaji. He made

12. Br. Ch. App. 34.

no attempt to mould or reform the political institutions of his state in a way that would benefit his people permanently. The feudal tendency among the Marathas which had again raised its head after Shivaji's death, was not only not repressed, but he himself became the greatest military vassal of his time. The armies he raised owed their first allegiance to him ; his successes in Malwa, Gujarat, Konkan, strengthened Shahu's authority not directly, but as represented by the Peshwa. The expansion of the Maratha power he envisaged, was the expansion effected by the Peshwa whose authority should be supreme over other chiefs. The weakness of this feudal organization made itself felt when the Maratha authority extended to the farthest confines of India.

APPENDIX

श्री गजानन

Recd. 17 June 1724.

छ ७ सवाल.

राजश्री बाजीराऊ पंडित यांसी

सुलतानजी निंबाळकर सरलष्कर दंडवत विनंति उपरी. गोसावी यांनीं पत्रें पाठविलीं प्रविष्ट होऊन लेखनार्थ अवगत जाहला. लिहिलें कीं नवाब निजामनमुलक रेवा तिरास असतां धारेसनिध घाट उतरोन आले; त्याची आमची सनिधता जाली. याकरितां भेटी घेणें लागले. भेटीचा सौरस्य उत्तम प्रकारचा जाला. आम्ही सडे होतो या करितां निरोप घेऊन पुढें बुऱ्हानपुरास आलो. नवाबही बुऱ्हानपुरास आले. कित्येक बोलीचालीचा प्रसंग स्नेह या राज्याचा दर्शविला व कित्येक सार्वभोमाकडील येकनिष्ठेचें वर्तमान सांगितलें. त्यास याची साह्यता सर्व प्रकारें केलियानें उत्तम गोष्टी आहे येसे जाणोन आम्ही यास आश्वासन दिलें आहे. तर गोसावी यांनीं फौजसहवर्तमान बागडा संनिध आले पाहिजे. येविसी राजश्री स्वामीसही पत्रें पाठविलीं आहेत. त्यांची आज्ञा आपणास येईल. आम्हीही गंगातीरास येतो. गोसावी यांची आमची भेटी होऊन तदनंतर मनसबा होणें तो होईल म्हणून कित्येक विशदें लिहिलें. येसियासी आपण जो मनसबा लिहिला तो विचारें करून केला असेल. जेणेंकरून स्वराज्याचे हेतू तें करणें उचित आहे.

[पुढील मजकूर निरुपयोगी सबब गाळला.]

BOMBAY CO. TO THE COURT OF DIRECTORS

Dated 14th April 1733.

The Sidi of Rajapore is lately deceased on which his eldest son whom he had appointed successor in the Govt. was immediately cut off by four officers who have put themselves at the head of an opposite faction and declared the youngest son a boy of seven years old Nabob in prejudice of an elder son who was likewise a party for him, so that all the Siddee's country is in a civil war, which we fear may give Angria an opportunity of possessing himself of some of the Sidi's fortresses as he has lately done of Rutnagheree, a fort on the top of a hill near the side betwixt Dabull and Gereah that belonged to Ram Rou's widow and commands a considerable district of country inland; the ambitious views of this our troublesome neighbour are very extensive."

BOMBAY CO. TO THE COURT OF DIRECTORS

18th August 1733.

Angria has reinforced his fleet with 5 large grabs and several gallivats, taken from the Sidi. We have therefore purchased the Rose Galley .... for in the beginning of May Badgee Row first General to the Sou Raja with 5 or 6000 men being joined with some troops of Angria's, marched directly to Rajapore and having intelligence with the chief officer, Shaikh Yacoot, Governor of the place who had under his command 6 or 7000 of the Sidi's forces, he marched out and joined Badgee Row as soon as he appeared and delivered up to him the town and the Sidi's fleet of grabs and galivats that lay in the port with all their guns, stores and ammunition; five of the grabs and several of the galivats were immediately given to Angria who carried them to Colaba and is now fitting them out with all expedition together with his own fleet to go as soon as weather will permit him, against the fort that is situated on an island in Rajahporee harbour."

BOMBAY CO. TO THE COURT OF DIRECTORS

Dated 1st February, 1734.

Upon our Gentlemen's arrival at Gingira they sent Capt. Inchbird with a message to Badgee Row and the Vizier Nizam-ul-mulk's agent came into Gingira from Badgee Row's camp where it was agreed that Sciddee Abdul Raman, the eldest son of the Sciddee Yacut Khan deceased, then in Badgee Row's camp, should be delivered to our gentlemen and by them introduced into the Gingira, which is the principal place of residence of the governing Sciddees and this was accordingly done.

Sundry other articles were proposed from one side and the other....but nothing concluded, Badgee Row of a sudden marching off his army and leaving Rajahporee for the Sciddees to take possession of, which they did, and some days afterwards the Sciddee Seyad (Saat) and Massoot embarked a sufficient number of troops on board their fleet and laid siege to the fort of Bancote in the river of (x x x) about five leagues to the southward of Rajahporee, garrisoned by Angria's forces which being attacked by the Sidi's fleet and some batteries from the shore, Angria's people in the night deserted it and made their escape to Southerndrook, and the Sciddees having put a sufficient garrison therein they proceeded up the river to another fort called Maar, formerly belonging to them but taken by the Sou Raja's troops who were then in garrison. This fort they took without much opposition and some other of less consequence in that neighbourhood.

Flushed with success they sent a detachment to besiege Rairee which had been likewise taken by Sou Raja's troops.

This was contrary to our opinion and advice and what was stipulated and agreed on with Sidi Saat and Massoot while they were here, as we were sensible that the Sou Raja would spare no pains or cost to maintain himself in the possession of that conquest.

On the news of the Sciddee's success against Bancote and Maar, reaching the Sou Raja's court and their laying siege to Rairee, Badgee Row was severely censured for his hasty retreat out of the Sciddee's territory and he was ordered by the Rajah to return immediately with his army against them.

On this Badgee Row wrote the President a letter complaining of the Sciddee's impatience and rashness in this enterprise while he was endeavouring to bring the Rajah to consent to an accommodation on the terms that the Sciddees desire except the surrender of Rajree and he desired the President to prevail with the Sciddees to lay aside the thought of besieging that fortress, otherwise he should be obliged to march against them a second time the consequence of which might be fatal to their other affairs ; a copy of which the President sent to Sidi Seyad with his opinion. But before the letter reached him 8 or 9000 of Sou Raja's troops marched against those of the Sciddees that laid siege to Rairee and defeated them obliging them to return to Maar where Sidi Seyad (Saat) with the rest of the army now lies encamped with about 12 to 15000 men....

Samuel Walker to the Bombay Council.

11 May 1741.

About four months ago Sambhajee wrote to the Sciddees at the time the Marathas took possession of Choule, representing the friendship which had formerly subsisted betwixt them, and setting forth the bad consequences which attended their disunion, which would be the ruin of both if not prevented by a timely accommodation, and desired their assistance in putting him in possession of Coleabby, and in return he would give them the amount of the rents and revenues of the countrys he had taken from them since the Moratta wars commenced, and in future to allow them the half of the produce of these countries, but does not choose to deliver up the fortifications. The Sciddees, it seems, refused to assist him against Monajee but promised a neutrality and represented to Sambhajee the impossibility of his accomplishing his designs upon that place, and if he moved dispossessing his brother, the consequence would be that place with the country to the northward would fall into a superior Power's hands. The Sciddees demanded from Sambhajee his complying with the Agreement made by Sciddee Saat, which was that Sambhajee should deliver a sum of money for Rents and Revenues of the country taken from the Sciddees in time past, and the half of the produce in future; they gave him to understand that tho' they were now in a low condition, yet they were capable of annoying his country, and that altho' they had lost Sciddee Saat, yet they had not lost his spirit, and that in case he did not comply with the treaty he made they would endeavour to oblige him.

It is said that Sambhajee has really given rupees twelve thousand and promised in future to give them the half of the produce of their country agreeable to the treaty he made with Sciddee Saat.

—*Public Dept. Diary*, No. 14, pp. 196-7.

---

11 May 1741

"Sidi Sambul expressed himself with as much gratitude as could be desired, saying it was great concern to him the misfortune of their state having lost the greatest and better part of their country, and what small part remained the Marathas had half of their produce, and that they had been obliged ever since the commencing of the war to keep a great body of forces for defending Gowalkot......"

(*Samuel Walker's report to the Bombay Council,*
Dated 11 May 1741, in Pub. Dept. Diary No. 14)

KESHORAM'S ARZDASHT TO MAHARAJA SAHIB :

You have come to learn by now the account of Malwa. First of all Kantha Maratha with 10,000 horse wandered in Malwa and then went to Gujarat. On hearing the news of his wanderings Raja Bahadur who camped at Mandsaur sent his palace servants etc. to Ujjain, and with his own force and Raja Anand Ram and Rao Gulab Ram, turned his attention to the chastisement of the villain. The villain, hence went from Malwa to Gujarat and stayed on the boundary of Gujarat near Banswara. Raja Bahadur encamped on the boundary of Amjhera. Chima Pundit (Chima Appa) brother of Bajirao and Udaji Pawar, etc., with a force of 22,000 crossed the Narbada all of a sudden, travelled 30 koss and on the 8th Jamad-ul-awal, Saneh 11 (29th November 1728) left some soldiers near Dhar fort lest Muhammad Umar Khan who was stationed at Dhar, might come from the fort and unite with Raja Bahadur. The rest gathered round the imperial army. First Rao Gulam Ram and Salabat Khan Jamadar killed most of the villains, but there is no remedy for fate, they were killed; Raja Anand Ram received two musket wounds and he with his brother Shambhuram, were captured by the Ghanims (plunderers). The Raja Bahadur discharged arrows from his own hand and killed many of them and when 4 quivers which were on his elephant were empty, he suddenly received a shot in his chest and sacrificed his life in royal work. From the day ......now Shree Maharaja is in the place of Raja Bahadur. You should take care of Kunwar Bhawani Ram, son of Raja Chhabilaram, Binay Ram, Mohanram and Shambhuram, sons of Raja Bahadur and their relatives. At that time all the four princes consoled their men and kept them in service as usual and began to engage new men in service. New men are being appointed to guard the city.

श्री

श्रीमंत राजश्री ंतप्रधान ता राजश्री आपा स्वामीचे

सेवेसी

विनंति सेवक सदासिव बल्लाळ सा नमस्कार विनंति. ता छ १७ साबान पावेतो स्वामीचें कृपा दृष्टिनें येथास्थित असे.........राणाजीस आज्ञेप्रा विनंती केली, मान्य केलें की रायांची स्वारी रेवा तीरीं येतांच जैसें लिहून पाठवितील त्याप्रमाणें सिध असो. परंतु सर्व हिंदुसमुदाय एकत्र होऊन जावे येसे बोलिले. राजश्री धोंडो गोविंद पावलियावर काय तह ठरेल तो लिहिला पाहिजे येसे राणाजीनें सांगितले.

(पुढील मजकूर गैरमहत्वाचा सबब गाळला.)

12 May 1740

In an interview which Capt. Inchbird, the English emissary had with Chimaji Appa on 12th May 1740, Chimaji is reported by the emissary to have remarked : "On the 12th instant in the morning Appah sent for me....and freely opened himself in regard to the treaty depending between them and the Portuguese with a long detail of what had past for many years, too tedious to rehearse ; the heads was (sic) heavy complaints against the Portuguese in regard to their religion, the sufferings of the poor Gentoo orphans, etc., inquisitions, imputing the justice of their chastisement to the Divine will...."

—(*Public Dept. Diary*, Vol. 13, pp. 223-4.)

ORIGINAL SOURCES.

This work is based mainly on the papers and despatches in the Peshwas' Daftar. Forty five volumes of selected correspondence have been published of which 16 containing about 2500 despatches relate to the subject under study. There are about the same number of unpublished records in addition to 'Rozkirds' in the Daftar. This is the first attempt to study the regime of the great Peshwa, Bajirao I, from contemporary records.

Another important source which the writer has been able to utilise exclusively through the kindness of his guide Sir Jadunath Sarkar, is the Jaipur Akhbarat. The Akhbarat are Persian news-letters sent to the Jaipur Princes by their agents with the emperor at Delhi and other important centres. But for this source Maratha activities in the north would have been confusing, if not inexplicable.

The Diaries of the Bombay Secretariat Records are useful in following the Sidi-Maratha and the Portuguese-Maratha wars. The letters sent by the Bombay Council to the Court of Directors were meant for their masters thousands of miles away and are in consequence full and give many details lacking elsewhere.

The Portuguese Records cannot be overlooked in studying Maratha expansion towards the west coast. In this field Pissurlencar is doing excellent work; his monographs on different topics are based on the Portuguese correspondence in the Goa archives; his books on the Fall of Bassein have been used for this thesis.

While the work is based on these new records, old papers published by Rajwade, Sane and Parasnis have not been overlooked. Chronicles and chronologies have been relegated to the background and have been marshalled only when their statements can be supported by contemporary evidence. Khafi Khan's work is familiar to students of Shivaji, but has missed the attention of scholars for the next twenty years. A close reading of Mirat-i-Ahmadi would repay the trouble for tracing Maratha activities in Gujarat. For the early history of the Nizam there is no better book than Hadiqat-ul-alam. All these Persian and Marathi sources have been used to make the present work as faultless as possible. The Persian manuscripts were read by the author with the help of a Munshi, while the Portuguese material was translated into English for him by his friends.

In the use of materials contemporary records by persons on the spot are always given preference to later histories or chronologies. But it is not always that one finds in contemporary records the springs of action of an individual or all the facts that go to make up an episode. In this situation one has to seek aid from chronicles, use the historical sense and exercise the historian's creative faculty in the selection and interpretation of facts. That is the high water-mark of scholarship. How far the writer has succeeded in the attempt he leaves it to his readers to judge.

Important original sources, manuscript and printed, have been indicated and the contents discussed in the note. Following is a detailed bibliography.

ORIGINAL SOURCES (Manuscripts)

I. MARATHI—Poona Daftar.

i. *Rumals* selected for further research, Nos. 1-4. These contain papers of the regime of Bajirao which have not been printed in the selections, but which are by no means unimportant.

ii. *Peshwa Rozkirds* or Diaries as they are popularly known, for the years 1720-1740. They contain the Peshwas' accounts and yield bits of very useful information.

II. ENGLISH—Secretariat Records, Bombay.

The Public Dept. Diaries, 4-14 and the Secretariat outward letter book, No. 7 contain correspondence relating to the Sidi-Maratha and the Portuguese-Maratha wars. Most of it is however printed by Banaji in the appendix of his thesis, *The Sidis and the English of Bombay*, and by Forrest in the *Maratha and Home Series*. Forrest has left out papers for the years 1737 and 1738.

III. PERSIAN—Jaipur State Records.

Jaipur Akhbarat—Persian news-letters sent to the Jaipur Rajas by their agents at the imperial capital and other centres. They have been copied out for Sir Jadunath Sarkar and form an important source of information for the first half of the 18th century. Copies in English translation were used for this work.

ORIGINAL SOURCES (Printed documents)

I. MARATHI.

APTE AND DIVEKAR,

Shiva Bharat.

Shiv Charitra Pradeep. This is a useful book. It contains the famous Jedhe Shakavali, as also the Gadadhar Pralhad Shakavali, the Deshpande Yadi, etc.

Also Shivkalin Patrasar Samgraha, etc.,

BHAVE.

Marathi Daftar, Rumals I & II, edited by Bhave.

PARASNIS.

Brahmendra Swamichen Charitra. In the appendix of the book is printed the correspondence between the Swami and his admirers and devotees. Some of the letters of Bajirao and Chimaji are very important. Grant Duff had seen them and made use of them in his history.

Bharat Warsha, and

Itihas Samgraha. These were two journals devoted to the study of history run by Parasnis. The Itihas Samgraha especially contains very useful material.

RAJWADE.

Marathyanchya Itihasachi Sadhanen, Vols. II, III, IV and VI. Vol. II contains a chronology of the Peshwas, and Vol. IV a bakhar, and Vols. III and VI correspondence.

PURANDARE.

Purandare Daftar, Vols. I and III, edited by K. V. Purandare.

SARDESAI.

Selections from the Peshwa Daftar, Nos. 3, 7-17, 22, 28, 29, 30, 33, 34, 31. (The dates of many of these papers require to be corrected.).

Shahu's campaign against the Sidi of Janjira and its Supplement,

Early activities of Shahu and Balaji Vishwanath,
Shahu in his private life,
Bajirao and his family,
Early strife between Bajirao and the Nizam,
Shahu's relations with Sambhaji of Kolhapur,
The Dabhades and the Conquest of Gujarat,
Bajirao's entry into Malwa and Bundelkhand,
Maratha conquests in the north,
Bajirao's advance upon Delhi,
The Bassein campaign, and its supplement,
Shahu and Bajirao, administrative,
Extracts from the Peshwas' Diaries,
Peshwa Balajirao and the Karnatak affairs,
Affairs of Northern India—Peshwa Madhavrao I,
Miscellaneous Papers of Shahu and his first two Peshwas.
Papers selected from the Jamav section.

2. *Kavyetihas Samgraha Patren Yadi*, etc., 1930 edition, by Sardesai and others.
3. *Aitihasik Patra Vyawahar*, edited by Sardesai and others.

WAD.

Selections from Satara Raja's Diaries,

Shahu Roznishi, edited by Wad,

Balaji Bajirao Roznishi, Vols. II and III.

Kaifiyats and Yadis, edited by Parasnis,

Treaties, Agreements and Sanads, selected by Wad and edited by Parasnis and Mawji.

JOURNALS.

Bharat Itihas Samshodhak Mandal Quarterly.

Nagari Pracharini Sabha.

BAKHARS.

Shivaji Maharaj yanche Charitra, Sabhasad,

Thorle Sahu Maharaj yanche Charitra, Chitnis,

Sambhaji and Rajaram yanchi charitren, Chitnis,

Peshwyanchi Bakhar, Sohoni,

Peshwyanchi Bakhar, (Rajwade Vol. IV.)

Marathi Samrajyachi Choti Bakhar,

Sashtichi Bakhar, (edited by Naik, very useful for the study of the Bassein campaign.)

Cheulchi Bakhar, (Vol. III, Rajwade).

ENGLISH.

FORREST.

Selections from State Papers, Bombay, Maratha Series, Vol. I, Part I, edited by Sir G. W. Forrest.

Selections from State Papers, Bombay, Home Series, edited by Sir G. W. Forrest.

GENSE AND BANAJI.

Gaikawads of Baroda, Vol. I.

MALCOLM, SIR JOHN.

A Memoir of Central India, Vols. I & II.

MANUCCI NICCOLAO

Storia Do Mogor, by Manucci, translated by Irvine, Vols. III and IV, useful.

ORME.

Historical Fragments.—deals with coast affairs upto 1684. It gives an account of Sambhaji's attack on Janjira in 1682. The Bangabashi edition of 1905 has been used for this work.

Foster, *English Factories in India*—a few references from these volumes have been taken to follow the progress of Shivaji in Konkan. The extracts are also to be found in *Patra Sar Samgraha* and *English Records on Shivaji*.

Jervis in his book '*Geographical and statistical memoirs of the Konkan*' gives the treaties concluded between the Sidis and the Marathas and the latter and the Portuguese. The first is wrongly dated 1732 Jervis reading 'Salas' (3) for 'Saba' (7).

Bombay Gazetteers—Poona, Satara, Nasik, Khandesh, Ratnagiri, Kolaba and Thana.

PERSIAN.

ANAND RAM MUKHLIS.

Tazkira in translation in Vol. VIII of Elliot and Dowson.

BHIMSEN.

Nuskha-i-Dilkasha. This is an account of Aurangzeb's reign extensively used by Sir Jadunath. References to Maratha activities have been utilised for this work.

GHULAM M HUSSEIN.

Siyar-ul-Mutakherin. Compiled late in the 18th century. Yields some good information

IBRAHIM KHAN.

Tarikh-i-Ibrahim Khan, (English translation, Vol. VIII of Elliot and Dowson),

KHAFI KHAN.

Muntakhab-ul-Lubab, (in English translation, Vol. VII of Elliot and Dowson),

MIR ALAM.

Hadiqat-ul-alam, History of Hyderabad written by Mir Alam about 1804—Hyderabad edition.

Mirat-i-Ahmedi, an authoritative history of Muslim rule in Gujarat. It was largely used in writing the historical portion of the Gazetteer of Gujarat; requires to be corrected in places.

PORTUGUESE

Como se Perdeu Baccaim, Pissurlencar.

LATER WORKS.

Among later works on the period are the two Histories of Grant Duff and Elphinstone. Grant Duff's book is the starting point of research in Maratha history, but owing to advance in historical research it has now only an antiquarian interest. Irvine's '*Later Mughals*,' two volumes, are indispensable for studying the Mughal-Maratha relations in the early decades of the 18th century, as also Sir Jadunath's *Fall of the Mughal Empire*, Vol. I. Sir Jadunath's *Aurangzeb*, Vols. IV and V are equally valuable. Dr. Khan's book on the history of *Nizam-ul-mulk Asaf Jah* completely ignores Marathi material and therefore loses much of its value. Compared to it Sir Jadunath's chapter on the *Hyderabad State* in Cambridge History of India, Vol. IV is masterly. Khan Bahadur Commissariat's *History of Gujarat* is a useful compendium. For the west coast affairs Grose, Anderson, Da Cunha are good in their own way. Grose voyaged to India in 1750 and gives his impressions. Anderson writes about the early days of the British power, while Da Cunha treats of the Antiquities of Chaul and Bassein. Danvers' history of the Portuguese in India is useful but makes dry reading. The chapter on the Portuguese in India by Sir Denison Ross in the Cambridge history Vol. V, is an important contribution to the study of the subject. Dr. H. N. Sinha's interesting book '*Rise of the Peshwas*' represents perhaps the first attempt in English at synthesis of original Marathi materials. Among works of research students for the period under study Dr. Raghubir Sinh's *Malwa in Transition*, Dr. Ashir Badi Lal's *The Nawabs of Oudh*, Dr. Banaji's *The Sidis of Janjira* and *The English of Bombay* and Miss Sulochana Rau's *Marathas in the South* deserve to be mentioned.

In Marathi the general history of the period is given by Rao Bahadur Sardesai in his Marathi Riyasat, Vol. V, of which he has brought out a revised version embodying the results of the latest researches since this thesis was written. The Bassein campaign has been treated at length by Y. N. Kelkar, while Maratha expansion in the north, 1720-1740, has been studied by the writer of this work in his monograph *Marathyanchya Uttarentil Mohima.* There are a number of popular biographies of Bajirao inspired by and based on Sardesai's book.

Two important articles appearing in the Vernacular Press, relating to episodes described in this work, deserve to be noticed. One is 'Bajirao in the land of the brave Bundelas' by Prof. Potdar and the other is 'A review of Sawarkar's poetry' by Mr. Priyolkar. The latter casts a revealing light on Portuguese intolerance towards their native subjects.

INDEX